Discard

# Alma Lynne's COUNTRY NEEDLECRAFTS

### From Cross-Stitch Bunnies to Easy Christmas Quilts, over 50 Projects to Warm Hearts and Homes

Rodale Press, Emmaus, Pennsylvania

If you have any questions or comments concerning this book,
please write to:
      Rodale Press, Inc.
      Book Readers' Service
      33 East Minor Street
      Emmaus, PA 18098

**Library of Congress Cataloging-in-Publication Data**

Alma Lynne.
    [Country needlecrafts]
    Alma Lynne's country needlecrafts : from cross-stitch
bunnies to easy Christmas quilts, over 50 projects to warm
hearts and homes
        p.   cm.
    ISBN 0–87596–636–5 hardcover
    1. Needlework.  2. Needlework—Patterns.  3. Alma Lynne.
I. Title.  II. Title: Country needlecrafts.
TT750.A46 1994
746.4—dc20                                        94–13872
                                                       CIP

**Distributed in the book trade by St. Martin's Press**

2  4  6  8  10  9  7  5  3  1  hardcover

**FOR RODALE PRESS**

**Editorial and Design Staff**
**Associate Editor:** Karen Bolesta
**Copy Editor:** Sarah Dunn
**Book and Cover Designer:** Patricia Field
**Technical Illustrator:** Charles Metz
**Photographer:** Mitch Mandel
**Photo Stylists:** Dee Schlagel and Marianne Grape Laubach
**Production Coordinator:** Jodi Schaffer


**Rodale Home and Garden Books**
**Editor-in-Chief:** William Gottlieb
**Executive Editor:** Margaret Lydic Balitas
**Senior Editor:** Cheryl Winters Tetreau
**Copy Manager:** Dolores Plikaitis
**Art Director:** Michael Mandarano
**Office Manager:** Karen Earl-Braymer
**Administrative Assistant:** Susan Nickol


**FOR ALMA LYNNE DESIGNS**

**Vice-President and Designer:** Alma Lynne Hayden
**President and Marketing Director:** Ed Hayden
**Production Coordinator:** Pam Swann
**Production Assistance:** Terry Belanger
**Administrative Assistants:** Donna Jordan and Virginia Gause

The author and editors who compiled this book have tried to
make all of the contents as accurate and as correct as possible.
Illustrations, photographs, and text have all been carefully
checked and cross-checked. However, due to the variability of
materials, personal skill, and so on, neither the author nor
Rodale Press assumes any responsibility for any damages or
other losses incurred that result from the material presented
herein. All instructions and diagrams should be carefully stud-
ied and clearly understood before beginning any project.

"Country Thoughts from Alma Lynne" on page 150 is adapted from
*Rodale's All-New Encyclopedia of Organic Gardening.* Rodale Press, 1992.

Once in a lifetime, if you're lucky, a white knight comes charging into your life armed with courage, vision, and best of all, a tender heart. To my white knight, my husband, Scoot, who could double for Prince Valiant in any lifetime, I lovingly dedicate this book.

# CONTENTS

ACKNOWLEDGMENTS .................................................................... vi
A SPECIAL MESSAGE TO MY NEEDLECRAFTING FRIENDS .................. vii
A VISIT WITH ALMA LYNNE ....................................................... viii
ON SANTA'S LAP PICTURE ............................................................ xii

## BUNNIES AND SEW FORTH

Alphabunnies Welcome Picture ........................................... 2
Little Gray Hares Sweaters .................................................. 12
Some Bunnies Sleeping Nursery Pillow .......................... 18
Flipper and Flopper ............................................................. 22
Roller Bunny Pillow ............................................................ 26
Horace and Hildegarde Wallhanging ............................. 30
Country Carrots Afghan ..................................................... 36

## BEARY WONDERFUL BEARS

Baby Bears Crib Garland .................................................... 42
Bear on Wheels Duet ......................................................... 46
Santa Bear ............................................................................ 52
Theodore in Springtime Picture ...................................... 58
A Beary Little Bear Ensemble .......................................... 64

## ANGELIC ANGELS

Love's Little Angel Picture ................................................ 70
Starlight Angel Stocking .................................................... 74
Land of Liberty Set ............................................................. 80
Loving Cupids Sweater ...................................................... 88
Pretty-in-Pink Angel .......................................................... 92
Harvest Angel Picture ........................................................ 96

# CHRISTMAS IS A-COMING

Sir Kringle .................................................104
The Christmas Kiss Picture ..........................112
Santa's on His Way Sweatshirt ....................120
Toy Soldier and Backyard Snowman Ornaments ..........124
Needle Little Christmas Tree-o ....................128
Merry Little Christmas Pillow ......................138
Roly-Poly Santa Sweater ............................142

# DAYS TO CELEBRATE

First Day of Spring Sweater ........................148
"It's My Birthday" Chair Tie-On ..................152
Julianne and Jonathan Jellybean ..................156
"A Day Off from Work" Sweaters ..................164
Rocky the Rocking Horse Baby Bib ..............174
Witch Charming Wallhanging ......................178
Country Claus ..........................................184

# HOME SWEET HOME

Jack-o'-Lantern Flag ..................................192
Patriotic Hearts Sweatshirt ..........................196
The Preacher's Kids ....................................200
Wash Day Picture ......................................210
Quilter's Charm Wallhanging ......................214
Guests of Honor Hand Towels ....................220
Old Glory Afghan ......................................226

LET'S START STITCHING ............................232
BUYER'S GUIDE ........................................240
SPECIAL THANKS ......................................240

# ACKNOWLEDGMENTS

Many very special people were involved in this project, both directly and indirectly. I take great joy in acknowledging their contributions.

To Scoot—my husband, my best friend, and my manager—for taking me out to eat a lot, for washing your own clothes when I didn't and not complaining, for saying "That's cute!" even when it wasn't, and for everything that I am when I'm with you.

To Clay and Seth, my wonderful sons who live at Clemson University most of the time—for making motherhood a beautiful experience, for not saying "Chicken again?", and for growing up so fine and tall in spite of the times I had to travel to shows.

To my momma, Elizabeth—for always encouraging me, for saving all those precious keepsakes, and for having me.

To Pam Swann, my left and right hands—for endless hours of beautiful stitching, for great graphics, for extraordinary creativity, and for being my friend first and my employee second.

To Donna Jordan, my administrative assistant—for never complaining, at least not so I could hear it, for daily enthusiasm, for keeping our office organized so we could concentrate on this project, and for always having pencils, pens, and treats in the "special drawer!"

To Virginia Gause, our very own "voice to the people"—for proofing beyond belief, for being nice to our customers who are so nice to us, and for conscientious work and a dedicated spirit.

To Terry Belanger, our token Yankee—for assisting our staff of Steel Magnolias, and for great organizing skills, exceptional graphics, and good jokes. Welcome to our "Stress Test Express."

To my stitching friends, Patricia Thompson, Sandy Albert, Diana Anderson, Michelle Bogovich, and Lisa Rabon—my gratitude to you can never be fully expressed.

And last, but certainly not least, to each of you who purchased this book—A GREAT BIG HUG!

# A Special Message to My Needlecrafting Friends

Being an only child definitely has its advantages, as I learned early in life. My momma saved everything I wore, touched, or played with. At the time, she was lovingly referred to as a pack rat, but I would prefer to think of her as a preserver of memories. Because of her  thoughtfulness, I can touch my memories with both heart and hand. I have teddy bears, quilts, dolls, baby clothes, and other wonderful treasures made by my momma and my Aunt Alma. Together, they shared a passion for handwork, and they showered their labors of love on me.

How fortunate I am to have inherited those priceless gifts, and even more fortunate to have the desire to do the same for my children. Now *I* am the preserver of memories, lovingly referred to as the pack rat, saving everything for my children and grandchildren. I want them to know the joy of seeing and touching, too.

Pass along your life's passion so that your sons and daughters might know and love their heritage. Long live the tradition of memory making through needlecrafts!

Your friend and fellow needleworker,

# A VISIT WITH ALMA LYNNE

## THE EARLY YEARS

So often, you buy a needlecraft book because you like the projects it contains, but you don't always have the chance to "meet" the person who authored the book. A project book is a very special purchase. You buy the book and stitch for hours, making gifts for your family, your friends, and yourself, filling each stitch with love. When I design, I fill each stitch with love, too, since so much of me goes into each design. The projects in this book seem to reflect who I am and I thought it would be nice if you had the opportunity to see behind the Alma Lynne name. Of course, since this is an autobiography, it is slightly biased. But I'm sure you'll forgive me!

I was born in Winston-Salem, North Carolina, in . . . well, the year really doesn't matter, does it? (I have two sons in college, if that gives you an idea.) Anyway, it all began

*A glimpse of me as a baby and as a baton-twirling contestant at age 7*

on February 23, when little Alma Lynne Thompson came into this world. (Named Alma after a favorite aunt, Lynne because mama decided that "Alma" alone was too grown up for an infant, and Thompson for obvious reasons.) My parents, Frank and Elizabeth, were never quite the same after I made my appearance. I've often wondered if *that's* why I'm an only child!

Momma was ecstatic and relieved that it was over. Daddy was extremely proud—even if I wasn't a boy, I weighed a whopping 8 pounds, 14 ounces, and that was good enough for him. If this girl was to be his special blessing, then at least she was a big girl. I'm sure he entertained visions of tag football games between father and son when he learned Momma was expecting. But I realize now that it never mattered that he didn't have the boy he hoped for—or any of those tag football games. I was the apple of his eye for the rest of his life.

My beautiful momma dedicated her younger years to me—staying home and driving me to dance lessons and baton-twirling lessons, and attending to the other studies that would make me a well-rounded southern young lady. The most important lesson I learned from her, though, was the art of needlework. Momma is still beautiful and lives close enough to me so I can keep my eye on her. (In her really younger years, she rode motorcycles, sidesaddle of course, with her brother across the sandhills of North and South Carolina.) In spite of her refined ways, Momma surprises me every once in a while with her spunk and energy.

I figure she's the one I got "it" from. What is "it"? Well, perhaps it's a nice way to describe being zany, high on life, fun-loving, and

maybe even cuckoo! Whatever you call "it," I've got "it" and my husband, Scoot, could tell you a lot more about "it." But, thank goodness, I'm writing this instead of him.

Anyway, Brownie Girl Scouts, art classes, junior choir, talent shows, and competitions (better known as beauty pageants) were added to my "well-rounded" list. And my love for art and needlework of all kinds continued to grow. By the time I was 20 years old, I had been, or was currently, Miss Myrtle Beach High School, Miss Myrtle Beach, Miss Southern Hospitality, Miss American Legion Post #41, Miss Bemco Mattress (Daddy was in furniture), Miss Sun Fun, and Miss Rambi Raceway. For southern belles, beauty pageants and talent shows were a way of life. It's not that we actually need a title like Miss Rambi Raceway, but, face it, it certainly adds humor to any later autobiographies should we be lucky enough to author our own book!

During this great beauty pageant era, Momma always had straight pins in her blouse and a pin-cushion on her wrist. There was never a hair out of place as she sewed, zipped, powdered, and gently pushed me onto the stage, while assuring me I was the prettiest one out there. She was right about that—I was the prettiest one

*On our way to a mother and daughter luncheon a few years back*

all right, because I was the *only* one entered!

But during it all, I had learned to sew, mend, and appliqué because I had watched Momma make my gowns. I still have them, too! Momma is a great needleworker and a wonderful teacher. My love for needlework and watercolor flourished under her influence and, after several years of study, I received my bachelor's degree in art and began a teaching career in the secondary schools. The teaching didn't last long, however, because I married and had two cute, sweet, perfect little boys.

During the boys' early years, I discovered counted cross-stitch. In between chasing my children and painting little watercolor pictures for extra spending money, I stitched every minute that I could while the babies napped. Momma suggested that I interpret my popular watercolors into charted designs and, since I always listen to my momma, I did just that! It was the beginning of Alma Lynne Designs. My husband, Scoot, is the president and marketing executive. And me? Well, I live a life of creating things that I love. We have been so fortunate to succeed in a business that we both enjoy. And our thanks to all of you who have shared this enthusiasm with us.

## HOW I DESIGN

I hope you are wondering about how I design. Maybe you imagine me in a lovely pink-striped studio, with lots of flowers everywhere, sunlight streaming in my window, and a little bird perched on my shoulder chirping out the tune "A Dream Is a Wish Your Heart Makes." Actually, it's not quite like that. In fact, it's not *anything* like that. The kitchen floor serves as my studio and my ideas come to me at the most inopportune times—in restaurants, airports, the van, and yes, even the ladies' room. I sketch on anything that's available at the time, including bathroom tissue. The most important element to my design comfort is a cold Tab (that's the diet drink of the 1960s) and a jar of peanut butter (the one that tastes like real peanuts).

If everything is in place and I'm situated just so on the kitchen floor with *Oprah* on, I can design until the cows come home. Once the design is conceived, the exciting part begins. It's so much fun to watch the image come to life as it's stitched or sewn. Then, the instructions are carefully written and checked until I'm sure every detail is correct. With a great sigh and high hopes, the project is photographed and everything is sent off to press.

## JUST FOR YOU

I've included a very special design in this book, one that's dear to my heart. As I was putting the finishing touches on these country needlecrafts, I happened to glance over at the kitchen table where I was assembling the projects. And, as quick as a wink, I realized that Sir Kringle was playing Santa Claus to many of the other projects gathered at his knee. Can you guess what happened next? I grabbed the nearest piece of paper and hit the floor to draw. My mind buzzed along with details, and my hand fought to keep up. And out of that one quick glance, I captured a moment many of us remember from childhood—visiting with Santa to share our wish list, reminding him that we still believed!

Everyone agreed that it would make the perfect first project in the book. And it would bring together the things I love most—children, teddy bears, and Santa Claus.

I charted the On Santa's Lap Picture and asked one of my faithful (and oh-so-speedy) stitchers to cross-stitch the design. She went to work immediately and, within a few days, delivered the finished piece to the framing shop. When I picked it up, I was elated! It

*My colored pencil sketch of the On Santa's Lap Picture*

was just as I had envisioned it when I had seen Sir Kringle that day.

I hope you enjoy seeing your Santa scene come to life as you cross-stitch this design. Wouldn't it make an ideal accent for your family room during the holidays? Or a special gift for someone who is starting to "teeter" about whether Santa is real or not? Who knows—that special someone may be able to say "I believe" for one more year. I know I still say it—I believe!

Have fun and be happy, my good friends. And remember, a gift of love, no matter how small, is one to treasure most of all.

# ON SANTA'S LAP PICTURE

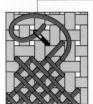

*The department store Santa is always a jolly fellow, listening with joy to youngsters reciting their memorized wish lists. What fun it must be to hear requests for curly-haired dolls, shiny fire engines, stuffed ponies—and, perhaps, baby sisters and brothers! Cross-stitch and enjoy this heart-warming glimpse of childhood.*

## SIZE

Design area is 6¾" × 9⅛" (over two threads) on 25-count linen

## MATERIALS

★ One 16¾" × 19⅛" piece of 25-count antique white Dublin linen
★ One skein of embroidery floss for each color listed in **Color Key**
★ One spool of blending filament for each color listed in **Color Key**
★ Size 26 tapestry needle

## DIRECTIONS

**1.** Prepare the edges of the linen as directed in "Preparing Fabric Edges" on page 232. Find the center of the linen and mark it with a pin. Find the center of the **On Santa's Lap Picture Chart** by connecting the arrows.

**2.** Matching the center of the chart and the linen, and using three strands of floss, begin stitching at the center point, working each cross-stitch over two threads. Work outward until the entire design is complete.

**3.** Backstitch Santa's glasses with three strands of gold blending filament. Using one strand of floss, backstitch the green areas with very dark blue-green, the blue areas and the fur with very dark antique blue, Santa's coat and hat and the girl's mitten with very dark garnet, the skin with medium pecan, the beard with dark beige-brown, the shoelaces with black, the lettering with medium antique blue, and all remaining areas with black-brown.

**4.** Using two strands of floss, work French knot buttons for the boy's jacket with very dark antique blue and for the shoelace grommets on Santa's boots with black. See "The Stitches" on page 233 for instructions on special stitches.

**5.** Wash and press the completed cross-stitch piece as directed in "Washing and Pressing" on page 233.

**6.** Mat and frame as desired.

### DESIGN OPTIONS

| Fabric Count | Design Area | Cutting Dimensions |
| --- | --- | --- |
| 22 | 3⅞" × 5⅛" | 13⅞" × 15⅛" |
| 18 | 4⅝" × 6⅜" | 14⅝" × 16⅜" |
| 14 | 6" × 8⅛" | 16" × 18⅛" |
| 11 | 7⅝" × 10⅜" | 17⅝" × 20⅜" |

## COLOR KEY

| | DMC | Anchor | J. & P. Coats | Color | | DMC | Anchor | J. & P. Coats | Color |
|---|---|---|---|---|---|---|---|---|---|
| ∕ | White | 2 | 1001 | White | + | 823 | 152 | 7982 | Dk. Navy Blue |
| Z | 310 | 403 | 8403 | Black | 8 | 838 | 380 | 5478 | Vy. Dk. Beige-Brown |
| • | 334 | 977 | 7977 | Med. Baby Blue | ⋇ | 839 | 360 | 5360 | Dk. Beige-Brown |
| 3 | 353 | 6 | 3006 | Peach | Ø | 840 | 379 | 5379 | Med. Beige-Brown |
| ✳ | 437 | 362 | 5942 | Lt. Tan | I | 841 | 378 | 5376 | Lt. Beige-Brown |
| 4 | 498 | 1005 | 3000 | Dk. Christmas Red | — | 842 | 388 | 5933 | Vy. Lt. Beige-Brown |
| ∕∕ | 500 | 683 | 6880 | Vy. Dk. Blue-Green | | 902 | 897 | 3083 | Vy. Dk. Garnet |
| ∧ | 501 | 878 | 6878 | Dk. Blue-Green | ‖ | 930 | 1035 | 7052 | Dk. Antique Blue |
| ⊃ | 502 | 877 | 6876 | Blue-Green | S | 931 | 1034 | 7051 | Med. Antique Blue |
| ⊠ | 725 | 305 | 2294 | Topaz | < | 932 | 1033 | 7050 | Lt. Antique Blue |
| L | 726 | 295 | 2295 | Lt. Topaz | U | 948 | 1011 | 2331 | Vy. Lt. Peach |
| ∩ | 738 | 361 | 5375 | Vy. Lt. Tan | ■ | 3371 | 382 | 5382 | Black-Brown |
| V | 739 | 387 | 5369 | Ultra Vy. Lt. Tan | Ɛ | 3750 | 1036 | — | Vy. Dk. Antique Blue |
| 7 | 754 | 1012 | 2331 | Lt. Peach | O | 3752 | 1032 | 7876 | Ultra Vy. Lt. Antique Blue |
| N | 760 | 1022 | 3069 | Salmon | Γ | 3753 | 1031 | 7031 | Vy. Lt. Antique Blue |
| 6 | 762 | 234 | 8510 | Vy. Lt. Pearl Gray | | 3772 | 1007 | 5579 | Med. Pecan |
| C | 775 | 128 | 7031 | Vy. Lt. Baby Blue | M | Kreinik Balger Silver Blending Filament #001 HL | | | |
| × | 814 | 45 | 3044 | Dk. Garnet | | Kreinik Balger Gold Blending Filament #002 HL | | | |
| ∖∖ | 815 | 43 | 3000 | Med. Garnet | | | | | |

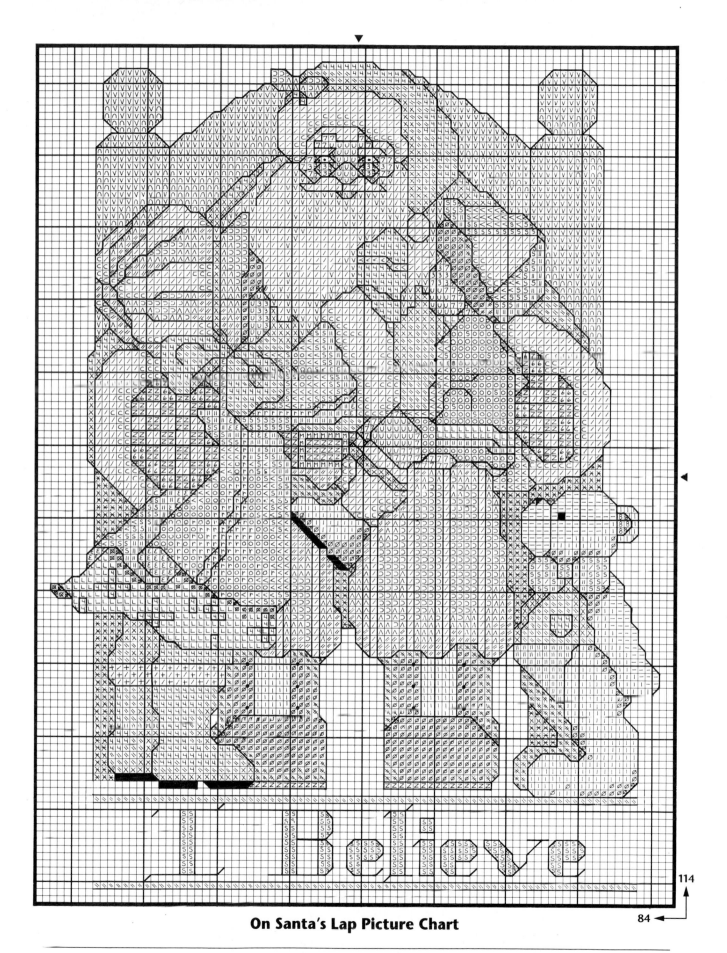

**On Santa's Lap Picture Chart**

# BUNNIES
## AND SEW FORTH

Is there anything sweeter than a soft, cuddly rabbit? I have simply fallen in love with the furry little creatures. Who can resist a country bunny curled up in an old oak basket? Or a momma bunny teaching woodland etiquette to her nest of babies? Certainly not me! I have a soft place in my heart for bunnies with big, droopy ears—just how do they manage to get around?

I had a wonderful time designing the bunnies in this chapter. Whether you stitch them or sew them, dress them up or dress them down, you're sure to find a very special one to love.

# ALPHABUNNIES WELCOME PICTURE

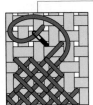

*Welcome guests to your cozy country living room with this adorable bevy of bunnies. These shy bumpkin bunnies are sure to hop their way into your heart as you cross-stitch them playing among the summer rosebuds.*

## SIZE

Design area is 4½" × 35¾" (over two squares) on 18-count Davosa

## MATERIALS

* 10-to-the-inch graph paper
* One 14½" × 45¾" piece of 18-count dusty rose Davosa
* One skein of embroidery floss for each color listed in **Color Key**\*
* Size 26 tapestry needle

\*Depending on the number of letters you will be stitching, you may need additional skeins of floss. It is best to purchase the floss at the same time to ensure similar dye lots.

## DIRECTIONS

**1.** Prepare the edges of the Davosa as directed in "Preparing Fabric Edges" on page 232. Find the center of the Davosa and mark it with a pin.

**2.** To create the picture, copy the needed letters from the **Alphabunnies Welcome Picture Charts** onto the graph paper, leaving three spaces between each letter. Count the total number of spaces on the chart both

horizontally and vertically and divide each by two to find the chart's center.

**3.** Matching the centers of the chart and the Davosa, and using three strands of floss, begin stitching at the center point, working each cross-stitch over two threads. Stitch the unsymboled letters with medium antique

### COUNTRY TIPS
*from Alma Lynne*

You can easily change the colors in this piece to coordinate with your decor. If you want a homespun look, use 20-count mushroom Valerie for the background fabric and a rich cranberry color for the lettering. I suggest DMC 814, Anchor 45, or J. & P. Coats 3044. You can make the lettering more prominent by backstitching with DMC 902, Anchor 897, or J. & P. Coats 3083. Don't forget to change the colors of the French knots to coordinate with the lettering.

I've charted the whole bunny alphabet for you, so let your imagination run (or should I say bounce?) wild. Spell out your child's name or stitch "BUNNIES" to accent a playroom. Will there be a little bundle of joy in your family soon? This would make a cute shower gift stitched with "BABY."

To determine the fabric needed for different words, count the entire number of spaces lengthwise and widthwise. Divide each number by the stitch count of the fabric you wish to use; this will give you the dimensions of your design area. Add 10" of extra fabric to each dimension to allow for framing; less if you plan to make a pillow. These will be your cutting dimensions.

blue. Work outward until the entire design is complete.

**4.** Work all backstitching with one strand of floss. Backstitch the flower stems with very dark blue-green, the bows on the bunnies with very dark rose, and the bunnies and whiskers with black-brown. Work the French knot flowers with two strands of floss in a variety of rose, medium pink, medium rose, and light rose.

**5.** Wash the completed cross-stitch piece, as directed in "Washing and Pressing" on page 233. Press your completed piece carefully, as directed.

**6.** Mat and frame as desired.

### DESIGN OPTIONS

| Fabric Count | Design Area | Cutting Dimensions |
|---|---|---|
| 22 | 2" × 14⅝" | 12" × 24⅝" |
| 18 | 2¼" × 18" | 12¼" × 28" |
| 14 | 3" × 23" | 13" × 33" |
| 11 | 3⅝" × 29¼" | 13⅝" × 39¼" |

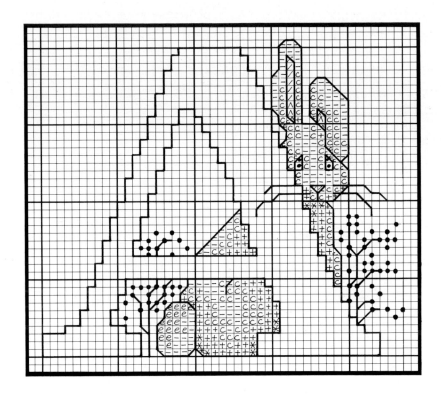

## Alphabunnies Welcome Picture Charts
### COLOR KEY

| | DMC | Anchor | J. & P. Coats | Color |
|---|---|---|---|---|
| e | Ecru | 387 | 5387 | Ecru |
| | 326 | 59 | 3401 | Vy. Dk. Rose |
| 3 | 335 | 38 | 3283 | Rose |
| | 500 | 683 | 6880 | Vy. Dk. Blue-Green |
| / | 776 | 24 | 3281 | Med. Pink |
| ✳ | 838 | 380 | 5478 | Vy. Dk. Beige-Brown |
| + | 840 | 379 | 5379 | Med. Beige-Brown |
| c | 841 | 378 | 5376 | Lt. Beige-Brown |
| — | 842 | 388 | 5933 | Vy. Lt. Beige-Brown |
| ∧ | 899 | 52 | 3282 | Med. Rose |
| | 931 | 1034 | 7051 | Med. Antique Blue |
| ⌐ | 3326 | 36 | 3126 | Lt. Rose |
| ● | 3371 | 382 | 5382 | Black-Brown |

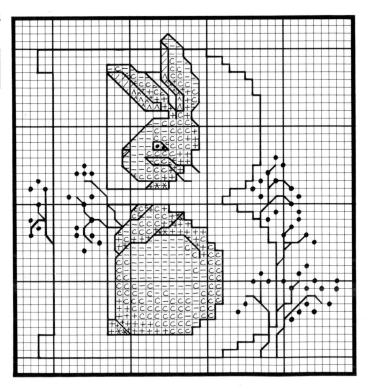

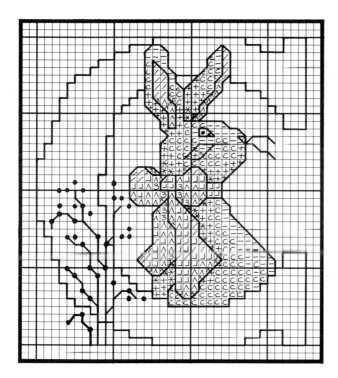

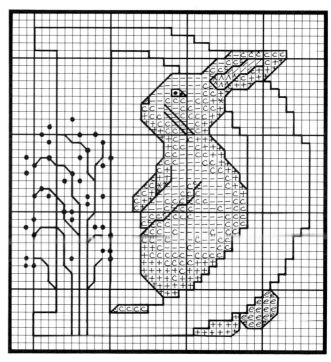

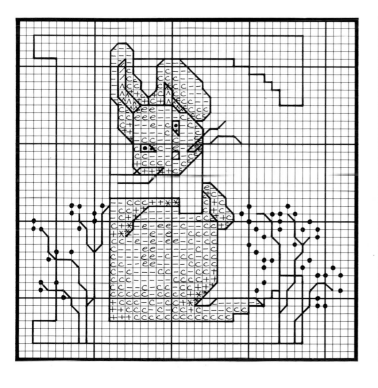

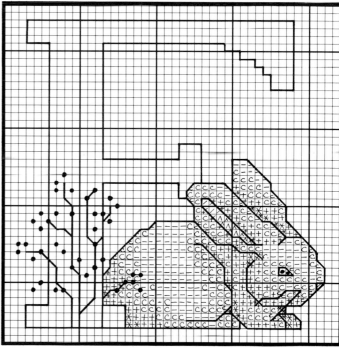

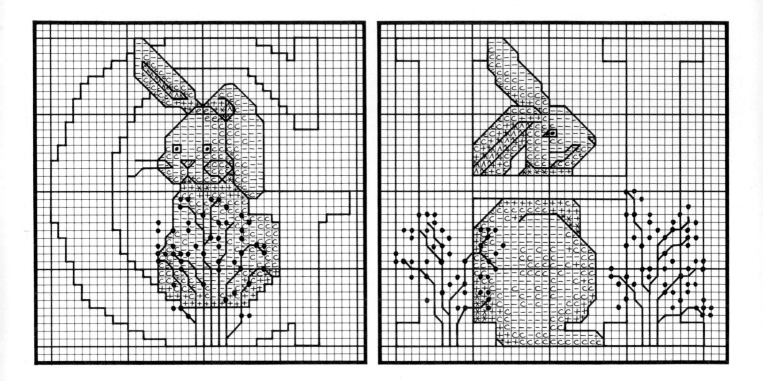

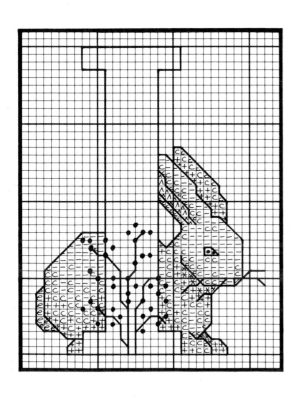

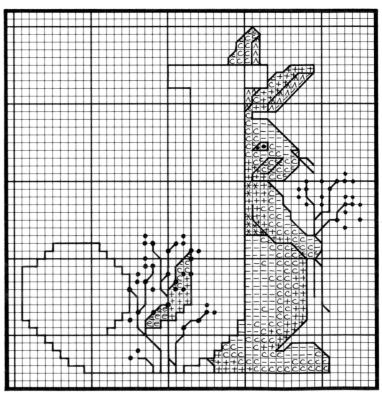

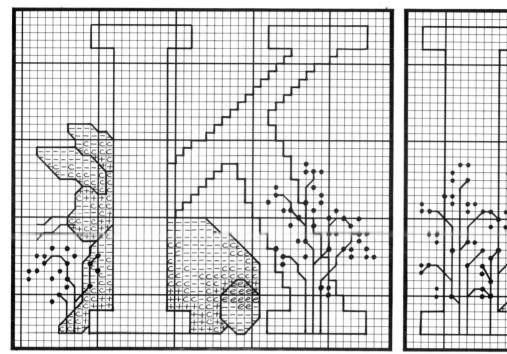

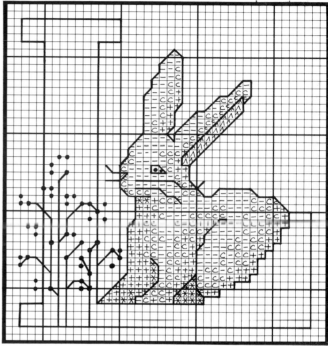

## Alphabunnies Welcome Picture Charts
### COLOR KEY

| | DMC | Anchor | J. & P. Coats | Color |
|---|---|---|---|---|
| e | Ecru | 387 | 5387 | Ecru |
| | 326 | 59 | 3401 | Vy. Dk. Rose |
| З | 335 | 38 | 3283 | Rose |
| | 500 | 683 | 6880 | Vy. Dk. Blue-Green |
| / | 776 | 24 | 3281 | Med. Pink |
| ✳ | 838 | 380 | 5478 | Vy. Dk. Beige-Brown |
| + | 840 | 379 | 5379 | Med. Beige-Brown |
| C | 841 | 378 | 5376 | Lt. Beige-Brown |
| — | 842 | 388 | 5933 | Vy. Lt. Beige-Brown |
| ∧ | 899 | 52 | 3282 | Med. Rose |
| | 931 | 1034 | 7051 | Med. Antique Blue |
| ⌐ | 3326 | 36 | 3126 | Lt. Rose |
| ● | 3371 | 382 | 5382 | Black-Brown |

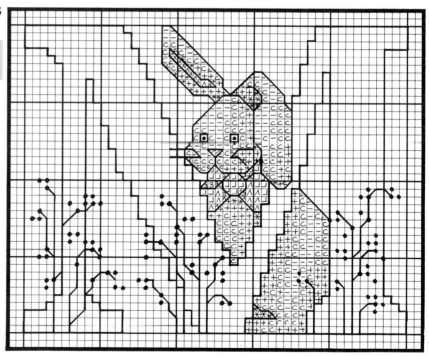

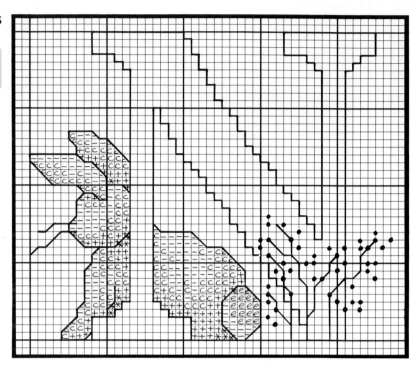

# Alphabunnies Welcome Picture Charts
## Color Key

| | DMC | Anchor | J. & P. Coats | Color |
|---|---|---|---|---|
| e | Ecru | 387 | 5387 | Ecru |
| | 326 | 59 | 3401 | Vy. Dk. Rose |
| 3 | 335 | 38 | 3283 | Rose |
| | 500 | 683 | 6880 | Vy. Dk. Blue-Green |
| / | 776 | 24 | 3281 | Med. Pink |
| ✳ | 838 | 380 | 5478 | Vy. Dk. Beige-Brown |
| + | 840 | 379 | 5379 | Med. Beige-Brown |
| C | 841 | 378 | 5376 | Lt. Beige-Brown |
| — | 842 | 388 | 5933 | Vy. Lt. Beige-Brown |
| ∧ | 899 | 52 | 3282 | Med. Rose |
| | 931 | 1034 | 7051 | Med. Antique Blue |
| ⌐ | 3326 | 36 | 3126 | Lt. Rose |
| ● | 3371 | 382 | 5382 | Black-Brown |

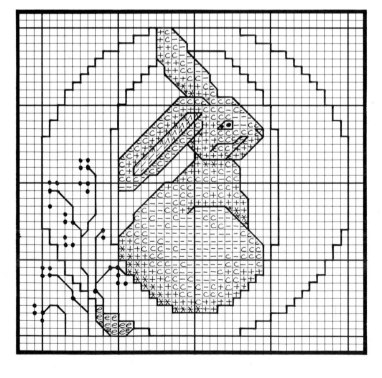

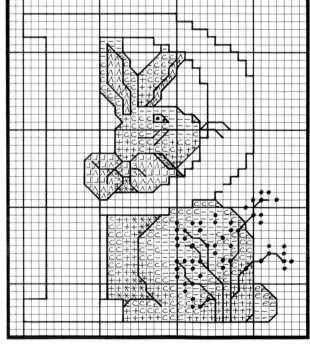

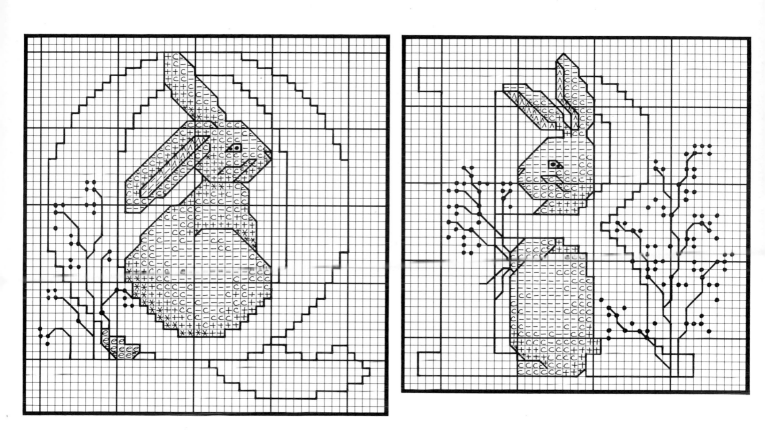

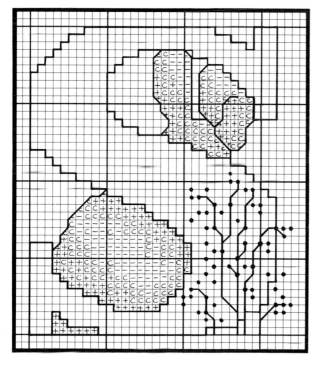

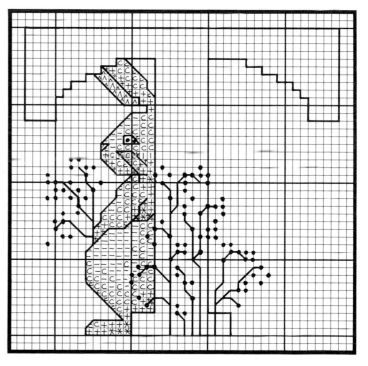

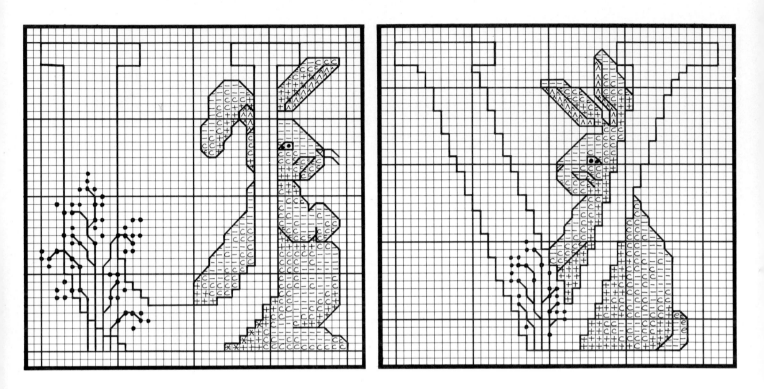

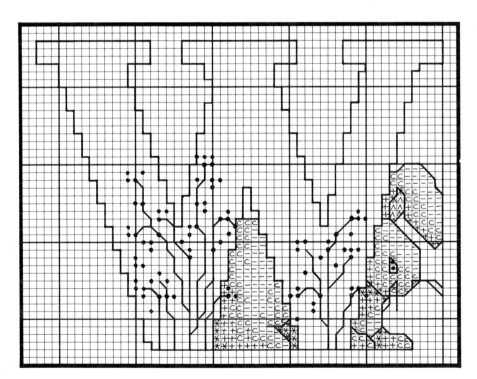

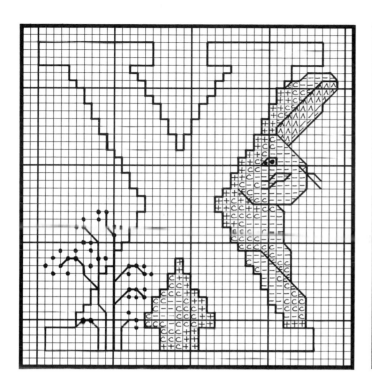

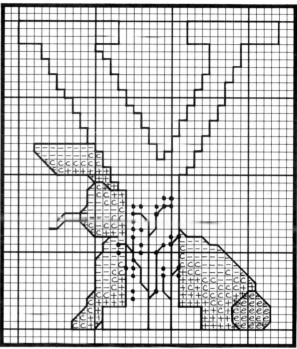

# Alphabunnies Welcome Picture Charts
## COLOR KEY

|   | DMC | Anchor | J. & P. Coats | Color |
|---|-----|--------|---------------|-------|
| e | Ecru | 387 | 5387 | Ecru |
|   | 326 | 59 | 3401 | Vy. Dk. Rose |
| 3 | 335 | 38 | 3283 | Rose |
|   | 500 | 683 | 6880 | Vy. Dk. Blue-Green |
| ∕ | 776 | 24 | 3281 | Med. Pink |
| ✳ | 838 | 380 | 5478 | Vy. Dk. Beige-Brown |
| + | 840 | 379 | 5379 | Med. Beige-Brown |
| C | 841 | 378 | 5376 | Lt. Beige-Brown |
| — | 842 | 388 | 5933 | Vy. Lt. Beige-Brown |
| ∧ | 899 | 52 | 3282 | Med. Rose |
|   | 931 | 1034 | 7051 | Med. Antique Blue |
| ⌐ | 3326 | 36 | 3126 | Lt. Rose |
| ● | 3371 | 382 | 5382 | Black-Brown |

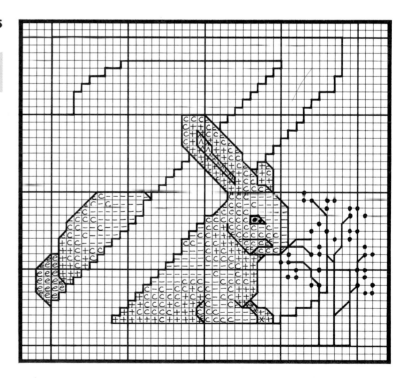

# LITTLE GRAY HARES SWEATERS

*Capture the charm of these young bunnies in duplicate stitch. Betsy Bunny is sometimes bashful, sometimes forthright, and always fun to be around. Best Bunnies go a-courting in the latest rabbitwear—she models a pink smock and heart-patterned petticoat; he shows off his dapper balloon pants and smart bow tie.*

## BETSY BUNNY SWEATER

### SIZE

Betsy design area is 6" × 10½" on 6 × 8 gauge

Heart border design area is 2⅛" × 3¼" on 6 × 8 gauge

### MATERIALS

★ One 6 × 8-gauge child's stockinette stitch white pullover sweater
★ One skein of embroidery floss for each color listed in **Color Key** (unless otherwise indicated)
★ Size 22 tapestry needle
★ Two ¼"-diameter light blue buttons
★ Matching thread
★ ½ yard of ⅜"-wide blue satin ribbon
★ 2 yards *each* of ⅝"-wide white, light blue, blue, pink, and pink polka-dot grosgrain ribbons for the froufrou
★ 8" length of ¾"-wide white Velcro strip for the froufrou

### DIRECTIONS

1. Plan the placement of the Betsy Bunny design on your sweater. On the model, I counted down 45 knit stitches from the center front neckline and marked it with a pin; this was the center stitch for my design. For your sweater, follow the directions above if you have at least 90 vertical stitches. If your sweater has more than 90 vertical stitches, find the center by counting the total number of vertical stitches (from the center front neckline to the top of the ribbing) and dividing that number by two. Find the center of the **Betsy Bunny Sweater Chart** by connecting the arrows.

2. Lay the sweater sleeves flat so the underarm seams are at the lower edges. Finger press folds at the opposite edges to find the sleeve centers. Measure 2" up from the top of the cuff ribbing along the sleeve center fold and mark it with a pin. Find the center of the **Betsy Bunny Sleeve Chart** by connecting the arrows.

3. Read the duplicate stitch basics in "The Stitches" on page 235. Matching the center of the **Betsy Bunny Sweater Chart** with the marked center stitch on the sweater, duplicate stitch the design using six strands of floss. Duplicate stitch the sleeve design in the same manner, using the **Betsy Bunny Sleeve Chart.**

4. Wash and press the completed duplicate stitch design as directed in "Washing and Pressing" on page 235.

5. Sew the button eyes in place over the medium navy blue stitches. Tie the satin rib-

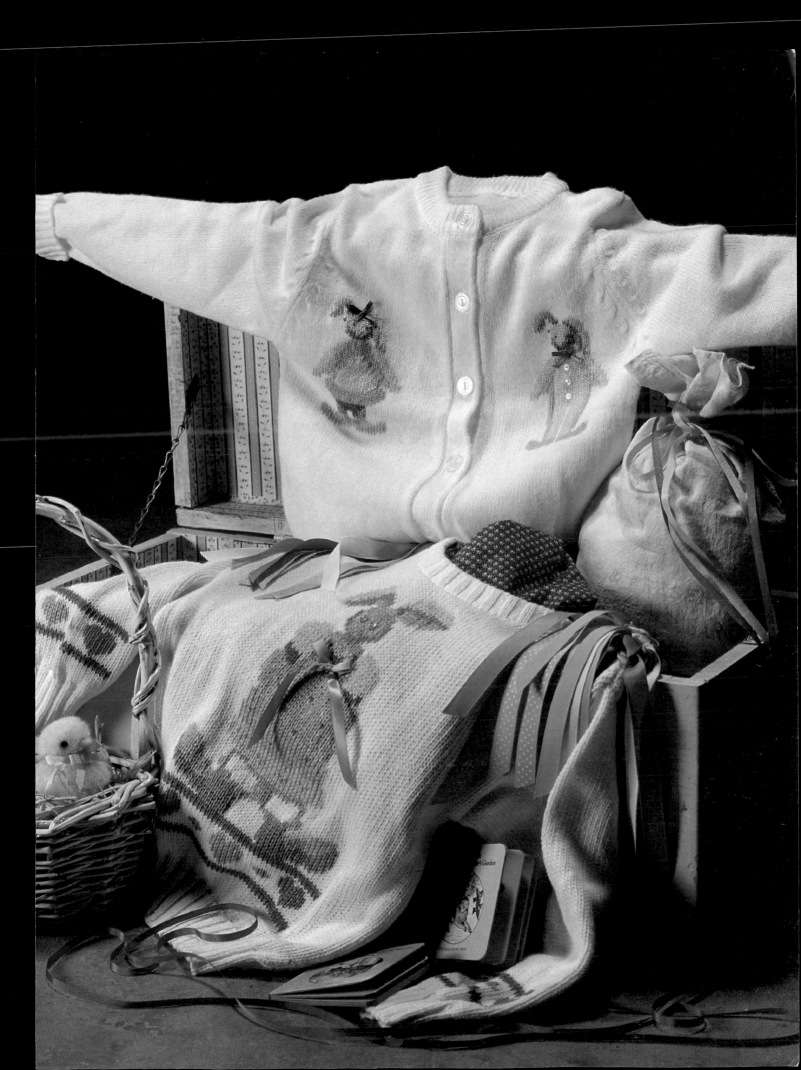

bon into a bow and hand tack it in place below Betsy Bunny's dress bodice. Clip the ribbon ends diagonally.

**6.** Cut the grosgrain ribbon lengths into ½-yard pieces. Using the ribbons and Velcro, add the froufrou to the shoulders as directed in "Froufrou" on page 239.

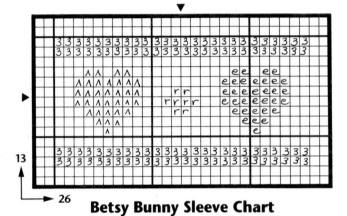

13
26

**Betsy Bunny Sleeve Chart**

## Betsy Bunny Sweater Charts
### COLOR KEY

|   | DMC | Anchor | J. & P. Coats | Color |
|---|-----|--------|---------------|-------|
|   | White | 2 | 1001 | White |
| V | 311 | 148 | 7980 | Med. Navy Blue |
| • | 318 | 399 | 8511 | Lt. Steel Gray |
| X | 322 | 978 | 7978 | Vy. Lt. Navy Blue |
| 3 | 334 | 977 | 7977 | Med. Baby Blue |
| ✳ | 414 | 235 | 8513 | Dk. Steel Gray |
| / | 415 | 398 | 8398 | Pearl Gray |
| ⌐ | 503 | 876 | 6879 | Med. Blue-Green |
| O | 762 | 234 | 8510 | Vy. Lt. Pearl Gray |
| Ɛ | 775 | 128 | 7031 | Vy. Lt. Baby Blue |
| \ | 776 | 24 | 3281 | Med. Pink (2 skeins) |
| ∧ | 899 | 52 | 3282 | Med. Rose |
| + | 3325 | 129 | 7976 | Lt. Baby Blue |
| e | 3326 | 36 | 3126 | Lt. Rose |

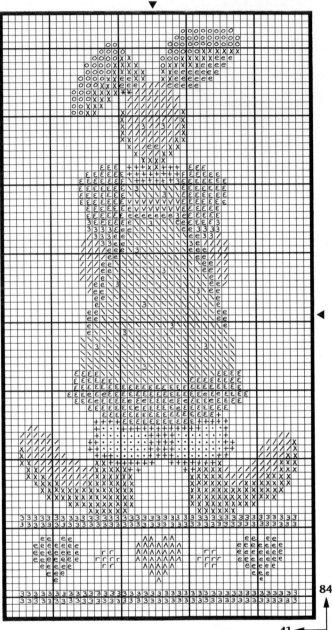

**Betsy Bunny Sweater Chart**

84
41

# COUNTRY THOUGHTS
*from Alma Lynne*

Wouldn't it be great if the Easter Bunny were your "best bunny"? Can you imagine what kind of dates you'd go on? One week you'd tour the chocolate factory, the next week you'd be off to the jellybean shop, and then you'd sneak off to twitch noses together in his egg-dyeing studio. What fun it would be!

I always wanted the Easter Bunny to be my boyfriend or, at least, my personal play mate. Each year, I did everything I could to convince Momma and the Easter Bunny that that was exactly what I wanted. Just think—a 6'-tall friend with baskets full of candy. One year, despite my head-turning tantrum at the department store, I went home without my

*A memento from one of my Eastertime visits to the big department stores in Winston-Salem, North Carolina*

intended playmate and without the gracious blessings of my mother. (And I even think my Easter basket had fewer treats that year! Am I right, Momma?)

I do have many wonderful memories of Easter, in spite of that one small incident. I thrived on the excitement of waking up on Easter morning and discovering a basketful of goodies at the foot of my bed. Momma always made a frilly new dress for me, and I loved getting all dolled up for the day. Best of all, I couldn't wait for the Easter egg hunt. I would peek under every bush and in the tall grass looking for that special gold egg. I knew that if I found it, I'd not only get a special treat but also be the envy of all the other egg hunters that day. I don't remember ever finding the prize egg, but I do remember the tummy aches from eating too many sweets!

I practically lived on solid chocolate bunnies (the ones with the big candy eyes) for weeks after Easter. Momma would try to ration the sweets, but I always found her hiding spot. I was so careful to rearrange the cabinets just the way she had them so she couldn't tell I'd been snitching candy. But she usually knew anyway—from the mushed chocolate on my little hands.

I loved all the other sweets at Easter, too. Yellow marshmallow peeps, spongy circus peanuts, and brightly colored malted-milk eggs were absolute staples in my basket. And, of course, the hard-boiled eggs we had decorated just hours before always found their way into the basket.

Easter is a wonderful time to relive the holidays of childhood. So get into the spirit of things and start to recelebrate the traditions of yesteryear with your children today.

# BEST BUNNIES SWEATER

## SIZE

Girl bunny design area is 3" × 4⅜" on 9 × 12 gauge

Boy bunny design area is 3" × 4⅞" on 9 × 12 gauge

## MATERIALS

★ One 9 × 12-gauge child's stockinette stitch white cardigan sweater
★ One skein of embroidery floss for each color listed in **Color Key**
★ Size 22 tapestry needle
★ 4 light blue glass seed beads
★ 2 pink seed beads
★ 5 ⅜"-diameter white buttons
★ ¼ yard of ⅛"-wide blue satin ribbon
★ Matching thread

## DIRECTIONS

**1.** Plan the placement of the designs on your sweater. On the model, I counted the total horizontal stitches on each side front and divided that number by two to find the horizontal center. Then I counted the total vertical stitches (from the shoulder seam to the top of the ribbing) and divided that number by two to find the vertical center. For your sweater, follow the directions above if you have at least 62 horizontal stitches on each side front. Find the horizontal and vertical centers of each side front and mark them with pins. Find the centers of the **Best Girl Bunny Chart** and the **Best Boy Bunny Chart** by connecting the arrows.

**2.** Read the duplicate stitch basics in "The Stitches" on page 235. Matching the center of the **Best Girl Bunny Chart** and the marked center stitch on the right side front of the sweater, duplicate stitch the design using four strands of floss. Repeat with the **Best Boy Bunny Chart** and the left side front of the sweater.

**3.** Wash and press the completed duplicate stitch design as directed in "Washing and Pressing" on page 235.

**4.** Sew the blue seed bead eyes and the pink seed bead noses in place as indicated by the large dots on the chart. Sew the buttons in place in the same manner. Cut the ribbon in half and tie each length in a bow. Hand tack one bow to the girl bunny's "hair" and one bow to the boy bunny's collar.

---

## COUNTRY TIPS
### *from Alma Lynne*

If you've stitched the Best Bunnies Sweater for a very small child, leave off the three-dimensional embellishments for safety reasons. Work the eyes and nose in French knots using three strands of floss. See "The Stitches" on page 235 for instructions. Duplicate stitch in a coordinating floss color to simulate the buttons on the bunnies' clothes.

If you've stitched the Betsy Bunny Sweater, sew pom-poms to the skirt over the medium navy blue stitches and add tiny white bows to the lower edge of Betsy's bloomers. Wouldn't Betsy look great with silly rabbit whiskers? Cut several 4" lengths of gray floss. Thread your needle with all six strands and pass the needle in at one side of Betsy's nose and out the other side, leaving a 2" tail at each end. Make your next pass one stitch down and the next pass one stitch out. Continue in this manner until you have a pleasing number of whiskers. Secure the whiskers in place on the inside of the sweater by hand tacking.

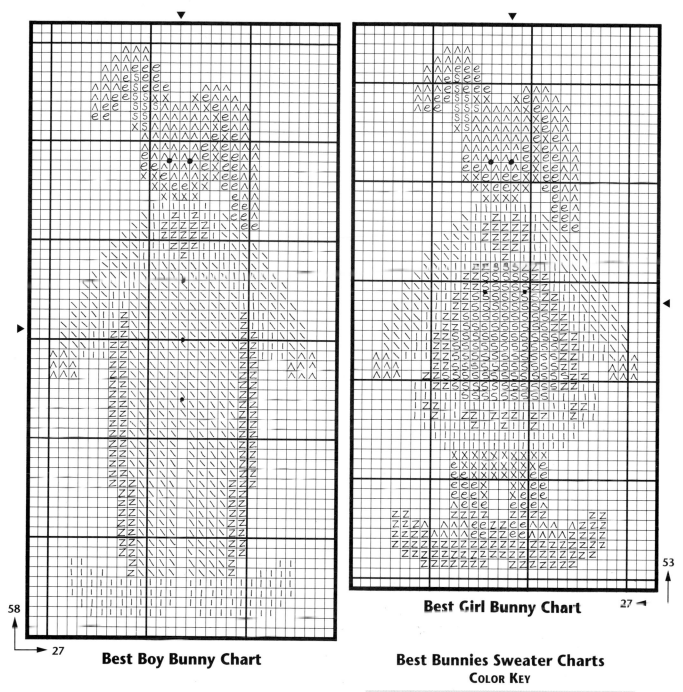

**Best Boy Bunny Chart**

**Best Girl Bunny Chart**

## Best Bunnies Sweater Charts
### COLOR KEY

|   | DMC | Anchor | J. & P. Coats | Color |
|---|-----|--------|---------------|-------|
| e | 318 | 399 | 8511 | Lt. Steel Gray |
| X | 414 | 235 | 8513 | Dk. Steel Gray |
| \ | 775 | 128 | 7031 | Vy. Lt. Baby Blue |
| S | 818 | 23 | 3281 | Baby Pink |
| ∧ | 3024 | 397 | 8397 | Vy. Lt. Gray-Brown |
| I | 3325 | 129 | 7976 | Lt. Baby Blue |
| Z | 3326 | 36 | 3126 | Lt. Rose |

# SOME BUNNIES SLEEPING NURSERY PILLOW

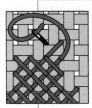

*What a sweet addition to your baby's room! Prop this pillow on a rocking chair as a gentle reminder that whispers are in order when baby is napping.*

## SIZE

Design area is 4½" × 7¾" (over two threads) on 28-count linen

Finished pillow is 14½" × 17¾", including ruffle

## MATERIALS

- ★ One 10½" × 13¾" piece of 28-count carnation pastel linen
- ★ One skein of embroidery floss for each color listed in **Color Key**
- ★ Size 26 tapestry needle
- ★ ¾ yard of 44"-wide blue print fabric for the borders, ruffle, and back
- ★ ⅜ yard of 44"-wide pink solid fabric for the piping
- ★ Matching thread
- ★ One 10½" × 13¾" piece of fleece
- ★ 1½ yards of ¼"-diameter cording
- ★ One 10½" × 13¾" piece of fusible interfacing
- ★ ⅜ yard of 44"-wide muslin for the covered pillow form
- ★ Polyester fiberfill
- ★ 1½ yards of 1"-wide pink grosgrain ribbon

## DIRECTIONS

**Note:** All seam allowances are ½". After sewing, trim all seam allowances to ¼" to reduce bulk.

**1.** Prepare the edges of the linen as directed in "Preparing Fabric Edges" on page 232. Find the center of the linen and mark it with a pin. Find the center of the **Some Bunnies Sleeping Nursery Pillow Chart** by connecting the arrows.

**2.** Matching the centers of the chart and the linen and, using two strands of floss, begin cross-stitching at the center point, working each cross-stitch over two linen threads. Work outward until the entire design is complete.

**3.** Backstitch the design with one strand of black.

**4.** Wash and press the completed cross-stitch as directed in "Washing and Pressing" on page 233.

**5.** With the design centered, trim the linen to 7" × 10¼". From the blue, cut two 2¾" × 10¼" border strips, two 2¾" × 10½" border strips, two 6" × 44" ruffle strips, and one 10½" × 13¾" pillow back. From the pink, cut one 2" × 51" bias strip for piping.

**6.** With right sides together and raw edges even, sew the 2¾" × 10¼" border strips to the top and bottom of the cross-stitch, as shown in **Diagram 1.** Press the seams toward the borders. Sew one 2¾" × 10½" border strip to each side in the same manner; see **Diagram 2.** Press the seams toward the borders.

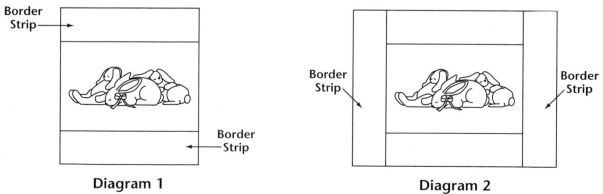

**Diagram 1**

Border Strip

Border Strip

**Diagram 2**

Border Strip

Border Strip

19

**7.** Make 51" of corded piping and sew the piping to the pillow front, as directed in "Sewing On the Piping" on page 238. Do *not* trim the seam allowance.

**8.** Sew the 10½" × 13¾" piece of fleece to the wrong side of the pillow top along all four edges.

**9.** With right sides together and raw edges even, sew the short ends of the two 6" × 44" strips together to form one continuous ruffle; see **Diagram 3.** Press the seams open. With wrong sides together, fold the loop in half

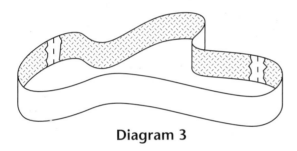

**Diagram 3**

lengthwise and press. Sew a line of gathering stitches ⅜" from the raw edges through both layers of the ruffle. Fold the ruffle in half to find the midpoints and place pins at these points. Match the midpoints of the ruffle and mark the quarterpoints with pins; see **Diagram 4.**

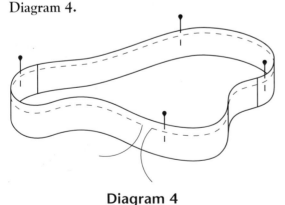

**Diagram 4**

## COUNTRY THOUGHTS
*from Alma Lynne*

My two boys loved to play outside when they were growing up. After dinner, they'd pile into the living room to watch television before bedtime. It wouldn't be very long before they were curled up next to each other, fast asleep. Talk about sweet little bunnies! I always kept a camera nearby to record these innocent moments. What fun it is to look back now and laugh over their angelic faces, still slightly smudged from afternoon play.

**10.** Sew the ruffle to the pillow top, referring to "Ruffles" on page 239.

**11.** Iron the fusible interfacing onto the wrong side of the pillow back.

**12.** Make a 9" × 12¼" covered pillow form and assemble the pillow, as directed in "Covered Pillow Forms" and "Assembling a Pillow" on page 239.

**13.** Cut the ribbon into three 18" lengths. Tie each length into a bow and trim the ends diagonally. Tack one bow to each upper corner of the linen and the remaining bow to the center bottom of the pillow just above the piping.

**DESIGN OPTIONS**

| Fabric Count | Design Area | Cutting Dimensions |
| --- | --- | --- |
| 22 | 2¾" × 4¾" | 12¾" × 14¾" |
| 18 | 3⅜" × 5¾" | 13⅜" × 15¾" |
| 14 | 4½" × 7¾" | 14½" × 17¾" |
| 11 | 5⅝" × 9⅝" | 15⅝" × 19⅝" |

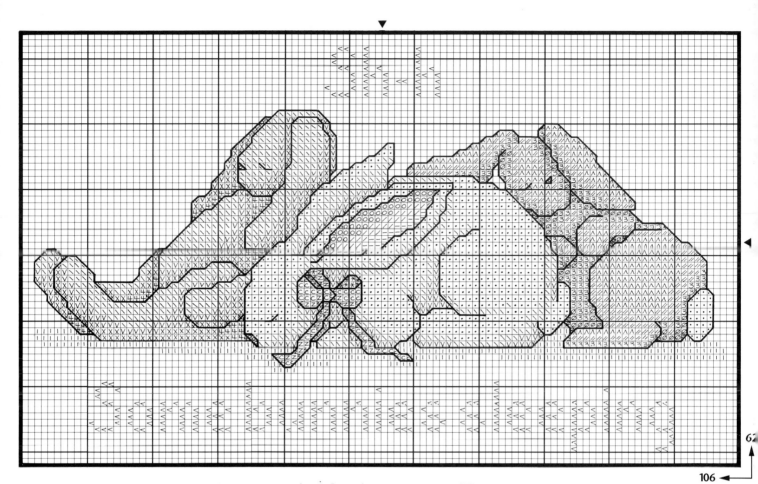

## Some Bunnies Sleeping Nursery Pillow Chart
### COLOR KEY

| | DMC | Anchor | J. & P. Coats | Color | | DMC | Anchor | J. & P. Coats | Color |
|---|---|---|---|---|---|---|---|---|---|
| • | White | 2 | 1001 | White | C | 747 | 158 | 7053 | Vy. Lt. Sky Blue |
| | 310 | 403 | 8403 | Black | ＼ | 762 | 234 | 8510 | Vy. Lt. Pearl Gray |
| × | 318 | 399 | 8511 | Lt. Steel Gray | O | 776 | 24 | 3281 | Med. Pink |
| Ꝡ | 414 | 235 | 8513 | Dk. Steel Gray | / | 818 | 23 | 3281 | Baby Pink |
| V | 415 | 398 | 8398 | Pearl Gray | — | 819 | 271 | 3280 | Lt. Baby Pink |
| < | 517 | 162 | 7162 | Dk. Wedgewood | Ø | 839 | 360 | 5360 | Dk. Beige-Brown |
| ✳ | 518 | 1039 | — | Lt. Wedgewood | 3 | 840 | 379 | 5379 | Med. Beige-Brown |
| Z | 519 | 1038 | — | Sky Blue | // | 841 | 378 | 5376 | Lt. Beige-Brown |
| I | 535 | — | 8400 | Vy. Lt. Ash Gray | ∧ | 842 | 388 | 5933 | Vy. Lt. Beige-Brown |

# FLIPPER AND FLOPPER

*These country cousins spend lazy summer days picking sweet blueberries and frolicking in the sunshine. They're a snap to sew and could easily be made in one evening—a great gift to brighten a nursery!*

## SIZE

12" tall

## MATERIALS FOR FLIPPER

* ★ ½ yard of blue floral chintz fabric
* ★ Matching thread
* ★ Polyester fiberfill
* ★ Matching buttonhole twist thread
* ★ Soft-sculpture doll needle
* ★ Four ½"-diameter white flower buttons
* ★ ¼ yard of 1½"-wide gathered white lace
* ★ ½ yard of ⅜"-wide rose satin ribbon

## MATERIALS FOR FLOPPER

* ★ ½ yard of blue-and-white striped chintz fabric
* ★ Matching thread
* ★ Polyester fiberfill
* ★ Matching buttonhole twist thread
* ★ Soft-sculpture doll needle
* ★ Four ½"-diameter white bunny buttons
* ★ ½ yard of 1"-wide blue satin ribbon

## DIRECTIONS

**Note:** All seam allowances are ¼".

1. Prepare the patterns as directed in "Preparing Patterns" on page 236, using the patterns on page 25.

2. From both the floral chintz and the striped chintz, mark and cut one body and one body reverse, two ears and two ears reverse, two front legs and two front legs reverse, and two back legs and two back legs reverse.

3. For each bunny, place the right sides together and sew the bodies together, leaving a 1½" opening. Clip the curves. Turn to the right side and press. Stuff to desired firmness. Whipstitch the opening closed.

4. Repeat Step 3 for each front leg and each back leg.

5. For each ear, place right sides together and sew, leaving a 1" opening. Clip the curves, then turn to the right side and press. Do not stuff. Whipstitch the opening closed.

6. Knot a 20" length of buttonhole twist at one end and thread it through the doll needle. Matching the large dots, run the needle from the outside of one front leg through to the inside of the leg, then through the body and the other front leg. Run the needle up through a hole of one button and down through the other hole, then back through the front leg, the body, and the other front leg. Thread another button on the buttonhole twist and pass the thread back through the legs and body several times to secure. Knot tightly.

**7.** Repeat Step 6 to attach the back legs.

**8.** Whipstitch the ears to the head where indicated on the pattern.

**9.** For Flipper, place the lace around her neck, overlapping the raw edges at the back of the neck; trim the excess. Hand tack in place. Tie the ribbon in a bow and clip the ends diagonally. Hand tack the bow to the neck front. For Flopper, tie the ribbon in a bow and clip the ends diagonally. Hand tack the bow to his neck front.

## COUNTRY THOUGHTS
### from Alma Lynne

I modeled Flipper and Flopper after bunnies my momma made for me many years ago. She was a natural at the sewing machine and made all my clothes—even my pageant gowns. She always drew her own patterns when she made dolls and toys and often used fabric scraps for her lovable creatures. In fact, the original Flipper and Flopper were made from 1940s drapery fabric. I dragged those bunnies from room to room as I played, and even to bed with me each night. Momma mended and mended them until they became so childworn that they had to be tucked away in a trunk. I'm so glad that she was a saver—because she carefully packed the mementos of my childhood in trunks and boxes, I can enjoy them again as an adult.

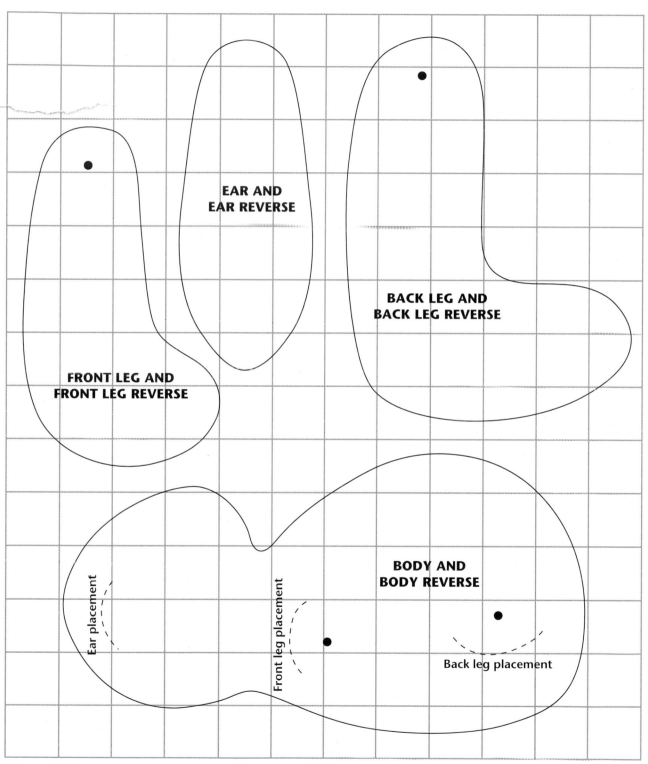

**EAR AND
EAR REVERSE**

**BACK LEG AND
BACK LEG REVERSE**

**FRONT LEG AND
FRONT LEG REVERSE**

**BODY AND
BODY REVERSE**

Ear placement

Front leg placement

Back leg placement

Enlarge 181%

**Flipper and Flopper Patterns**

1 square = 1"

# ROLLER BUNNY PILLOW

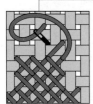

*He's polka-dotted, he's checkered, and he's on wheels! He's Roller Bunny, of course—a good-natured friend to country folk across the land. Let him roll into your home as a whimsical addition to your bunny collection.*

## SIZE

Design area is 7¼" square (over two squares) on 14-count Aida

Finished pillow is 16½" square, including ruffle

## MATERIALS

* One 13½" square of 14-count ivory Aida
* One skein of embroidery floss for each color listed in **Color Key**
* Size 22 or 24 tapestry needle
* ⅜ yard of rose pindot fabric for the borders and ruffle
* ⅞ yard of navy plaid fabric for the piping, ruffle, and back
* Matching thread
* 12½" square of fleece
* 1½ yards of ⅜"-diameter cording
* 12½" square of fusible interfacing
* ⅜ yard of 44"-wide muslin for the covered pillow form
* Polyester fiberfill

## DIRECTIONS

**Note:** All seam allowances are ½". After sewing, trim all seam allowances to ¼" to reduce bulk.

**1.** Prepare the edges of the Aida as directed in "Preparing Fabric Edges" on page 232. Find the center of the Aida and mark it with a pin. Find the center of the **Roller Bunny Pillow Chart** by connecting the arrows.

**2.** Matching the centers of the chart and the Aida, and using two strands of floss, begin cross-stitching at the center point, working each cross-stitch over two Aida squares. Work outward until the entire design is complete.

**3.** Backstitch with one strand of black.

**4.** Wash and press the completed cross-stitch piece as directed in "Washing and Pressing" on page 233.

**5.** With the design centered, trim the Aida to an 8½" square.

**6.** From the pindot, cut two 3" × 8½" border strips, two 3" × 12½" border strips, and two 3" × 44" ruffle strips. From the plaid, cut two 6" × 44" ruffle strips, one 2" × 52" bias strip for piping, and one 12½" pillow back.

**7.** With right sides together and raw edges even, sew one 3" × 8½" border strip to each side of the completed cross-stitch, as shown in **Diagram 1** on page 28. Press the seams toward the borders. Sew the 3" × 12½" border strips to the top and bottom of the cross-stitch in the same manner; see **Diagram 2** on page 28. Press the seams toward the borders.

**8.** Sew the 12½" square of fleece to the wrong side of the pillow top along all four edges.

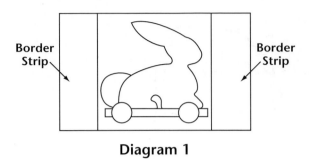

**Diagram 1**

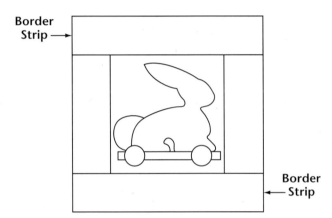

**Diagram 2**

**9.** Make 52" of corded piping and sew the piping to the pillow front, as directed in "Making Corded Piping" on page 238 and "Sewing On the Piping" on page 238. Do *not* trim the seam allowance.

**10.** With right sides together and raw edges even, sew the short ends of the two 6" × 44" plaid strips together to form one continuous loop; see **Diagram 3.** Press the seams open. Repeat with the two 3" × 44" pindot strips. With right sides together and one long edge of the strips aligned, sew the continuous loops together along the long edge, as shown in **Diagram 4.** Turn the loop right side out, fold it in half lengthwise with wrong sides together, and press. Sew a line of gathering stitches ⅜" from the raw edges through both layers of the ruffle. Fold the ruffle in half to find the midpoints and place pins at these points. Match the midpoints of the ruffle and mark the quarterpoints with pins; see **Diagram 5.**

**11.** Sew the ruffle to the pillow top, referring to "Ruffles" on page 239.

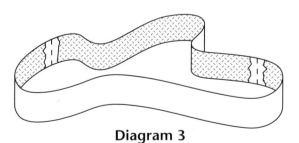

**Diagram 3**

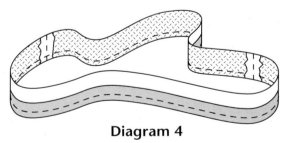

**Diagram 4**

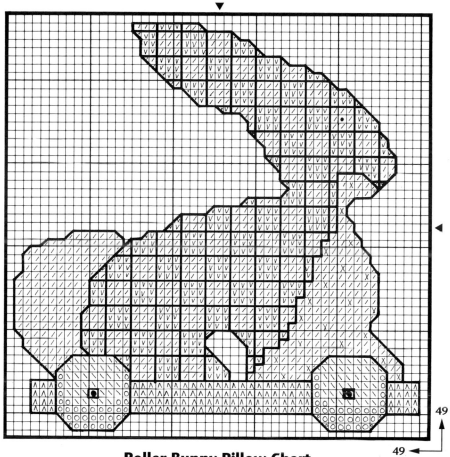

**Roller Bunny Pillow Chart**

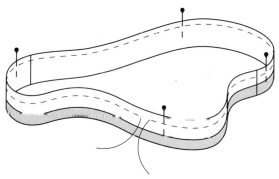

**Diagram 5**

## COLOR KEY

| | DMC | Anchor | J. & P. Coats | Color |
|---|---|---|---|---|
| / | White | 2 | 1001 | White |
| X | 223 | 895 | 3240 | Med. Shell Pink |
| ● | 310 | 403 | 8403 | Black |
| V | 823 | 152 | 7982 | Dk. Navy Blue |
| ∧ | 840 | 379 | 5379 | Med. Beige-Brown |
| O | 841 | 378 | 5376 | Lt. Beige-Brown |
| \ | 842 | 388 | 5933 | Vy. Lt. Beige-Brown |

**12.** Iron the 12½" square of fusible interfacing onto the wrong side of the pillow back.

**13.** Make an 11"-square covered pillow form and assemble the pillow, as directed in "Covered Pillow Forms" and "Assembling a Pillow" on page 239.

## DESIGN OPTIONS

| Fabric Count | Design Area | Cutting Dimensions |
|---|---|---|
| 22 | 2¼" × 2¼" | 12¼" × 12¼" |
| 18 | 2¾" × 2¾" | 12¾" × 12¾" |
| 14 | 3½" × 3½" | 13½" × 13½" |
| 11 | 4½" × 4½" | 14½" × 14½" |

# HORACE AND HILDEGARDE WALLHANGING

*Big brother and li'l sis pose for a fabric "portrait." Gather calico scraps and start stitching! Add three-dimensional bows to gussy up your wallhanging.*

## SIZE

Wallhanging is 28½" × 31½"

## MATERIALS

★ ⅝ yard of 44"-wide navy floral fabric for the first border strips, bows, dress, and hatband
★ ¼ yard of 44"-wide cream print fabric for the second border strips and Horace's shirt and hat
★ 1⅜ yards of 44"-wide rose print fabric for the fourth border strips, center panel, and backing
★ ½ yard of 44"-wide navy print fabric for the third border strips and overalls
★ ⅛ yard of 44"-wide mint print fabric for the dress collar and cuffs and Hildegarde's bonnet
★ 1 yard of fusible webbing
★ ¼ yard of 44"-wide tea-dyed muslin for the bunny bodies*
★ Matching thread
★ 15" × 18" piece of tear-away stabilizer
★ Dark brown thread
★ 29" × 32" piece of fleece
★ ⅜ yard of ½"-wide navy grosgrain ribbon
★ Two 2½"-diameter pink buttons

*See "Tea Dyeing" on page 239 for instructions on tea dyeing.

## DIRECTIONS

**Note:** Wash, dry, and press all your fabrics before beginning this project. All seam allowances are ¼".

1. Prepare all patterns as directed in "Preparing Patterns" on page 236, using the patterns on pages 34 and 35.

2. From the navy floral, cut two 1½" × 17" first border strips, two 1½" × 18" first border strips, two 6" × 26" bow strips, and one 6" × 42" bow strip. From the cream print, cut four 2" × 20" second border strips. From the rose print, cut one 15" × 18" center panel piece, two 1½" × 29" fourth border strips, two 1½" × 30" fourth border strips, and one 29" × 32½" backing piece. From the navy print, cut two 4" × 23" third border strips and two 4" × 27" third border strips.

3. Fuse the fusible webbing to the remaining pieces of the cream print, navy floral, and navy print, as directed in "Fusible Webbing" on page 235. Also, fuse the fusible webbing to the muslin and the mint print.

4. Refer to "Machine Appliqué" on page 235 for directions on marking and cutting appliqué pieces. From the cream print, mark and cut one boy's shirt and one boy's hat. From the navy floral, mark and cut one girl's hatband and one girl's dress. From the navy print, mark and cut one boy's overalls. From the muslin, mark and cut one boy's right ear, one boy's face, one boy's left ear, one boy's hand, one boy's left foot, one boy's right foot, one girl's right ear, one girl's face, one girl's left ear, one girl's left arm and left foot, one

**Appliqué Placement Diagram**

girl's right arm, and one girl's right foot. From the mint print, mark and cut one girl's bonnet, one girl's collar, one girl's right cuff, and one girl's left cuff. Remove the paper backing from the appliqué pieces.

**5.** Center the appliqué pieces on the center panel, referring to the **Appliqué Placement Diagram,** layering as indicated by the dashed lines. Fuse in place as directed in "Fusible Webbing" on page 235.

**6.** Center and pin the tear-away stabilizer to the back of the center panel. Machine appliqué all edges of Horace and Hildegard using matching thread and following the solid lines on the **Accent Stitching Diagram** as a guide. Work long running stitches with dark brown thread as indicated by the dashed lines.

**7.** With right sides together and raw edges even, sew one 1½" × 18" first border strip to

**Accent Stitching Diagram**

the top and bottom of the center panel, as shown in **Diagram 1.** Press the seams toward the border. Sew one 1½" × 17" first border strip to each side of the center panel in the same manner; see **Diagram 2.** Press the seams toward the floral print.

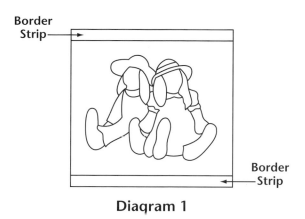

**Diagram 1**

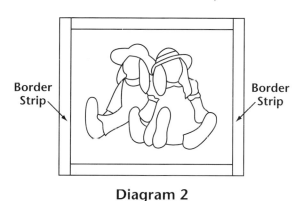

**Diagram 2**

**8.** Repeat Step 7 for the second, third, and fourth border strips.

**9.** Place the wallhanging top and backing right sides together, then place them on top of the fleece. Pin all three layers together. Sew around the outer edge, leaving an 8" opening along the bottom edge. Grade the seam allowance to reduce bulk. Turn the wallhanging right side out and whipstitch the opening closed.

**10.** Fold each bow strip in half lengthwise with right sides together. For each bow, sew across one short end and along the long raw edge. Trim the seam allowances and corners. Turn and press. Whipstitch the opening closed. Tie each strip in a bow. Hand tack one smaller bow to each upper corner of the center panel, allowing the bow ends to hang freely. Hand tack the large bow to the bot-

## COUNTRY TIPS
*from Alma Lynne*

Horace and Hildegarde can celebrate any holiday with a quick color scheme change. For Valentine's Day, make Horace's overalls red corduroy and his shirt white cotton. Hilde's dress could be a pretty red print and her hat could be accented with heart-shape charms.

For Easter, pastel colors are just the ticket. Make Hilde's dress out of a frilly white eyelet backed with soft blue and accented with medium blue collar and cuffs. Horace could wear stone-washed denim and a pastel plaid sports shirt. Machine appliqué brightly colored Easter eggs on the wide border.

Next comes the July 4th picnic! Horace could sport blue-and-white ticking bibs and a star-patterned shirt. Use burlap for his "straw" hat. Hildegarde will look dynamite in a red striped dress and matching sunhat. Instead of adding bows, make 3"-wide stuffed stars and hand tack them around the border.

For Halloween, dress Hilde and Horace as scarecrows. Hilde can wear a classic plaid wool jumper. Horace can chase autumn's chill away with tan overalls and a flannel shirt. And, the best part, stuff a little straw in their sleeves before machine appliquéing.

At Christmas, pull out all the stops for a fancy holiday party. Hilde looks simply smashing in a burgundy velvet dress. Embroider tiny holly leaves on her white collar and cuffs. Horace is regal in black wool overalls and ruffled tuxedo shirt (just add a bit of scalloped lace to the "buttonband" on his shirt). You could even add gold lamé piping between the center panel and the first border to give the wallhanging added glitz.

Whatever you decide, have fun while you're creating. Pick a theme and let your imagination roll! Horace and Hilde could even visit the 1960s in tie-dye shirts and peace-sign necklaces. Make a Victorian wallhanging in somber colors and elegant fabrics. I've given all the basics you'll need to get started—all you have to do is add the inspiration.

tom of the center panel, then hand tack the bow tails to the wallhanging, as shown in **Diagram 3.**

**11.** Tie the navy ribbon into a bow and hand tack it to the left side of Hildegarde's hatband. Sew the two buttons to Hildegarde's dress where indicated by the large dots on the pattern.

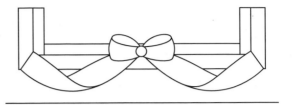

**Diagram 3**

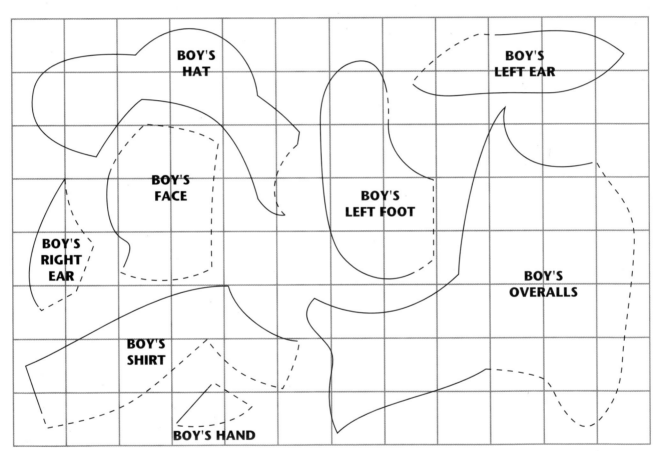

Enlarge 181%

**Horace and Hildegarde Wallhanging Patterns**

1 square = 1"

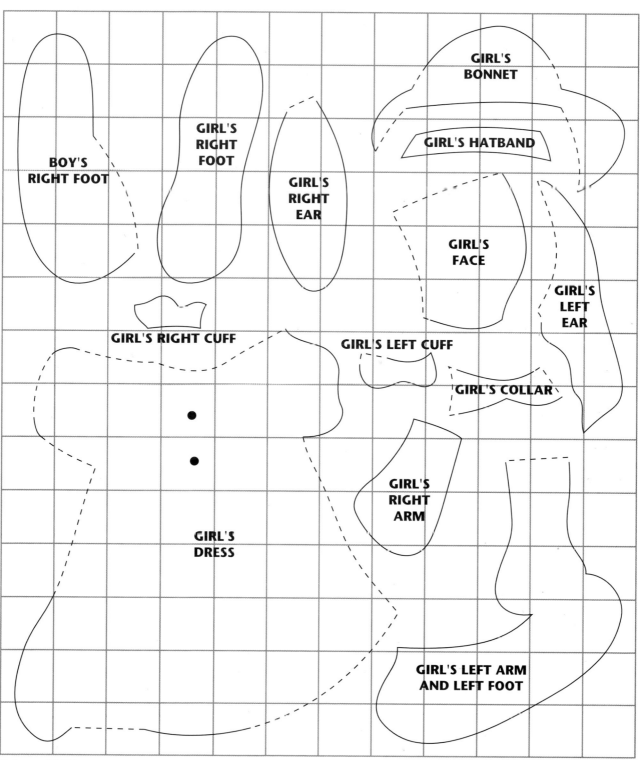

Enlarge 181%

**Horace and Hildegarde Wallhanging Patterns**

1 square = 1"

# COUNTRY CARROTS AFGHAN

*Cozy up with this afghan as you page through the spring seed catalogs. Then plant a whole garden of yummy carrots for this sweet bunny.*

## SIZE

Country carrots design area is 11" × 17" on 6 × 8 gauge

Heart and Checks design area is 4½" × 5" on 6 × 8 gauge

## MATERIALS

- ★ One 6 × 8-gauge Piper Glen afghan*
- ★ One skein of embroidery floss for each color listed in **Color Key** (unless otherwise indicated)
- ★ Size 22 tapestry needle
- ★ One 1½"-diameter white pom-pom
- ★ One 9 mm green bead
- ★ 1⅜ yards of ⅛"-wide green satin ribbon

*See "Buyer's Guide" on page 240 for ordering information.

## DIRECTIONS

**1.** Find the center of the afghan's center stitching area and the center of each corner stitching area; mark each center with a pin. Find the centers of the **Country Carrots Motif Chart** and the **Heart and Checks Motif Chart** by connecting the arrows.

**2.** Read the duplicate stitch basics in "The Stitches" on page 235. Matching the centers of the charts and the stitching areas, duplicate stitch the design using six strands of floss.

**3.** Wash and press the completed duplicate stitch design as directed in "Washing and Pressing" on page 235.

**4.** Sew the pom-pom over the white stitches on the bunny's tail. Sew the bead eye to the face as indicated by the large dot on the chart.

**5.** From the ribbon, cut one 32" length. Cut the remaining length in half. With the 32" length, make a four-loop bow, as shown in **Diagram 1.** Use the remaining lengths to wrap around the bow to secure it; tie them in a knot as shown. Clip all ribbon ends diagonally. Sew the ribbon to the bunny's neck.

◄——— 4" ———►

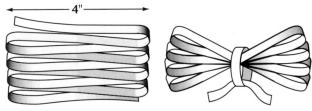

**Diagram 1**

### COUNTRY THOUGHTS
*from Alma Lynne*

A pretty garden, whether filled with flowers or vegetables, is a slice of heaven in a southerner's yard. And the little bunnies seem to enjoy the garden almost as much as I do.

There are a few hints I've learned to keep rabbits out of my garden. Dust cat box litter on the plants or lightly sprinkle cayenne pepper to discourage the invasion. Planting onions or soybeans nearby will also do the trick.

I have to admit, though, I love to have the little creatures around. I get such a kick out of watching them from my window. Maybe next year, I'll plant extra seeds just for them!

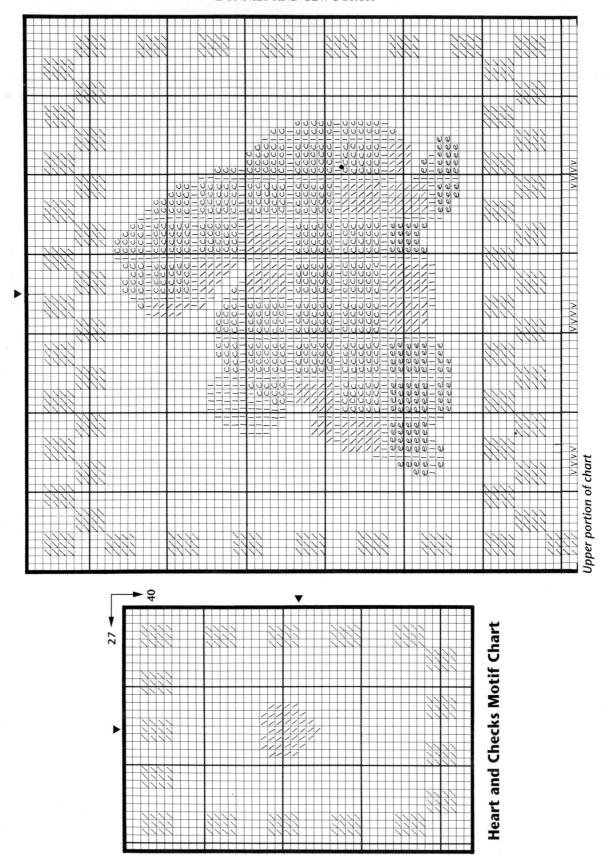

*Upper portion of chart*

**Heart and Checks Motif Chart**

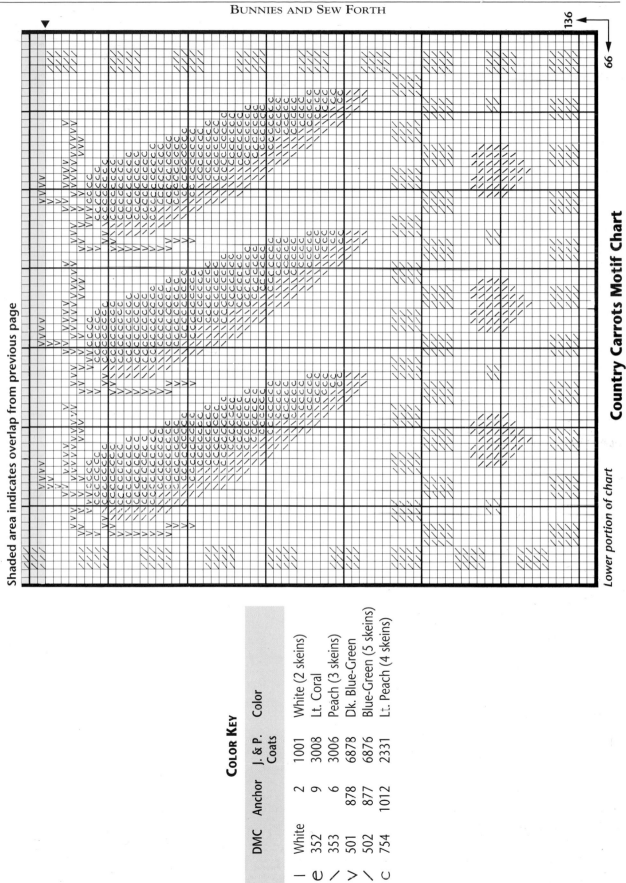

Shaded area indicates overlap from previous page

136

66

**Country Carrots Motif Chart**

*Lower portion of chart*

**COLOR KEY**

| | DMC | Anchor | J. & P. Coats | Color |
|---|---|---|---|---|
| | White | 2 | 1001 | White (2 skeins) |
| e | 352 | 9 | 3008 | Lt. Coral |
| / | 353 | 6 | 3006 | Peach (3 skeins) |
| > | 501 | 878 | 6878 | Dk. Blue-Green |
| \ | 502 | 877 | 6876 | Blue-Green (5 skeins) |
| C | 754 | 1012 | 2331 | Lt. Peach (4 skeins) |

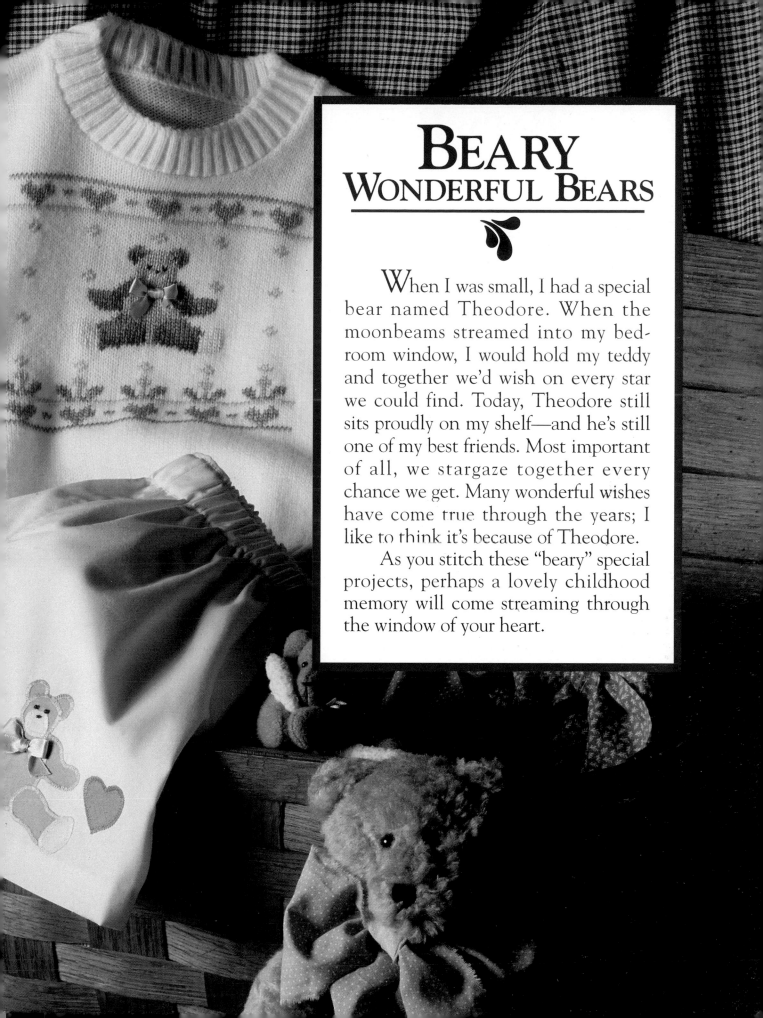

# BEARY
# WONDERFUL BEARS

When I was small, I had a special bear named Theodore. When the moonbeams streamed into my bedroom window, I would hold my teddy and together we'd wish on every star we could find. Today, Theodore still sits proudly on my shelf—and he's still one of my best friends. Most important of all, we stargaze together every chance we get. Many wonderful wishes have come true through the years; I like to think it's because of Theodore.

As you stitch these "beary" special projects, perhaps a lovely childhood memory will come streaming through the window of your heart.

# BABY BEARS CRIB GARLAND

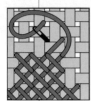

*These chubby bears celebrate the pleasures of babyhood—full bottles, soft diapers, and time for cuddling! Stitch each one or any combination of the four for an oh-so-cute garland to brighten baby's room.*

## SIZE

Design area for each pillow is 5" square (over two squares) on 18-count Tabby Cloth Finished size of each pillow is 6" square

## MATERIALS

- ★ Four 11" squares of 18-count daffodil Tabby Cloth
- ★ One skein of embroidery floss for each color listed in **Color Key**
- ★ Size 24 or 26 tapestry needle
- ★ Eight 7" squares of fusible interfacing
- ★ ¾ yard of light blue print fabric for the piping and backing
- ★ Matching thread
- ★ 3½ yards of ⅜"-diameter cording
- ★ Polyester fiberfill
- ★ Light blue heavy-duty quilting thread
- ★ 3 yards of ⅜"-wide blue satin ribbon
- ★ 1 yard of ⅜"-wide yellow satin ribbon

## DIRECTIONS

**Note:** All seam allowances are ½". After sewing, trim all seam allowances to ¼" to reduce bulk.

**1.** Prepare the edges of each Tabby Cloth square as directed in "Preparing Fabric Edges" on page 232. Find the center of each square and mark with a pin. Find the center of each of the **Baby Bears Crib Garland Charts** by connecting the arrows.

**2.** Matching the center of the chart and the square, and using two strands of floss, begin stitching at the center point, working each cross-stitch over two threads. Work outward until the entire design is complete.

**3.** Work all backstitching with one strand of floss. Backstitch the bears and the diaper pins with black-brown, the diapers and the bottles with light navy blue, and the bottle nipples with medium rose.

**4.** Wash and press each completed cross-stitch piece as directed in "Washing and Pressing" on page 233.

**5.** With the design centered, trim each completed cross-stitch piece to 7" square. Iron a 7" square of fusible interfacing to the wrong side of each cross-stitched square for stability.

**6.** From the light blue, cut four 7" squares for the pillow backs and one 2" × 120" bias strip for the piping.

**7.** Make 120" of corded piping as directed in "Making Corded Piping" on page 238, and cut it into four 30" lengths. Sew one length of piping to each pillow front as directed in "Sewing On the Piping" on page 238. Do *not* trim the seam allowances.

**8.** Iron a 7" square of fusible interfacing to the wrong side of each pillow back.

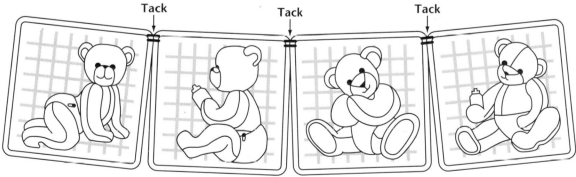

**Diagram 1**

**9.** Assemble each pillow as directed in "Assembling a Pillow" on page 239.

**10.** Using quilting thread, tack the pillows together with two or three stitches at the upper corners; see **Diagram 1.**

**11.** From the blue and yellow ribbons, cut three 12" lengths each. Holding one blue and one yellow length as if they were one, tie a bow and cut the ends diagonally. Repeat for the remaining two bows. Tack one bow to each of the joined upper corners of the pillows.

Tack                                                                                    Tack

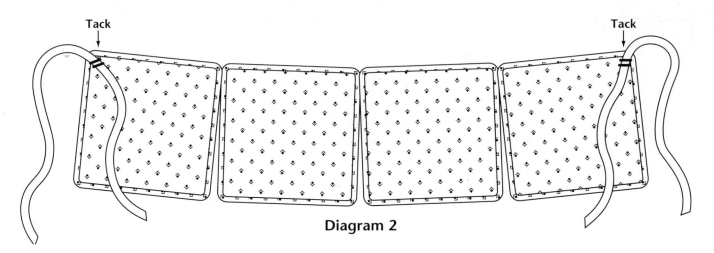

**Diagram 2**

**12.** Cut the remaining blue ribbon in half to make the garland ties. Tack the center of one length to the back of one end pillow at the upper outside corner. Repeat for the remaining length. See **Diagram 2.**

### DESIGN OPTIONS

| Fabric Count | Design Area | Cutting Dimensions |
|---|---|---|
| 22 | 2" × 2" | 12" × 12" |
| 18 | 2½" × 2½" | 12½" × 12½" |
| 14 | 3¼" × 3¼" | 13¼" × 13¼" |
| 11 | 4⅛" × 4⅛" | 14⅛" × 14⅛" |

## COUNTRY TIPS
*from Alma Lynne*

I've charted the background lines in the design with the symbols Z and \\, each representing shades of blue. If you wish to make these lines in pink for a little girl, stitch the symbol Z in light rose and the symbol \\ in rose. Change the piping and backing fabric to a pretty pink floral and the blue ribbons to a soft pink. It's as easy as changing baby's diaper, isn't it?

### COLOR KEY

| | DMC | Anchor | J. & P. Coats | Color |
|---|---|---|---|---|
| • | White | 2 | 1001 | White |
| | 312 | 979 | 7979 | Lt. Navy Blue |
| U | 322 | 978 | 7978 | Vy. Lt. Navy Blue |
| \\ | 334 | 977 | 7977 | Med. Baby Blue |
| | 335 | 38 | 3283 | Rose |
| 3 | 433 | 358 | 5471 | Med. Brown |
| X | 434 | 310 | 5000 | Lt. Brown |
| V | 435 | 1046 | 5371 | Vy. Lt. Brown |
| O | 436 | 1045 | 5943 | Tan |
| / | 437 | 362 | 5942 | Lt. Tan |
| — | 738 | 361 | 5375 | Vy. Lt. Tan |
| I | 739 | 387 | 5369 | Ultra Vy. Lt. Tan |
| \ | 775 | 128 | 7031 | Vy. Lt. Baby Blue |
| 8 | 801 | 359 | 5472 | Dk. Coffee Brown |
| | 899 | 52 | 3282 | Med. Rose |
| Z | 3325 | 129 | 7976 | Lt. Baby Blue |
| ∧ | 3326 | 36 | 3126 | Lt. Rose |
| ■ | 3371 | 382 | 5382 | Black-Brown |

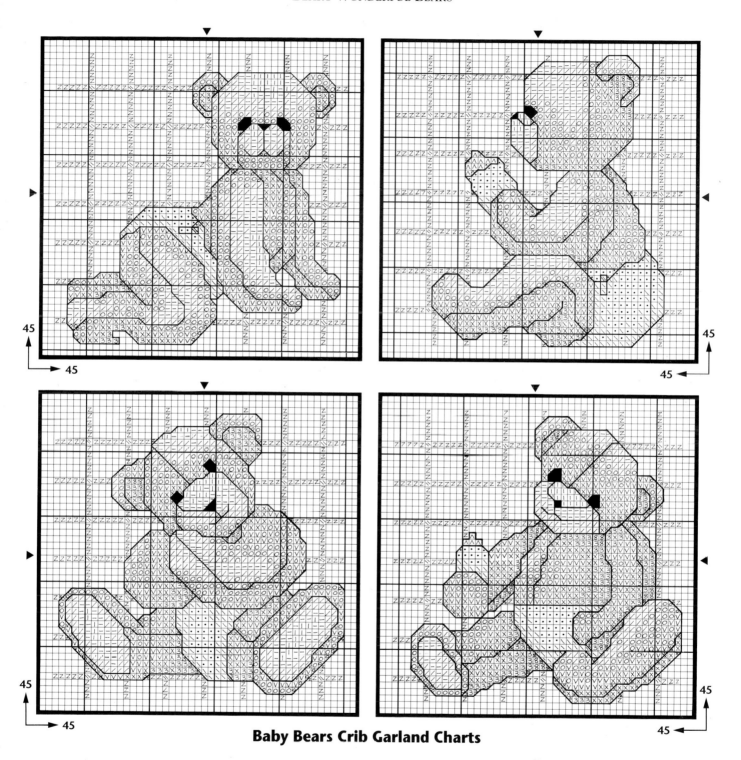

**Baby Bears Crib Garland Charts**

# BEAR ON WHEELS DUET

*Take a trip on the Nostalgia Express when you stitch this favorite childhood pull-toy. Accent the bear on wheels with primitive stars and a rustic alphabet and you have the makings of a country classic.*

## BEAR ON WHEELS PICTURE

### SIZE

Design area is 7" × 7¼" on 14-count Aida

### MATERIALS

★ One 17" × 17¼" piece of 14-count ivory Aida
★ One skein of embroidery floss for each color listed in **Color Key**
★ Size 22 or 24 tapestry needle

### DIRECTIONS

1. Prepare the edges of the Aida as directed in "Preparing Fabric Edges" on page 232. Find the center of the Aida and mark it with a pin. Find the center of the **Bear on Wheels Chart** by connecting the arrows.

2. Matching the centers of the chart and the Aida, and using two strands of floss, begin stitching at the center point, working outward until the entire design is complete.

3. Using one strand of floss, backstitch the border lines with dark garnet; work all remaining backstitches with black. Work the French knots for the wheel axles with two strands of black.

4. Wash and press the completed cross-stitch as directed in "Washing and Pressing" on page 233.

5. Mat and frame as desired.

### DESIGN OPTIONS

| Fabric Count | Design Area | Cutting Dimensions |
| --- | --- | --- |
| 22 | 4½" × 4⅝" | 14½" × 14⅝" |
| 18 | 5½" × 5⅝" | 15½" × 15⅝" |
| 14 | 7" × 7¼" | 17" × 17¼" |
| 11 | 8⅞" × 9⅛" | 18⅞" × 19⅛" |

## BEAR ON WHEELS PILLOW

### SIZE

Design area is 5½" square (over two threads) on 27-count Linda cloth

Finished pillow size is 11½" square, including ruffle

### MATERIALS

★ One 11½" square of 27-count celery green Linda cloth
★ One skein of embroidery floss for each color listed in **Color Key**
★ Size 26 tapestry needle
★ ⅝ yard of 44"-wide dark green plaid fabric for the borders, ruffle, and backing
★ ⅜ yard of 44"-wide burgundy print fabric for the piping

* Matching thread
* One 9½" square of fleece
* 1⅛ yards of ¼"-diameter cording
* One 9½" square of fusible interfacing
* ⅜ yard of 44"-wide muslin for the covered pillow form
* Polyester fiberfill
* 1 yard of ⅝"-wide burgundy grosgrain ribbon

## DIRECTIONS

**Note:** All seam allowances are ½", unless otherwise indicated. After sewing, trim all seam allowances to ¼" to reduce bulk.

**1.** Prepare the edges of the Linda cloth as directed in "Preparing Fabric Edges" on page 232. Find the center of the Linda cloth and mark it with a pin. The center of the bear-on-wheels portion of the **Bear on Wheels Chart** is indicated by the gray square; the star background will continue above the center for eight rows.

**2.** Matching the centers of the chart and the Linda cloth, and using two strands of floss, begin stitching at the center point, working the bear-on-wheels and the star background around the bear. Continue the background by stitching eight additional rows of stars above the center point.

**3.** Backstitch the bear with one strand of black.

**4.** Wash and press the completed cross-stitch piece as directed in "Washing and Pressing" on page 233.

**5.** With the design centered, trim the Linda cloth to a 6½" square. From the green, cut two 2½" × 6½" strips and two 2½" × 9½" strips for the border, two 5½" × 44" strips for the ruffle, and one 9½" square for the pillow back. From the burgundy print, cut one 1½" × 40" bias strip for the piping.

**6.** With right sides together and raw edges even, sew the 2½" × 6½" border strips to the top and bottom of the completed cross-stitch, as shown in **Diagram 1.** Press the seams toward the borders. Sew one 2½" × 9½" border strip to each side of the cross-stitch in the same manner; see **Diagram 2.** Press the seams toward the borders.

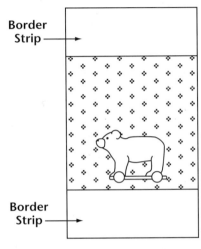

**Diagram 1**

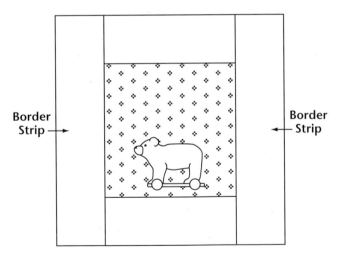

**Diagram 2**

**7.** Make 40" of corded piping and sew the piping to the pillow front, as directed in "Making Corded Piping" on page 238 and "Sewing On the Piping" on page 238. Do *not* trim the seam allowance.

**8.** Sew the 9½" square of fleece to the wrong side of the pillow top along all four edges, using a ⅜" seam allowance.

**9.** With right sides together and raw edges even, sew the short ends of the two 5½" × 44" strips together to form one continuous ruffle; see **Diagram 3.** Press the seams open. With wrong sides together, fold the loop in half lengthwise and press. Sew a line of gath-

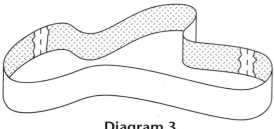

**Diagram 3**

ering stitches ⅜" from the raw edges through both layers of the ruffle. Fold the ruffle in half to find the midpoints, and place a pin at these points. Match the midpoints of the ruffle and mark the quarterpoints with pins; see **Diagram 4.**

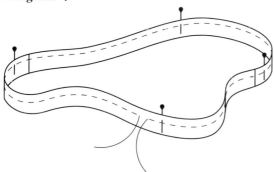

**Diagram 4**

**10.** Sew the ruffle to the pillow top, referring to "Ruffles" on page 239.

**11.** Iron the fusible interfacing onto the wrong side of the pillow back.

## COUNTRY TIPS
*from Alma Lynne*

Try using the Bear on Wheels to inspire a corner in your home. Stitch a row of golden stars on rustic linen for a country shelf edging. Use the tiny tulip motif on Ribband for a pretty basket trim. Or stitch the entire center portion of the design, then use the letters in the border to spell out popular country sentiments like "Hello Friends" or "For a Special Friend."

I always encourage stitchers to use my designs in creative ways. It's not necessary for you to always cross-stitch a chart as presented; select the individual motifs you like best, then stitch them on tote bags, jelly jar lids, bookmarks—whatever strikes your fancy!

**12.** Make an 8"-square covered pillow form and assemble the pillow, as directed in "Covered Pillow Forms" and "Assembling a Pillow" on page 239.

**13.** Cut the ribbon in half. Tie each length into a bow and trim the ends diagonally. Tack one bow to the upper left corner and one bow to the lower right corner of the Linda cloth.

### DESIGN OPTIONS

| Fabric Count | Design Area | Cutting Dimensions |
| --- | --- | --- |
| 22 | 3⅜" × 3⅜" | 13⅜" × 13⅜" |
| 18 | 4" × 4" | 14" × 14" |
| 14 | 5¼" × 5¼" | 15¼" × 15¼" |
| 11 | 6⅝" × 6⅝" | 16⅝" × 16⅝" |

## COLOR KEY

| | DMC | Anchor | J. & P. Coats | Color |
|---|---|---|---|---|
| • | White | 2 | 1001 | White |
| ■ | 310 | 403 | 8403 | Black |
| Ø | 433 | 358 | 5471 | Med. Brown |
| V | 434 | 310 | 5000 | Lt. Brown |
| L | 435 | 1046 | 5371 | Vy. Lt. Brown |
| C | 436 | 1045 | 5943 | Tan |
| ＼ | 437 | 362 | 5942 | Lt. Tan |
| 4 | 498 | 1005 | 3000 | Dk. Christmas Red |
| Z | 500 | 683 | 6880 | Vy. Dk. Blue-Green |
| ⊃ | 501 | 878 | 6878 | Dk. Blue-Green |
| 7 | 676 | 891 | — | Lt. Old Gold |
| — | 738 | 361 | 5375 | Vy. Lt. Tan |
| X | 801 | 359 | 5472 | Dk. Coffee Brown |
| O | 814 | 45 | 3044 | Dk. Garnet |
| 6 | 816 | 1005 | 3021 | Garnet |

**Bear on Wheels Chart**

98 ← 101

# SANTA BEAR

 *Santa Bear is comin' to town! And he's wearing the new out-fit Mrs. Bear just finished. His spiffy knickers and gold-accented poet's shirt are right in style. Add a sporty vest with con-trasting lapels and he's ready for his dashing midnight ride!*

## SIZE

19" tall

## MATERIALS

* ⅞ yard of 44"-wide brown wool fabric for the body
* ⅞ yard of 44"-wide Christmas print fabric for the shirt and toy sack cuff
* ½ yard of 44"-wide black-and-white check fabric for the knickers
* ¼ yard of 44"-wide black corduroy for the boots
* ¾ yard of 44"-wide burgundy corduroy for the hat, cummerbund, and vest lining
* ⅝ yard of 44"-wide dark green solid fabric for the toy sack, vest, and hat cuff
* Matching thread
* Polyester fiberfill
* 1 skein of black embroidery floss for facial embroidery
* Brown buttonhole twist thread
* Soft-sculpture doll needle
* ⅜ yard of 1"-wide burgundy satin ribbon for the shirt cuffs
* 1 yard of ½"-wide black satin ribbon for the knicker cuffs
* 2 snaps

* Two ½"-diameter pearl shank buttons for the vest lapels
* ½ yard of ⅜"-wide white grosgrain ribbon for the beard
* 1 package of white curly hair for the beard
* ½ yard of ⅜"-wide green satin ribbon for the hat
* One ½"-diameter gold jingle bell for the hat
* 1 pair of gold wire glasses to fit a 3"–4" doll head
* 1 yard of ⅜"-diameter gold metallic cording for the toy sack

## DIRECTIONS

**Note:** All seam allowances are ¼". Santa Bear is for decorative purposes only; his clothing cannot be removed.

**1.** Prepare all patterns as directed in "Preparing Patterns" on page 236, using the patterns on pages 56 and 57.

**2.** Referring to "Cut-and-Sew Method" on page 236, from the wool, cut one head gusset, one side head and one side head reverse, two bodies and two bodies reverse, two ears and two ears reverse, two legs and two legs reverse, and two arms and two arms reverse. From the Christmas print, cut two shirts and one 6" × 23½" piece for the toy sack cuff. From the black-and-white check, cut two knickers. From the black corduroy, cut two boots and two boots reverse. From the burgundy corduroy, cut two hats. Also cut one vest back, and one vest front and one vest front reverse for the vest lining. Cut one 4½" × 16½" piece with the corduroy wales running crosswise for Santa Bear's cummerbund. From the green solid, cut one vest

## COUNTRY THOUGHTS
*from Alma Lynne*

If you want a cute bear to give as a gift, use the Santa Bear patterns to get started. For a baby gift, make the bear out of pink or blue seersucker. Tie a bright ribbon bow around the neck for added charm.

For an older child, use a wild print from your local fabric store. Of course you'll find teddy bear prints and puppy dog fabric, but you'll also find skateboard prints, neon fabrics, and soft fake furs. Take a few hours and browse to create a one-of-a-kind gift. You'll discover all sorts of special accents on the store shelves—faceted jewel eyes, elegant metallic laces, doll hats, chairs, and more!

For a neighbor or special friend, choose a rich moiré taffeta fabric and add a Victorian crazy quilt vest. Finish with a purchased bonnet and beaded handbag. Or design a classic country bear using mismatched homespun fabrics. When you attach the arms and legs, accent your sewing stitches with antique buttons. Then add a jute bow around the neck!

back, one vest front and one vest front reverse, two hat cuffs, and one 12" × 24" piece for the toy sack.

**3.** With right sides together, sew two bodies together along the center front and back seam to form the front of Santa Bear's body. Clip the curves and press. Repeat with the two remaining bodies to form the back of Santa Bear's body.

**4.** With right sides together, sew the two bodies together at the sides and neck, leaving the bottom edge open for turning. Clip the curves and press. Turn and stuff the body firmly. Whipstitch the opening closed.

**5.** With right sides together, pin the head gusset to one side head, matching the notches at the nose and neck. Sew along the top of the head between these two points. Repeat for the other side head. Clip the curves and press.

**6.** With right sides together, pin and sew from the dot at the tip of the nose to the front neck edge. Leave the neck area open for turning. Clip the curves, turn, and press. Stuff firmly. Whipstitch the neck edge closed.

**7.** With right sides together, sew around the curved edge of two ears, leaving the straight edge open for turning. Repeat for the other ear. Clip the curves, turn, and press the ears flat. Fold ¼" on the open end of the ears to the inside. Whipstitch the opening closed. Hand sew the ears to the head where indicated on the Side Head pattern.

**8.** Hand sew the head to the body at the neck, using the buttonhole twist.

**9.** Using six strands of floss, embroider the eyes and nose in satin stitch and the mouth in stem stitch, referring to the **Face Embroidery Diagram** for placement and to "Facial Features" on page 237 for stitch details.

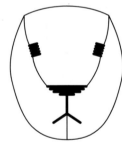

**Face Embroidery Diagram**

**10.** With right sides together, sew two legs together, leaving an opening at the upper back for turning. Clip the curves. Turn, press, and stuff firmly. Whipstitch the openings closed. Repeat for the remaining leg and the arms.

**11.** Knot a 20" length of buttonhole twist at one end and thread it through the doll needle. Matching the large dots, run the needle from the outside of one arm through to the inside of the arm, then through the body and the other arm. Pass the needle back through the arms and body several times to secure. Knot tightly. Repeat for the legs. Set Santa Bear aside.

**12.** With right sides together, sew the shirt front and back along the shoulder and underarm seams. Clip the underarm seam. Turn and press. Turn under ¼" on the neck and wrist edges and press.

**13.** Run gathering threads around the neck and wrist edges. Place the shirt on Santa Bear. Pull the gathering threads tightly to fit the neck and wrists and knot them tightly.

**14.** Cut the burgundy ribbon in half. Wrap one length around each wrist, covering the shirt sleeve by ½". Whipstitch the ribbon ends together.

**15.** With right sides together, sew one boot and one boot reverse together, leaving the top edge open. Clip the curves, turn, and press lightly. Repeat for the remaining boot. Place the boots on Santa Bear's feet.

**16.** With right sides together, sew the knickers front and back together along the sides and inseams. Clip the inseam curve. Turn and press. Turn under ¼" on the waist and ankle edges.

**17.** Run gathering threads around the waist and ankle edges. Place the knickers on Santa Bear and pull the gathering threads to fit. Knot the thread.

**18.** Cut the black ribbon in half. Wrap one length around each ankle, covering the knickers by ¼"; tie it in a bow and clip the ends diagonally.

**19.** Fold the cummerbund in half lengthwise with right sides together. Sew across one short raw edge and the long raw edge. Turn it right side out, press, and whipstitch closed. Wrap the cummerbund around Santa's waist

and overlap the ends. Mark positions for two snaps at the center back and sew on the snaps.

**20.** With right sides together and matching side seams, sew the vest fronts to the vest back at the sides; press the seams open. Repeat for the vest lining. With right sides together, sew the vest to the vest lining, leaving the shoulder edges open. Trim the seams, clip the curves, and notch the underarm. Carefully turn the vest right side out. With right sides together, sew the shoulder seams of the vest fabric only, being careful not to catch the vest lining in the seam. Whipstitch the shoulder seams of the lining closed.

**21.** Place the vest on Santa Bear. Turn the lapels back 1" to expose the lining; tack them in place by sewing one pearl button on each lapel, being sure to sew through all clothing layers.

**22.** To make Santa Bear's beard, place the white ribbon on a flat surface. Separate the beard hair to a width of approximately 10". Place the beard in the center of the ribbon, being careful to cover the top edge of the ribbon; see the **Beard Assembly Diagram.**

**Beard Assembly Diagram**

**23.** Hand tack the beard to the ribbon by taking tiny stitches through the nonvisible areas of the beard. Place the center of the beard under Santa Bear's mouth and bring the ribbon ends over his ears to the back of his head. Hand tack the ribbon ends in place. Trim and groom the beard if necessary.

**24.** To make Santa Bear's hat, fold one hat cuff in half lengthwise with wrong sides together. Press the fold flat. With right sides together and notches matched, sew the hat cuff to one hat. Press the hat flat, having the seam toward the hat. Repeat for the remaining hat cuff and hat. With right sides together, sew the hats together along the two long edges. Trim the seam allowance at the tip of the hat. Turn and press.

**25.** Tie the green ribbon in a bow and trim the ends diagonally. Hand tack the bow and the jingle bell to the tip of the hat.

**26.** Place the glasses on Santa Bear's face.

**27.** To make the toy sack, fold the 12" × 24" piece in half crosswise with right sides together and sew the side seams. Turn the sack right side out and press.

**28.** Sew the short ends of the sack cuff together to form a loop. Hem one long edge by turning under ¼" and sewing. Do not turn right side out. Slip the cuff over the toy sack, having right sides together and seams aligned. Sew around the upper edge. Turn the cuff to the inside and press. Fold half of the cuff to the outside of the sack and press. Hand tack the cuff in place at the side seams. Wrap the gold cord around the sack and tie it in a bow.

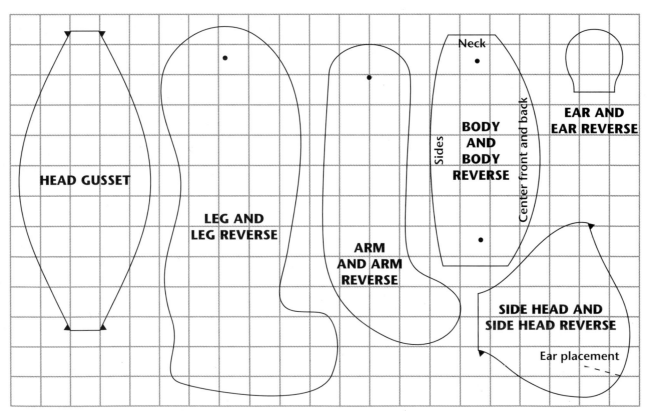

Enlarge 320%

**Santa Bear Patterns**
1 square = 1"

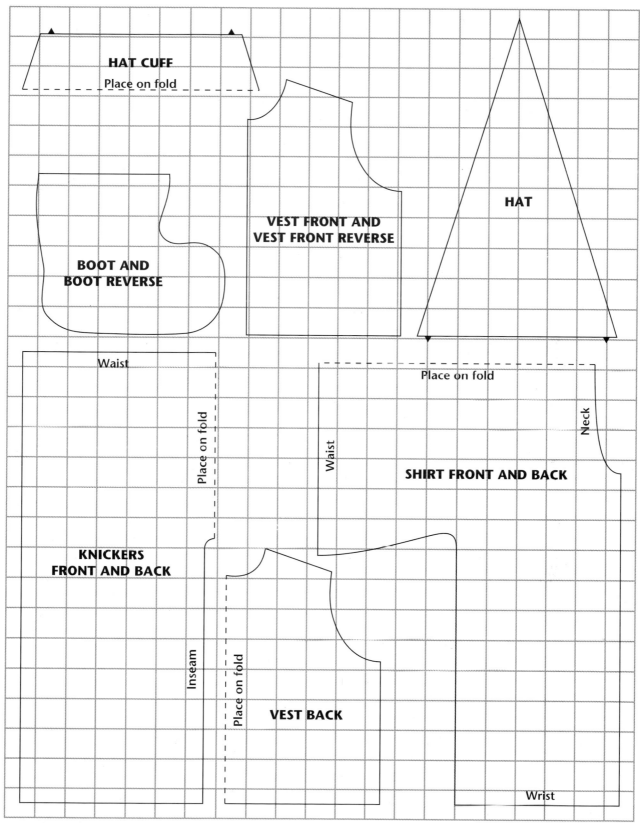

**HAT CUFF**
Place on fold

**BOOT AND BOOT REVERSE**

**VEST FRONT AND VEST FRONT REVERSE**

**HAT**

Waist

Place on fold

Place on fold

Waist

Neck

**SHIRT FRONT AND BACK**

**KNICKERS FRONT AND BACK**

Inseam

Place on fold

**VEST BACK**

Wrist

Enlarge 320%

**Santa Bear Outfit Patterns**

1 square = 1"

# THEODORE IN SPRINGTIME PICTURE

*Is spring your favorite time of year? Celebrate its glorious arrival by cross-stitching Theodore with his freshly potted geraniums. Tie on a gentleman's bow and he's ready to head outside to enjoy the warm sunshine.*

## SIZE

Design area is 8¾" × 10¼" (over two threads) on 28-count linen

## MATERIALS

★ One 18¾" × 20¼" piece of 28-count periwinkle pastel linen
★ One skein of embroidery floss for each color listed in **Color Key**
★ Size 26 tapestry needle

## DIRECTIONS

**1.** Prepare the edges of the linen as directed in "Preparing Fabric Edges" on page 232. Find the center of the linen and mark it with a pin. Find the center of the **Theodore in Springtime Picture Chart** by connecting the arrows.

**2.** Matching the centers of the chart and the linen, and using two strands of floss, begin cross-stitching at the center point, working each cross-stitch over two threads. Work the entire window frame, the hearts, and Theodore's shadow in half cross-stitch. Work outward until the entire design is complete.

**3.** Work all backstitching with one strand of floss. Backstitch Theodore with black-brown, his bow with medium navy blue, the flower pot with light navy blue, the window with dark pewter gray, the hearts with baby pink, and the leaves with very dark pistachio green.

**4.** Wash and press the completed cross-stitch as directed in "Washing and Pressing" on page 233.

**5.** Mat and frame as desired.

### DESIGN OPTIONS

| Fabric Count | Design Area | Cutting Dimensions |
|---|---|---|
| 22 | 5⅝" × 6½" | 15⅝" × 16½" |
| 18 | 6⅞" × 8" | 16⅞" × 18" |
| 14 | 8¾" × 10¼" | 18¾" × 20¼" |
| 11 | 11⅛" × 13" | 21⅛" × 23" |

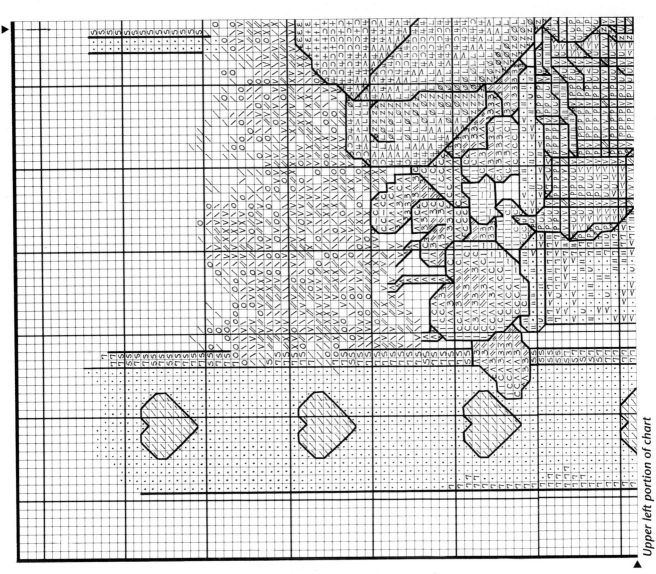

*Upper left portion of chart*

## Theodore in Springtime Picture Chart
### COLOR KEY

| | DMC | Anchor | J. & P. Coats | Color |
|---|---|---|---|---|
| • | White | 2 | 1001 | White |
| | 311 | 148 | 7980 | Med. Navy Blue |
| ‖ | 312 | 979 | 7979 | Lt. Navy Blue |
| 3 | 319 | 218 | 6246 | Vy. Dk. Pistachio Green |
| C | 320 | 215 | 6017 | Med. Pistachio Green |
| < | 322 | 978 | 7978 | Vy. Lt. Navy Blue |
| X | 326 | 59 | 3401 | Vy. Dk. Rose |
| // | 335 | 38 | 3283 | Rose |

| | DMC | Anchor | J. & P. Coats | Color |
|---|---|---|---|---|
| ∧ | 367 | 217 | 6018 | Dk. Pistachio Green |
| I | 368 | 214 | 6016 | Lt. Pistachio Green |
| — | 369 | 1043 | 6015 | Vy. Lt. Pistachio Green |
| | 413 | 401 | 8514 | Dk. Pewter Gray |
| S | 415 | 398 | 8398 | Pearl Gray |
| L | 433 | 358 | 5471 | Med. Brown |
| > | 434 | 310 | 5000 | Lt. Brown |
| 4 | 435 | 1046 | 5371 | Vy. Lt. Brown |

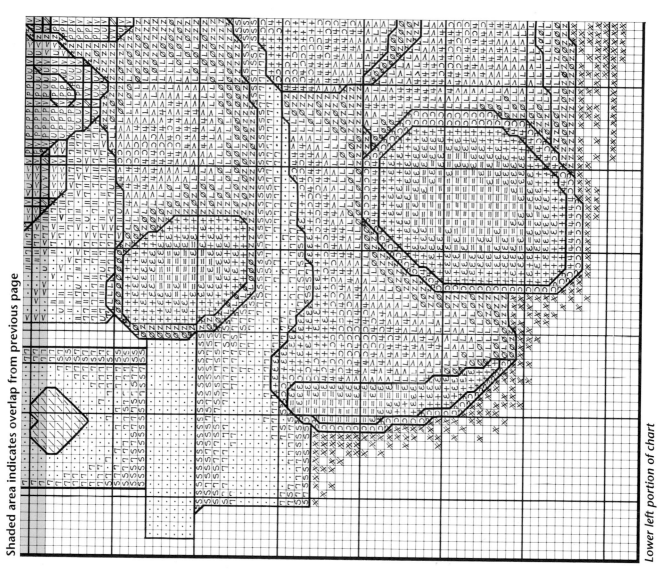

Shaded area indicates overlap from previous page

Lower left portion of chart

## Theodore in Springtime Picture Chart
### Color Key

| | DMC | Anchor | J. & P. Coats | Color |
|---|---|---|---|---|
| ⊃ | 436 | 1045 | 5943 | Tan |
| + | 437 | 362 | 5942 | Lt. Tan |
| ⋇ | 535 | — | 8400 | Vy. Lt. Ash Gray |
| ε | 738 | 361 | 5375 | Vy. Lt. Tan |
| = | 739 | 387 | 5369 | Ultra Vy. Lt. Tan |
| 7 | 762 | 234 | 8510 | Vy. Lt. Pearl Gray |
| P | 775 | 128 | 7031 | Vy. Lt. Baby Blue |
| O | 776 | 24 | 3281 | Med. Pink |

| | DMC | Anchor | J. & P. Coats | Color |
|---|---|---|---|---|
| Ø | 801 | 359 | 5472 | Dk. Coffee Brown |
| / | 818 | 23 | 3281 | Baby Pink |
| \\ | 890 | 218 | 6021 | Ultra Dk. Pistachio Green |
| Z | 898 | 360 | 5476 | Vy. Dk. Coffee Brown |
| V | 899 | 52 | 3282 | Med. Rose |
| U | 3325 | 129 | 7976 | Lt. Baby Blue |
| \ | 3326 | 36 | 3126 | Lt. Rose |
| ● | 3371 | 382 | 5382 | Black-Brown |

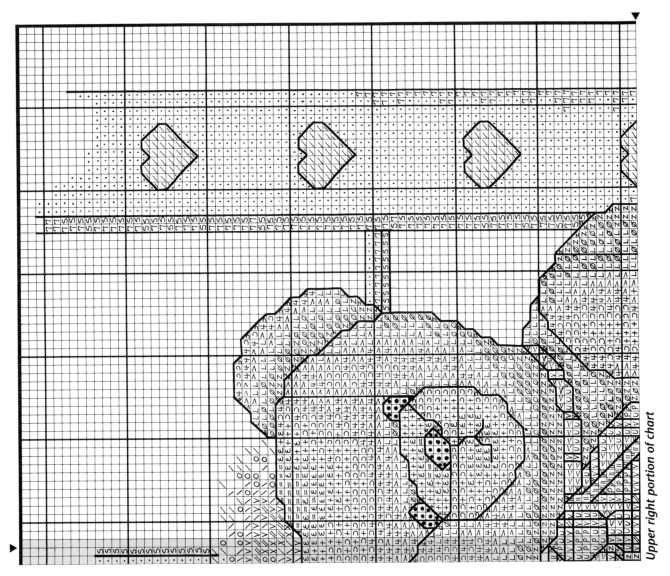

*Upper right portion of chart*

## Theodore in Springtime Picture Chart
### COLOR KEY

| | DMC | Anchor | J. & P. Coats | Color |
|---|---|---|---|---|
| • | White | 2 | 1001 | White |
| | 311 | 148 | 7980 | Med. Navy Blue |
| ‖ | 312 | 979 | 7979 | Lt. Navy Blue |
| 3 | 319 | 218 | 6246 | Vy. Dk. Pistachio Green |
| C | 320 | 215 | 6017 | Med. Pistachio Green |
| < | 322 | 978 | 7978 | Vy. Lt. Navy Blue |
| × | 326 | 59 | 3401 | Vy. Dk. Rose |
| // | 335 | 38 | 3283 | Rose |

| | DMC | Anchor | J. & P. Coats | Color |
|---|---|---|---|---|
| ∧ | 367 | 217 | 6018 | Dk. Pistachio Green |
| ·I | 368 | 214 | 6016 | Lt. Pistachio Green |
| — | 369 | 1043 | 6015 | Vy. Lt. Pistachio Green |
| | 413 | 401 | 8514 | Dk. Pewter Gray |
| S | 415 | 398 | 8398 | Pearl Gray |
| L | 433 | 358 | 5471 | Med. Brown |
| > | 434 | 310 | 5000 | Lt. Brown |
| 4 | 435 | 1046 | 5371 | Vy. Lt. Brown |

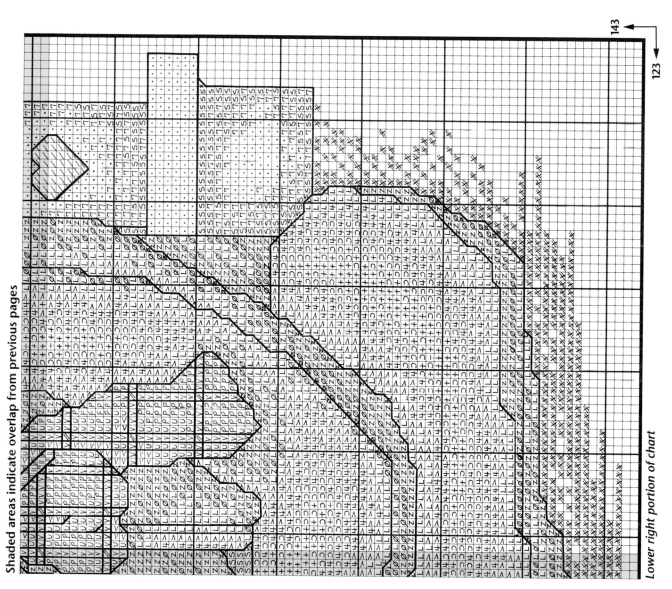

## Theodore in Springtime Picture Chart
### COLOR KEY

| | DMC | Anchor | J. & P. Coats | Color | | DMC | Anchor | J. & P. Coats | Color |
|---|---|---|---|---|---|---|---|---|---|
| ⊃ | 436 | 1045 | 5943 | Tan | Ø | 801 | 359 | 5472 | Dk. Coffee Brown |
| + | 437 | 362 | 5942 | Lt. Tan | / | 818 | 23 | 3281 | Baby Pink |
| ✕ | 535 | — | 8400 | Vy. Lt. Ash Gray | \\ | 890 | 218 | 6021 | Ultra Dk. Pistachio Green |
| Ɛ | 738 | 361 | 5375 | Vy. Lt. Tan | Z | 898 | 360 | 5476 | Vy. Dk. Coffee Brown |
| = | 739 | 387 | 5369 | Ultra Vy. Lt. Tan | V | 899 | 52 | 3282 | Med. Rose |
| 7 | 762 | 234 | 8510 | Vy. Lt. Pearl Gray | U | 3325 | 129 | 7976 | Lt. Baby Blue |
| P | 775 | 128 | 7031 | Vy. Lt. Baby Blue | \ | 3326 | 36 | 3126 | Lt. Rose |
| O | 776 | 24 | 3281 | Med. Pink | ● | 3371 | 382 | 5382 | Black-Brown |

# A BEARY LITTLE BEAR ENSEMBLE

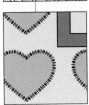

*The little darling who receives this ensemble as a gift just won't want to grow out of it. You can easily finish both pieces in one weekend! Just duplicate stitch innocent looking teddy with country-style hearts and tulips. Then machine appliqué the same bear in fabric.*

## BEARY LITTLE BEAR SWEATER

### SIZE

Design area is 8½" × 10⅞" on 6 × 8 gauge

### MATERIALS

★ One 6 × 8-gauge child's stockinette stitch white pullover sweater
★ One skein of embroidery floss for each color listed in **Color Key**
★ Size 22 tapestry needle
★ ¼ yard of ⅜"-wide green satin ribbon
★ One black seed bead

### DIRECTIONS

1. Plan the placement of the Beary Little Bear design on your sweater. You will need room for at least 72 vertical stitches on the sweater front. On the model, I counted down 42 vertical stitches from the center front neckline and marked it with a pin; this was the center stitch of my design. For your sweater, you may follow the directions above or you can center the design vertically by counting the number of vertical stitches and dividing by two; mark the center stitch with a pin. Find the center of the **Beary Little Bear Sweater Chart** by connecting the arrows.

2. Read the duplicate stitch basics in "The Stitches" on page 235. Matching the center of the chart with the marked stitch on the sweater, duplicate stitch the design using six strands of floss.

3. Wash and press the completed duplicate stitch design as directed in "Washing and Pressing" on page 235.

4. Tie the ribbon in a bow and sew it to the bear's neck for a bow tie. Clip the ribbon ends diagonally. Sew the bead to the bear's nose at the large dot.

## BEARY LITTLE BEAR SHORTS

### SIZE

Beary Little Bear motif is 3" × 6"

### MATERIALS

★ One pair of white shorts with at least 7"-wide leg openings*
★ Small scraps of tan, muslin, and pink fabrics
★ ¼ yard of fusible webbing
★ One 4" × 7" piece of tear-away stabilizer
★ Matching thread
★ ¼ yard of ⅜"-wide green satin ribbon
★ Three dark brown seed beads

*The shorts can be made from patterns available at most fabric shops. Complete all machine appliqué before assembling shorts.

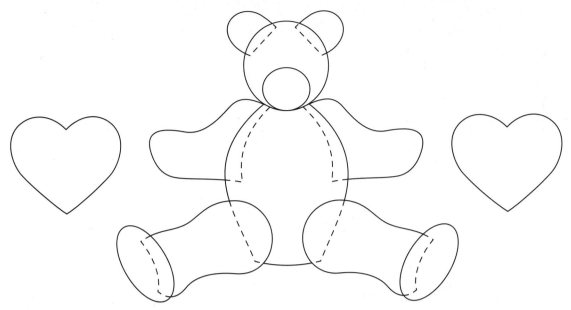

## Full-Size Beary Little Bear Appliqué Pattern

**1.** Prepare the pattern pieces as directed in "Preparing Patterns" on page 236, using the patterns on the opposite page.

**2.** Fuse the fusible webbing to the fabrics, referring to "Fusible Webbing" on page 235.

**3.** Refer to "Machine Appliqué" on page 235 for directions on marking and cutting appliqué pieces. From the tan, mark and cut the bear's ears, head, body, arms, and legs.

From the muslin, mark and cut the bear's muzzle and foot pads. From the pink, mark and cut two hearts. Remove the paper backing from the appliqué pieces.

**4.** Arrange the appliqué pieces on the lower portion of the left shorts leg, layering as indicated by the dashed lines. Fuse in place as directed in "Fusible Webbing" on page 235.

**5.** Center and pin the tear-away stabilizer to the back of the appliqué. Machine appliqué along all edges using matching thread.

**6.** Tie the ribbon in a bow and hand tack it to the bear's neck for a bow tie.

**7.** Sew the bead eyes and nose in place as shown in **Diagram 1.**

### COUNTRY TIPS
*from Alma Lynne*

Add Beary Little Bear appliqué accents to lots of things—your child's school bag, denim jacket, bath towel, bedroom curtains, and more! You could plan your baby's nursery using this motif. Make a baby quilt featuring this sweet little guy, then accent the room with a stenciled Beary Little Bear border, a stuffed bear mobile, and bear crib bumpers. Use the heart pattern to sponge paint closet doors, a white dresser, and even a paper lampshade. And don't forget to sew a heart-shape pillow for your rocking chair!

**Diagram 1**

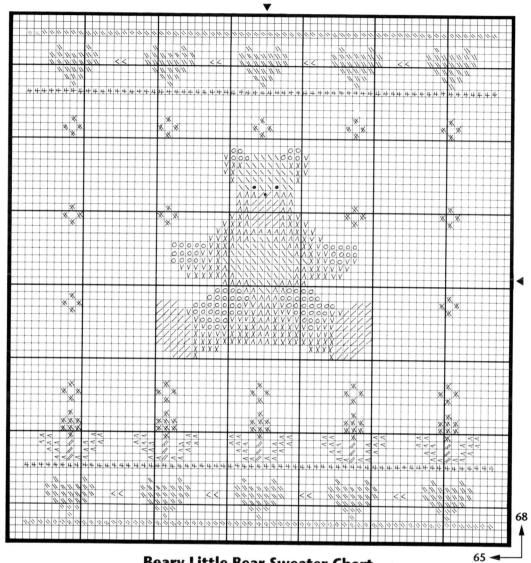

68

65

## Beary Little Bear Sweater Chart
### Color Key

| | DMC | Anchor | J. & P. Coats | Color |
|---|---|---|---|---|
| X | 433 | 358 | 5471 | Med. Brown |
| V | 434 | 310 | 5000 | Lt. Brown |
| O | 435 | 1046 | 5371 | Vy. Lt. Brown |
| ∧ | 436 | 1045 | 5943 | Tan |
| \ | 437 | 362 | 5942 | Lt. Tan |
| < | 502 | 877 | 6876 | Blue-Green |
| // | 503 | 876 | 6879 | Med. Blue-Green |
| / | 739 | 387 | 5369 | Ultra Vy. Lt. Tan |
| • | 898 | 360 | 5476 | Vy. Dk. Coffee Brown |
| \\ | 899 | 52 | 3282 | Med. Rose |
| 4 | 3325 | 129 | 7976 | Lt. Baby Blue |
| ✳ | 3326 | 36 | 3126 | Lt. Rose |

# ANGELIC
## ANGELS

Long believed to bring peace into a home at the holidays, angels have become popular decorator accents throughout the year. The special guardian angels in this chapter are heaven-sent for you to make and enjoy. Since angels come in all styles, these projects do, too! You'll find a rustic country angel, an innocent childlike angel, cupid angels, a pretty guardian angel, and other angelic angels to keep your hands busy. And when the halos and wings are in place, display your angel so that she may add a blessing to all who enter your home and your heart.

# LOVE'S LITTLE ANGEL PICTURE

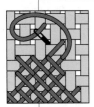

*Cupid recruited this pretty love angel to spread romance and kisses on Valentine's Day. Her delicate wings simply sparkle when love is nearby.*

## SIZE

Design area is 3⅞" × 5⅛" (over two threads) on 28-count Annabelle

## MATERIALS

★ One 13⅞" × 15⅛" piece of 28-count white Annabelle
★ One skein of embroidery floss for each color listed in **Color Key**
★ One spool of blending filament for each color listed in **Color Key**
★ Size 26 tapestry needle

## DIRECTIONS

**1.** Prepare the edges of the Annabelle as directed in "Preparing Fabric Edges" on page 232. Find the center of the Annabelle and mark it with a pin. Find the center of the **Love's Little Angel Picture Chart** by connecting the arrows.

**2.** Matching the centers of the chart and the Annabelle, and using two strands of floss or blending filament, begin stitching at the center point, working each cross-stitch over two threads. Combine two strands of pearl blending filament with the floss for the wing stitches. For the symbol ⟍, use one strand of crimson blending filament with one strand of deep rose floss. Work outward until the entire design is complete.

**3.** Work all backstitching with one strand of floss. Backstitch the hair with very dark beige-brown, eyes with blue-green, wings with medium rose, and banner with very dark rose. Backstitch the cheeks, neck, arms, and feet with light pecan. Backstitch the dress, hearts on dress, heart and wand, pantaloons, and bows with deep rose. Backstitch "LOVE" on the banner with one strand each of deep rose and crimson blending filament.

**4.** Wash and press the completed cross-stitch as directed in "Washing and Pressing" on page 233.

**5.** Mat and frame as desired.

---

### COUNTRY THOUGHTS
*from Alma Lynne*

We started fun traditions for each holiday when my boys were young. Valentine's Day is always special since we declared it "Red Day." A red shirt is certainly the first item of business and, from there, it gets wacky! My husband, Scoot, wears a red polka-dot tie and sons Clay and Seth always manage to slip into red socks and red shoelaces.

We sip strawberry milk and munch on strawberry pancakes for breakfast. At lunch, we enjoy sandwiches cut with a heart-shaped cookie cutter and raspberry parfaits. For dinner, it's spaghetti with red clam sauce and cherry cobbler for dessert. We exchange little presents—wrapped in red tissue, of course! Then, as the evening draws to a close, we settle in for an *I Love Lucy* marathon or a classic movie like *An Affair to Remember*.

## COLOR KEY

| | DMC | Anchor | J. & P. Coats | Color |
|---|---|---|---|---|
| • | White | 2 | 1001 | White |
| ⊖ | 309 | 42 | 3284 | Deep Rose |
| | 326 | 59 | 3401 | Vy. Dk. Rose |
| ∧ | 335 | 38 | 3283 | Rose |
| O | 353 | 6 | 3006 | Peach |
| ■ | 502 | 877 | 6876 | Blue-Green |
| 7 | 754 | 1012 | 2331 | Lt. Peach |
| I | 775 | 128 | 7031 | Vy. Lt. Baby Blue |
| \ | 776 | 24 | 3281 | Med. Pink |
| U | 818 | 23 | 3281 | Baby Pink |
| < | 819 | 271 | 3280 | Lt. Baby Pink |
| | 838 | 380 | 5478 | Vy. Dk. Beige-Brown |

| | DMC | Anchor | J. & P. Coats | Color |
|---|---|---|---|---|
| ✕ | 839 | 360 | 5360 | Dk. Beige-Brown |
| ¢ | 840 | 379 | 5379 | Med. Beige-Brown |
| V | 841 | 378 | 5376 | Lt. Beige-Brown |
| + | 842 | 388 | 5933 | Vy. Lt. Beige-Brown |
| e | 899 | 52 | 3282 | Med. Rose |
| — | 948 | 1011 | 2331 | Vy. Lt. Peach |
| | 3064 | 883 | 3883 | Lt. Pecan |
| 3 | 3325 | 129 | 7976 | Lt. Baby Blue |
| ⊃ | 3326 | 36 | 3126 | Lt. Rose |

Kreinik Balger Pearl Blending Filament #032 HL
Kreinik Balger Crimson Blending Filament #031 HL

## DESIGN OPTIONS

| Fabric Count | Design Area | Cutting Dimensions |
|---|---|---|
| 22 | 2½" × 3¼" | 12½" × 13¼" |
| 18 | 3" × 4" | 13" × 14" |
| 14 | 3⅞" × 5⅛" | 13⅞" × 15⅛" |
| 11 | 4⅞" × 6½" | 14⅞" × 16½" |

**Love's Little Angel Picture Chart**

72

54

# STARLIGHT ANGEL STOCKING

Heaven-sent and country-bound, this old-fashioned angel is made from somber antique cotton fabrics found in a second-hand store. Hang the starlight stocking from a rustic mantel, then fill it with good wishes, glad tidings, and hopes for peace on earth.

## SIZE

Finished stocking is 20" long

## MATERIALS

* ⅞ yard of 44"-wide maroon solid fabric for the stocking
* ⅜ yard of 44"-wide green-and-maroon check fabric for the stocking cuff, hanger, stocking toe, and angel's dress
* ½ yard of fleece for the stocking lining
* ½ yard of fusible webbing
* One 10" square of 44"-wide muslin for the wings and stars
* One 5" square of tan solid fabric for the hair
* One 6" square of peach solid fabric for the face, hands, and feet
* One 12" square of dark green solid fabric for the bows, trim on the dress, and sleeves
* One 6" square of cream print fabric for the apron
* One 2" square of black solid fabric for the shoes
* Matching thread
* Black, razor-point, permanent pen for the faux quilting stitches

## DIRECTIONS

**Note:** Wash, dry, and press all your fabrics before beginning this project. All seam allowances are ¼".

**1.** Prepare all patterns as directed in "Preparing Patterns" on page 236, using the patterns on pages 78 and 79.

**2.** From the maroon solid, mark and cut four stockings. From the green-and-maroon check, cut one 11" × 18" strip for the stocking cuff and one 3" × 6" strip for the hanger. From the fleece, cut two stockings.

**3.** Fuse the fusible webbing to the remaining pieces of fabric, referring to "Fusible Webbing" on page 235 for directions.

**4.** Refer to "Machine Appliqué" on page 235 for directions on marking and cutting appliqué pieces. From the green-and-maroon check, cut one lower ruffle, one right sleeve, one left sleeve, and one stocking toe. From the muslin, cut one pair of wings and three stars. From the tan solid, cut one curly locks and one bangs. From the peach solid, cut one face, one pair of hands, and one pair of legs. From the dark green solid, cut one left bow, one right bow, one collar, one left sleeve trim, one right sleeve trim, and one ruffle. From the cream print, cut one dress. From the black solid, cut one pair of slippers.

**5.** Arrange the appliqué pieces on one stocking front, having the top of the wings 6" from the top of the stocking. Refer to the **Appliqué Placement Diagram** on page 76 and layer the pieces in the following order: wings, curly locks, face, bangs, left bow, right

bow, dress, hands, left sleeve, left sleeve trim, right sleeve, right sleeve trim, collar, feet, slippers, lower ruffle, and ruffle. Fuse in place as directed in "Fusible Webbing" on page 235 Fuse the toe to the stocking front.

**6.** Layer one unembellished stocking, one fleece stocking, and then the stocking front; baste around all edges to form the stocking front. Repeat for the remaining stockings and fleece to form the stocking back.

**7.** With right sides together, sew the stocking front to the stocking back, leaving

**Appliqué Placement Diagram**

the top edge open. Grade the seam allowance to reduce bulk. Clip and notch curves. Do *not* turn to the right side.

**8.** With right sides together, fold the hanger in half lengthwise. Sew along the long raw edge. Turn to the right side and press. Fold the hanger in half crosswise and pin it to the outside of the stocking at the back seam, having the raw edges aligned. Baste the hanger in place.

**9.** With right sides together, sew the short ends of the cuff together to form a loop. Press the seams open. Fold the loop in half lengthwise with wrong sides together. Slip the cuff over the stocking and hanger, having the raw edges aligned and the seam of the cuff at the back seam of the stocking. Sew around the top edge of the stocking. Trim the seam allowance.

## COUNTRY THOUGHTS
*from Alma Lynne*

I'm sure you remember a favorite Christmas from your childhood. I certainly do! I was the *only* child and the proverbial "apple of my mom and dad's eye."

I wasn't spoiled in the least, however. Oh no, not me!

Everything I pointed to at the department store that year showed up under the Christmas tree. My stocking was crammed full of even more surprises. I thought I was the luckiest child in the world. My stocking got a lot of use over the years. It was filled with toys and games for the first few years, then on to tiny notebooks and colored ink pens, and then frilly hair ribbons and bows as I got older. To this day, my Christmas stocking hangs on the mantel year-round.

My mother made the stocking for me right after I was born. It's hand-appliquéd and crazy quilted with silky threads and delicate embroidery stitches. And very colorful, to say the least. The seams show signs of wear, probably from being stuffed too full once or twice. I don't think I'll mend it though, since those weak seams hold memories, too.

**10.** Turn the stocking to the right side and fold the cuff and hanger to the outside and press.

**11.** Center and fuse two stars to the cuff front as directed in "Fusible Webbing" on page 235.

**12.** Use the razor-point pen to embellish the angel, star, and toe with "quilting stitches," referring to the **Faux Quilting Diagrams** for placement. For the angel and stars, the "quilting stitches" should be ⅛" long, ⅛" apart, and about ⅛" from the appliqué edge. For the toe, make your "quilting stitches" about ⅝" long.

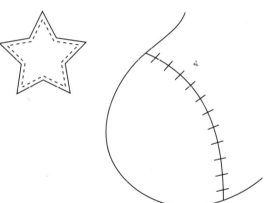

**Faux Quilting Diagrams**

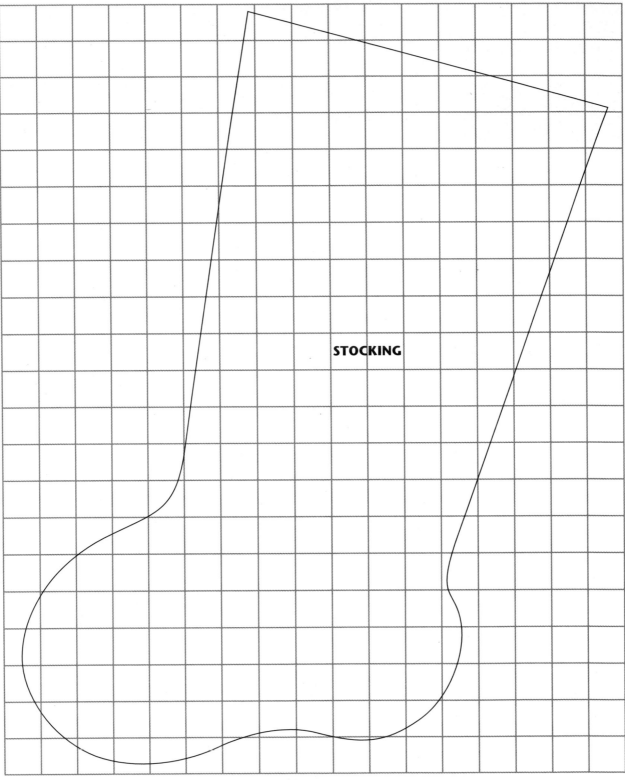

STOCKING

Enlarge 263%

**Starlight Angel Stocking Pattern**

1 square = 1"

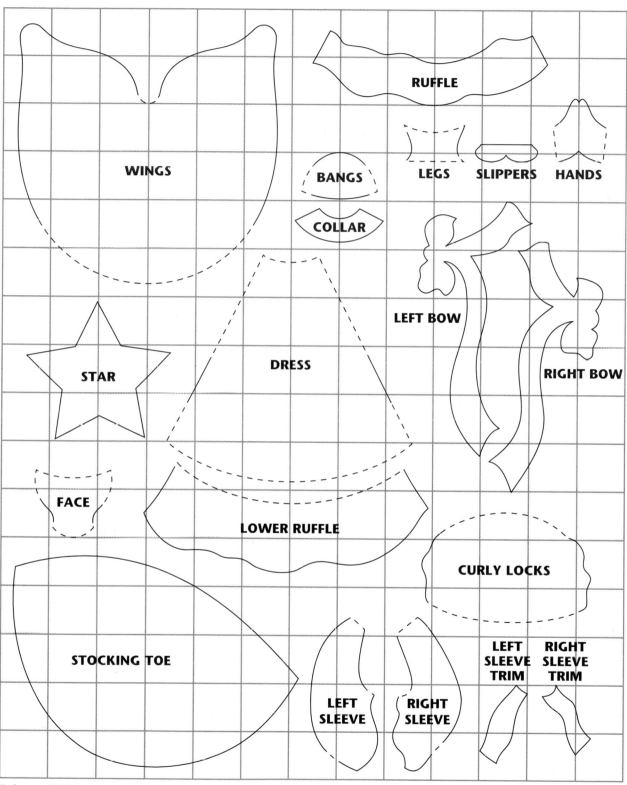

**WINGS**

**RUFFLE**

**BANGS**

**LEGS**  **SLIPPERS**  **HANDS**

**COLLAR**

**LEFT BOW**

**STAR**

**DRESS**

**RIGHT BOW**

**FACE**

**LOWER RUFFLE**

**CURLY LOCKS**

**STOCKING TOE**

**LEFT SLEEVE TRIM**  **RIGHT SLEEVE TRIM**

**LEFT SLEEVE**  **RIGHT SLEEVE**

Enlarge 200%

**Starlight Angel Appliqué Patterns**

1 square = 1"

# LAND OF LIBERTY SET

*Oh, say, can you see…a red, white, and blue doll as lovely as she? Lady Liberty will be a stunning addition to your collection of Americana folk art. Use rough-woven fabric for her body and "antiqued" flags for her freedom-inspired clothing. This country verse works up quickly in backstitch to complement a patriotic decorating scheme. Or finish it as a pillow to send to a serviceperson overseas.*

## LADY LIBERTY ANGEL

### SIZE

Finished doll is 18" tall

### MATERIALS

- ½ yard of 44"-wide tea-dyed Osnaburg fabric for the doll body and wings*
- Matching thread
- Polyester fiberfill
- Matching buttonhole twist thread
- Two 4" × 5" tea-dyed American flags for hearts on wings*
- Two 4" × 5" pieces of fusible webbing
- Two 4" × 5" pieces of tear-away stabilizer
- Four 12" × 18" tea-dyed American flags for the dress*
- One 9" × 13" piece of lightweight fusible interfacing
- ½ yard of tea-dyed eyelet lace for collar *
- Five ½"-diameter white star buttons
- ½ yard of ¼"-wide cream grosgrain ribbon for the waist tie
- One tube of fabric paint *each* in black, white, and maroon
- Small paintbrush
- Powdered blusher
- One ball of cotton twine for hair
- One 12" piece of cardboard
- One 3"-diameter twig wreath
- One small bunch of dried red berries
- Hot-glue gun
- Two 3" × 4" paper American flags
- Two 6" twigs
- ¾ yard of ⅝"-wide maroon grosgrain ribbon

*See page 239 for directions on tea dyeing.

### DIRECTIONS

**Note:** Lady Liberty Angel is for decorative purposes only; her clothing cannot be removed.

1. For instructions on constructing the Lady Liberty Angel, see "Draw-and-Sew Method" on page 236. Use the patterns on pages 84 and 85 for the doll's body and clothing. Follow the directions to make the body, head, legs, and arms.

2. Flatten the top of the legs so the seams are centered in the front and back. Baste across the upper edge. Sew along the indicated lines on the arms to define the angel's fingers.

3. Using the buttonhole twist, hand sew the head, arms, and legs to the angel's body where indicated by the dots on the pattern.

4. Fuse the fusible webbing to the front of one 4" × 5" flag and to the back of the

An angel known as "Liberty"
Watches over you and me
Night and day she helps us be
Forever thankful to be free.

remaining flag, as directed in "Fusible Webbing" on page 235. Using the heart pattern on page 85 as a guide, mark and cut one heart from the center of each flag. Fuse one heart to each upper portion of the wings front, as indicated on the pattern. Center and pin the tear-away stabilizer to the back of the heart appliqués. Machine appliqué around the hearts using matching thread. With right sides together, sew the wings front and back together, leaving an opening for turning. Clip the curves, turn to the right side, and lightly stuff. Whipstitch the opening closed. Using the twine, tie the layers together at 1" intervals, staggering each row; refer to the **Wing Tying Diagram.** Set the wings aside.

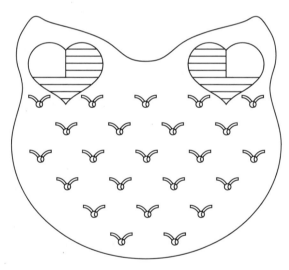

**Wing Tying Diagram**

**5.** Prepare the bodice and sleeve patterns as directed in "Preparing Patterns" on page 236. **Note:** All clothing seam allowances are ¼", unless otherwise indicated.

**6.** For the bodice, cut off the star field and the stripes below the star field from one 12" × 18" flag. Fold the remaining stripes section into quarters and finger-press the folds well. Mark and cut one bodice piece, align-

---

## COUNTRY THOUGHTS
### *from Alma Lynne*

Isn't it wonderful that we celebrated our nation's 200th birthday in 1976— and we're still celebrating? The Bicentennial was an inspiration to the entire country and reminded us of our good fortune to live here.

The colors of our flag can be seen everywhere—from folk-art dolls to Uncle Sam Santas. We celebrate our freedom each time we incorporate those three special colors into our needlecrafts. And besides, are there any prettier colors than red, white, and blue?

---

ing the center and shoulder edges with the pressed folds and having the stripes running vertically. Cut one sleeve from the star field of each of two additional 12" × 18" flags.

**7.** Cut along the center back fold to form the back opening. Turn the back opening and neck edges ⅛" to the wrong side and hem.

**8.** Fuse the fusible interfacing to the wrong side of the sleeves for stiffness. Run a gathering thread a scant ¼" from the sleeve cap, then pull up the gathers to fit the armholes. Set the sleeves into the armholes, matching the dots at the shoulders and leaving ½" smooth at the underarm.

**9.** With the right sides of the bodice together, sew the underarm seams from the wrist edge to the waist edge. Turn under ¼", then ½", at the wrist edges of the sleeves and press; hem. Turn under ¼", then another ¼", at the lower edge of the waist and press; hem. Turn right side out.

**10.** Hand sew the lace to the neck edge of the bodice, turning the raw ends under at the back opening. Sew two star buttons to the bodice, one ½" below the other. Place the bodice on the angel and whipstitch the back opening closed.

**11.** For the skirt, place the two remaining flags together with the star fields matching. Sew the flags together along the short edges to form a loop; press the seams open.

**12.** Turn under ¼", then another ¼", along the lower (striped) edge of the skirt and press; hem.

**13.** To make the waist casing, turn under ½" along the upper (starred and striped) edge and press. Sew ⅜" from the folded edge, leaving an opening near the center back (where the stripes meet).

**14.** For the waist tie, insert the ¼" ribbon in the casing, leaving the ends free. Place the skirt on the angel, tucking the bodice inside. Adjust the skirt to fit snugly and tie the ribbon in a knot; trim the ends and tuck them inside the skirt. Hand sew the casing closed.

**15.** Referring to the pattern for placement and using the fabric paint, make black dots for eyes. Dip one end of a toothpick in white paint and make a small dot for each pupil. Make a maroon dot for the mouth. Lightly blush each cheek with blusher.

**16.** For the hair, wrap the cotton twine around the cardboard 90 times. Cut through the wrapped twine along one end of the cardboard. Bunch and center the twine on the angel's head, then hand sew it in place, forming a part with your stitches. Braid each side of the hair, securing each braid by wrapping thread around the end; knot tightly. Hand sew each braid to the angel's face at the neck.

**17.** Place the wreath on the angel's head. Hot-glue the berries and the three remaining star buttons to the wreath. Flip the hair braids up and around the wreath to the back of the head and hand sew the ends in place.

**18.** Hot-glue one paper flag to each twig. Place one flag in each hand and wrap the angel's fingers around the twig. Whipstitch the fingers to the arm to hold the flag in place; see the **Flag Position Diagram.**

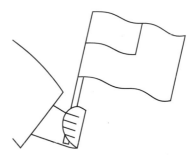

**Flag Position Diagram**

**19.** Position the wings on the angel's back, as shown in the **Wing Placement Diagram,** and sew them in place along the center of the angel's back.

**20.** Wrap the maroon ribbon around the angel's waist and tie it in a bow; clip the ribbon ends diagonally.

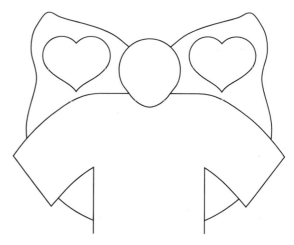

**Wing Placement Diagram**

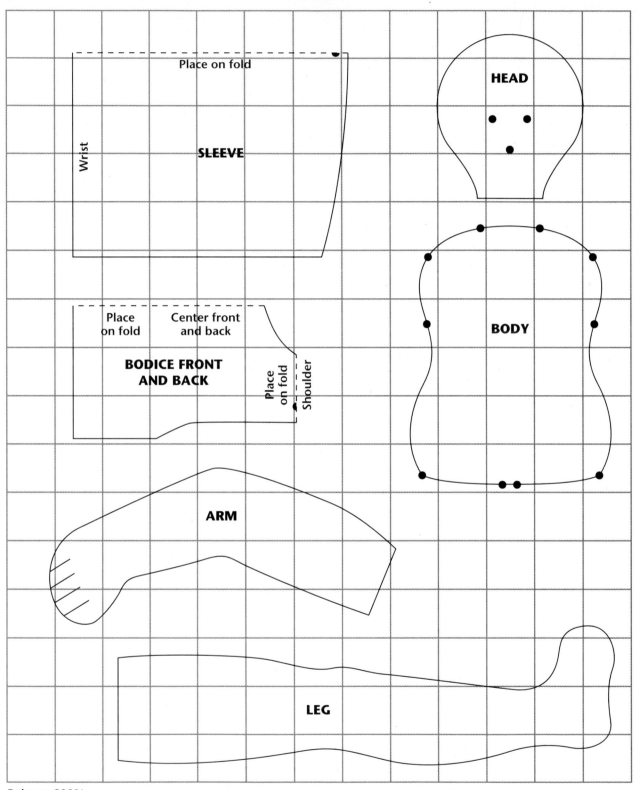

Enlarge 200%

**Lady Liberty Angel Patterns**

1 square = 1"

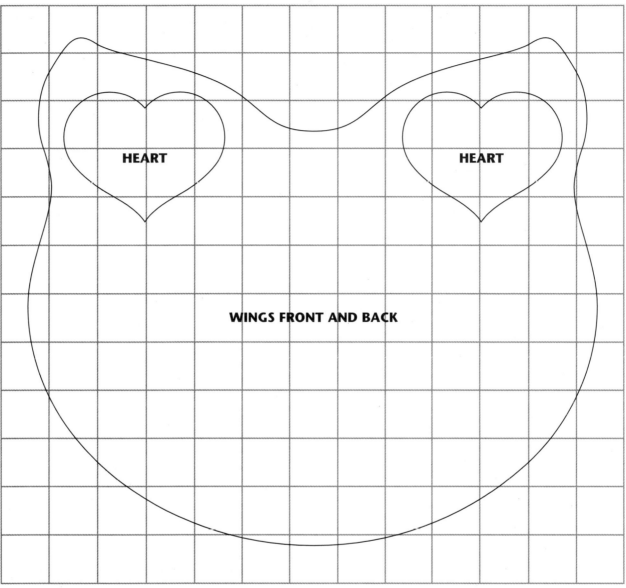

**HEART**

**HEART**

**WINGS FRONT AND BACK**

Enlarge 200%

**Lady Liberty Angel Patterns**

1 square = 1"

# LIBERTY DECLARATION PICTURE

## SIZE

Design area is 6¼" × 11⅜" (over two threads) on 18-count Davosa

## MATERIALS

* ★ One 16¼" × 21⅜" piece of 18-count new khaki Davosa
* ★ One skein of embroidery floss for each color in **Color Key**
* ★ Size 26 tapestry needle

## DIRECTIONS

**1.** Prepare the edges of the Davosa as directed in "Preparing Fabric Edges" on page

### DESIGN OPTIONS

| Fabric Count | Design Area | Cutting Dimensions |
|---|---|---|
| 22 | 2½" × 4⅝" | 12½" × 14⅝" |
| 18 | 3⅛" × 5⅝" | 13⅛" × 15⅝" |
| 14 | 4" × 7¼" | 14" × 17¼" |
| 11 | 5" × 9¼" | 15" × 19¼" |

### COLOR KEY

| | DMC | Anchor | J. & P. Coats | Color |
|---|---|---|---|---|
| ╱ | 823 | 152 | 7982 | Dk. Navy Blue |
| ✕ | 902 | 897 | 3083 | Vy. Dk. Garnet |
| | 3371 | 382 | 5382 | Black-Brown |

232. Find the center of the Davosa and mark it with a pin. Find the center of the **Liberty Declaration Picture Chart** by connecting the arrows.

**2.** Matching the centers of the chart and the Davosa, and using two strands of floss, begin stitching at the center point, working backstitches with black-brown. Work outward until the entire design is complete.

**3.** Work a French knot for the period with two strands of black-brown.

**4.** Wash and press the completed cross-stitch piece as directed in "Washing and Pressing" on page 233.

**5.** Mat and frame as desired.

## COUNTRY TIPS
### *from Alma Lynne*

If you make patriotic dolls, you can use this quick-to-stitch declaration as a flag or hanging banner for the doll to hold proudly. Stitch the Liberty Declaration verse over one thread on 26-count fabric, using one strand of floss. Hem the fabric edges, then stiffen the piece with a liquid starch product. Use a twig for the flagpole or hand tack a narrow ribbon to each upper corner for the banner hanger. Place the flag or banner in the doll's hand and secure it in place by hand tacking or with hot glue.

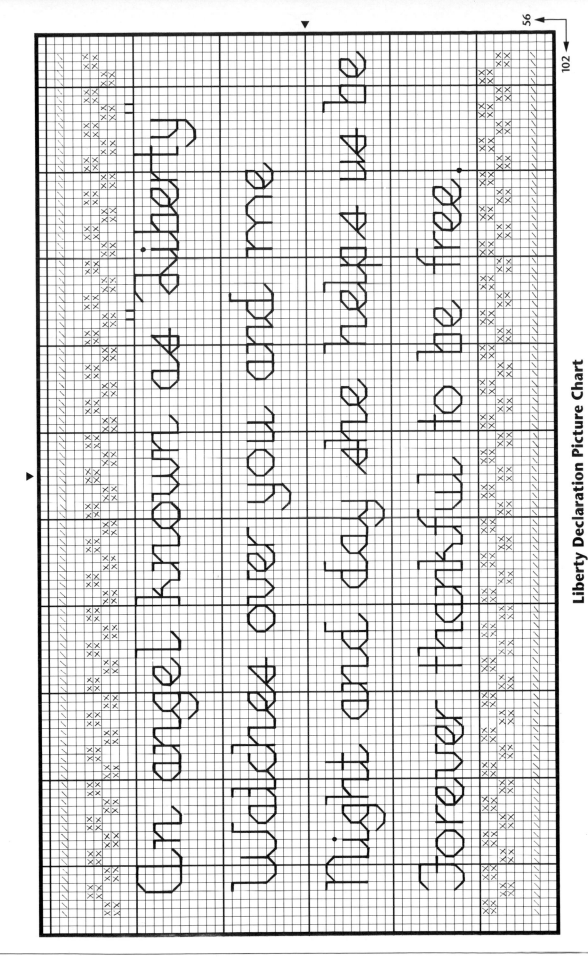

**Liberty Declaration Picture Chart**

An angel known as liberty

Watches over you and me

Night and day she helps us be

Forever thankful to be free.

# Loving Cupids Sweater

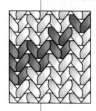

*Two little cherubs flutter about with oh-so-precious cargo—a heart just waiting for love. This easy design can be duplicate stitched in just a few hours!*

## Size

Design area is 11" × 16" on 6 × 8 gauge

## Materials

* One 6 × 8-gauge adult's stockinette stitch white pullover sweater
* One skein of embroidery floss for each color listed in **Color Key** (unless otherwise indicated)
* One spool of blending filament for each color listed in **Color Key**
* Size 22 tapestry needle
* ⅝ yard of 8"-wide pregathered white lace for the froufrou
* ½ yard of 1"-wide white Velcro strip for the froufrou
* 1 yard of 1"-wide white satin ribbon for the froufrou
* ¾ yard of ½"-wide rose satin ribbon for the froufrou
* 2 yards *each* of ⅛"-diameter pink and white pearls-on-a-string for the froufrou

## Directions

**1.** Plan the placement of the Loving Cupids design on your sweater. On the model, I counted the total number of vertical stitches from the center front neckline to the top of the ribbing, then divided that number by three. I placed a pin one-third of the way down, marking the center stitch of the design. For your sweater, you may follow the directions above if you have at least 156 vertical stitches. If you have fewer than 156 vertical stitches, you should center the design by counting the total number of vertical stitches, then dividing that number by two; mark the center with a pin. Find the center of the **Loving Cupids Sweater Chart** by connecting the arrows.

**2.** Read the duplicate stitch basics in "The Stitches" on page 235. Matching the center of the chart with the marked center stitch on the sweater, duplicate stitch the design using six strands of floss. For the symbol ∨, combine three strands of blending filament with the six strands of floss. Stitch the unsymboled area inside the large heart with medium rose.

**3.** Wash and press the completed duplicate stitch design as directed in "Washing and Pressing" on page 235.

**4.** Cut the lace, ribbons, pearls-on-a-string, and Velcro lengths in half. Cut the pearls-on-a-string in half again.

**5.** Separate the Velcro strips; fold the "loop" strips in half to find the centers and mark them with a pin. Place one strip over the shoulder area as shown in **Diagram 1,** matching the marked center with the shoulder seam and aligning one long edge of the

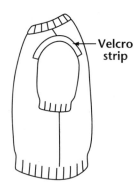

← Velcro strip

**Diagram 1**

strip with the sleeve seam. Whipstitch the strip in place. Repeat for the other shoulder.

**6.** Place one "hook" strip over the gathered portion of one lace length and sew it in place. Place two lengths each of pink and white pearls-on-a-string side by side. Wrap thread around the center of the two lengths to secure it, then hand tack the center to the center of the lace/Velcro strip. Tie one white ribbon into a bow and hand tack it over the pearls. Tie one rose ribbon into a bow and hand-tack it at one end of the lace/Velcro strip. Clip the ribbon ends diagonally. Repeat for the other Velcro strip and trims.

## COUNTRY THOUGHTS
### from Alma Lynne

Cupid entered my life when I met my husband, Scoot. On our first date, we shared a chocolate soda, sipping through red-and-white striped straws, just like the boy and girl in the drugstore posters. We're both hopeless romantics and, even to this day, we try to outdo each other with cards and little surprises—like chocolate kisses and flowers. Isn't love grand? And now that I think about it, Scooty sort of looks like these cupids! My inspiration for this design? Scooty, of course!

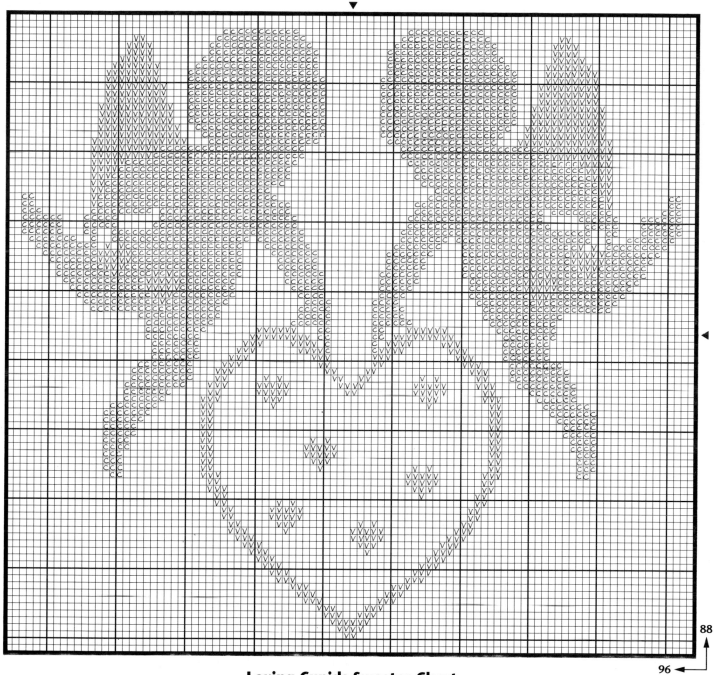

88

96

## Loving Cupids Sweater Chart
### COLOR KEY

| | DMC | Anchor | J. & P. Coats | Color |
|---|---|---|---|---|
| C | 899 | 52 | 3282 | Med. Rose (13 skeins) |
| V | 899 | 52 | 3282 | Med. Rose (4 skeins) and Kreinik Balger Pearl Blending Filament #032 HL |

# PRETTY-IN-PINK ANGEL

*This delicate sprite sprinkles kindness and love on the posies she delivers. Her simple style makes this project an easy one for the beginner. With just a few quick seams, you can create a sweet outfit for this country angel.*

## SIZE

Finished doll is 15" tall

## MATERIALS

★ ¾ yard of 44"-wide Osnaburg fabric for the doll body and wings
★ ½ yard of 44"-wide light pink solid fabric for the dress
★ One 9½" × 20" piece of cream print fabric for the apron
★ ½ yard of ⅝"-wide pink satin ribbon for the waist sash
★ ¾ yard of ¼"-wide flat cream lace for the apron
★ 1½ yards *each* of ¼"-wide pink, blue, green, and white satin ribbons for the bows
★ Matching thread
★ Polyester fiberfill
★ Matching buttonhole twist thread
★ One ball of cotton twine for the hair
★ One 3" piece of cardboard
★ Blue colored pencil
★ Black, fine-point, permanent pen
★ Powdered blusher
★ One 2"-high basket with handle
★ Small bunch of silk and dried flowers for the basket
★ Hot-glue gun

## DIRECTIONS

**Note:** Pretty-in-Pink Angel is for decorative purposes only; her clothing cannot be removed. All seam allowances are ¼".

1. Prepare all patterns as directed in "Preparing Patterns" on page 236, using the patterns on page 95.

2. Referring to "Draw-and-Sew Method" on page 236, from the Osnaburg, mark and cut two bodies, two wings, four arms, and four legs. From the pink solid, cut two blouses and one 9½" × 26" piece for the skirt. From the cream print, cut one 9½" × 18" piece for the apron.

3. With right sides together, sew the body pieces together, leaving an opening for turning. Clip the curves. Turn to the right side and stuff firmly. Whipstitch the opening closed.

4. Repeat Step 3 for each arm and leg.

5. Knot a 20" length of buttonhole twist at one end and thread through the doll needle. Matching the large dots, run the needle from the outside of one arm through to the inside of the arm, then through the body and the other arm. Make several passes through the arms and body to secure. Knot tightly. Repeat for the legs.

6. Repeat Step 3 for the wings, but stuff them lightly. Topstitch around all edges of the wings ½" from the outer edge. Tie the 1"-wide pink ribbon in a bow and hand tack it to the lower point of the wings; clip the ribbon ends diagonally. Set the wings aside.

7. With the right sides of the blouses together, sew along one back slit, around the neckline, and along the opposite back slit. Clip the neckline curves. Turn to the right side and press. Fold the blouse in half at the shoulder seam to form a blouse front and back. Sew the underarm seams. Clip the curves. Turn under ¼" on the lower edge and hem. Turn the blouse and run a gathering thread around each wrist edge.

## COUNTRY THOUGHTS
### from Alma Lynne

Angels are very special to me. I feel the presence of my own angel daily. Of course, my special angels are my children—Clay, 22, and Seth, 19.

The topic of angels always brings to mind a priceless moment from when my little ones were attending elementary school. Christmastime is celebrated annually with a nativity play and that particular year, Clay and Seth were wise men from the East. When it was their turn, they walked silently and solemnly across the stage toward the manger. All of a sudden, another little wise man stepped on Seth's robe, ripping the hem and pulling off his rope belt. Seth tripped forward, completely off balance, and his crown came to rest on the bridge of his nose. It was quite a sight—and a pretty funny one at that—to everyone except Seth. The next thing I knew, Seth was taking the "Alfalfa-getting-ready-to-bop-Butch-a-good-one" stance. He wound up his balled-up fist and I prayed he would come to his senses.

From out of nowhere, a little blonde angel appeared and whispered to Seth, "Don't forget the star. Hurry up or you'll be late." WHEW! A real little angel that must have been heaven-sent. And just in time, too. Seth hurried on his way, and I somehow managed to catch my breath to enjoy the rest of the production.

8. Place the blouse on the angel and pull the gathering threads tightly to fit the wrists and knot them. Overlap the edges of the blouse back and whipstitch closed.

9. With right sides together, sew the short ends of the skirt together. Turn under ½" on the lower edge and hem. Turn the waist under ½" and run a gathering thread around the edge.

10. Place the skirt on the angel, tucking in the blouse. Pull the gathering threads tightly to fit the angel's waist, then knot the gathering threads to secure.

11. Turn under ¼" along one long edge of the apron and press. Topstitch the lace to the folded edge; this will be the lower edge of the apron. Turn under ¼" on the remaining three sides of the apron and hem.

12. Run a gathering thread around the waist. Place the apron on the angel and pull the gathering threads tightly to fit the angel's waist. Knot the gathering threads to secure.

13. Place the ⅝"-wide pink ribbon around the angel's waist for a sash and tie a bow in the back. Clip the ribbon ends diagonally.

14. Cut a ¼-yard length of each of the remaining ribbons. Holding the ribbons together as if they were one, tie a bow and leave long tails. Hand tack the bow's knot to the sash. Clip the ribbon ends diagonally.

15. For the hair, wrap the cotton twine around the cardboard 115 times. Cut through the wrapped twine along one end of the cardboard. Bunch and center the twine on the angel's head, then hand sew it in place, forming a part with your stitches. Cut a 15"

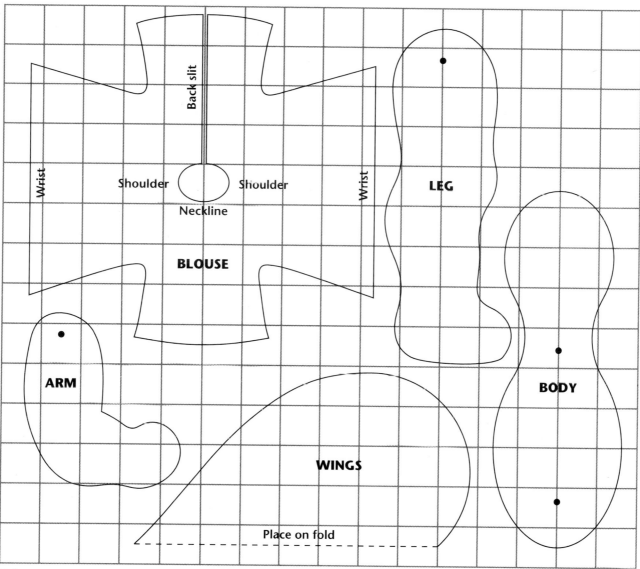

**Enlarge 241%**

**Pretty-in-Pink Angel Patterns**

1 square = 1"

length of twine and wind it around three pencils held together. Slide the loops off the pencils and hand tack them to the front of the hair to form curly bangs. Braid each side of the hair and secure by wrapping thread around the end; knot tightly. Cut the remaining blue ribbon in half. Tie each length around a braid and make a bow; clip the ribbon ends diagonally.

**16.** Use the colored pencil to make ⅛" circles for the eyes. Use the marker to make a

dot for the pupils and a curved line for the eyelashes. Lightly blush the cheeks.

**17.** Hold the remaining ribbon lengths together as if they were one and tie in a bow; clip the ends diagonally. Hot-glue the bow to the basket and the flowers inside the basket. Hand tack the basket to the angel's hand.

**18.** Using the buttonhole twist and the doll needle, hand sew the wings to the angel's back, referring to the photo for placement.

# HARVEST ANGEL PICTURE

*With wings as subtle as twilight in autumn and hair the color of Indian corn, this beautiful guardian angel brings good fortune to the crop harvest. Watch her come to life as you cross-stitch the subtle shading of her country-plaid frock.*

## SIZE

Design area is 7" × 10" (over two threads) on 20-count Valerie

## MATERIALS

★ One 17" × 20" piece of 20-count bone Valerie
★ One skein of embroidery floss for each color in **Color Key**
★ Size 26 tapestry needle

## DIRECTIONS

**1.** Prepare the edges of the Valerie as directed in "Preparing Fabric Edges" on page 232. Find the center of the Valerie and mark it with a pin. Find the center of the **Harvest Angel Picture Chart** by connecting the arrows.

**2.** Matching the centers of the chart and the Valerie, and using two strands of floss, begin stitching at the center point, working over two threads. Work outward until the entire design is complete.

## COUNTRY TIPS
### from Alma Lynne

In some regions of the country, autumn is celebrated without traditional cornhusk decorations and frosty pumpkins. Since autumn might be sunny and warm where you live, I thought I would adapt this pretty harvest angel to suit a milder climate. Just by substituting a few colors, the new harvest angel will be carrying peaches instead of apples, will be a golden blonde rather than a redhead, and will be wearing a country blue frock instead of a green one. Make the following substitutions and watch your warm-weather Harvest Angel celebrate her own version of fall.

|   | DMC | Anchor | J. & P. Coats | Color |
|---|-----|--------|---------------|-------|
| > | 948 | 1011 | 2331 | Vy. Lt. Peach |
| β | 754 | 1012 | 2331 | Lt. Peach |
| 2 | 353 | 6 | 3006 | Lt. Peach Flesh |
| S | 746 | 275 | 2275 | Off-White |
| c | 677 | 886 | 5372 | Vy. Lt. Old Gold |
| < | 676 | 891 | — | Lt. Old Gold |
| × | 729 | 890 | 2875 | Med. Old Gold |
| // | 680 | 901 | 2876 | Dk. Old Gold |
| e | 3752 | 1032 | 7876 | Vy. Lt. Antique Blue |
| z | 932 | 1033 | 7050 | Lt. Antique Blue |
| U | 931 | 1034 | 7051 | Med. Antique Blue |
| 4 | 930 | 1035 | 7052 | Dk. Antique Blue |

**3.** Work all backstitching with one strand of floss. Backstitch the stems with very dark blue-green, the eyes with medium brown, the skin with light brown, and the hair with dark red-copper. Backstitch the apron, dress, shoes, and wings with dark beige-brown. Work the French knots for the flowers with two strands of very dark shell pink and for the apple stems with two strands of black-brown.

**4.** Wash and press the completed cross-stitch piece as directed in "Washing and Pressing" on page 233.

**5.** Mat and frame as desired.

## DESIGN OPTIONS

| Fabric Count | Design Area | Cutting Dimensions |
|---|---|---|
| 22 | 3⅛" × 4½" | 13⅛" × 14½" |
| 18 | 3¾" × 5⅝" | 13¾" × 15⅝" |
| 14 | 4⅞" × 7¼" | 14⅞" × 17¼" |
| 11 | 6⅛" × 9⅛" | 16⅛" × 19⅛" |

## COLOR KEY

| | DMC | Anchor | J. & P. Coats | Color |
|---|---|---|---|---|
| • | White | 2 | 1001 | White |
| B | 221 | 897 | 3243 | Vy. Dk. Shell Pink |
| 2 | 223 | 895 | 3240 | Med. Shell Pink |
| 3 | 353 | 6 | 3006 | Peach |
| X | 402 | 1047 | — | Vy. Lt. Mahogany |
| | 433 | 358 | 5471 | Med. Brown |
| \\ | 434 | 310 | 5000 | Lt. Brown |
| ∧ | 435 | 1046 | 5371 | Vy. Lt. Brown |
| 6 | 436 | 1045 | 5943 | Tan |
| L | 437 | 362 | 5942 | Lt. Tan |
| 5 | 500 | 683 | 6880 | Vy. Dk. Blue-Green |
| Z | 501 | 878 | 6878 | Dk. Blue-Green |
| e | 502 | 877 | 6876 | Blue-Green |
| U | 503 | 876 | 6879 | Med. Blue-Green |
| 4 | 504 | 1042 | 6875 | Lt. Blue-Green |

| | DMC | Anchor | J. & P. Coats | Color |
|---|---|---|---|---|
| ⊘ | 640 | 903 | 5393 | Vy. Dk. Beige-Gray |
| V | 642 | 392 | 5832 | Dk. Beige-Gray |
| / | 644 | 830 | 5830 | Med. Beige-Gray |
| 7 | 754 | 1012 | 2331 | Lt. Peach |
| I | 822 | 390 | 5933 | Lt. Beige-Gray |
| | 839 | 360 | 5360 | Dk. Beige-Brown |
| > | 902 | 897 | 3083 | Vy. Dk. Garnet |
| + | 918 | 341 | 3340 | Dk. Red-Copper |
| // | 919 | 340 | 2326 | Red-Copper |
| C | 920 | 1004 | 3337 | Med. Copper |
| S | 921 | 1003 | — | Copper |
| < | 922 | 1003 | 3336 | Lt. Copper |
| — | 948 | 1011 | 2331 | Vy. Lt. Peach |
| | 3371 | 382 | 5382 | Black-Brown |

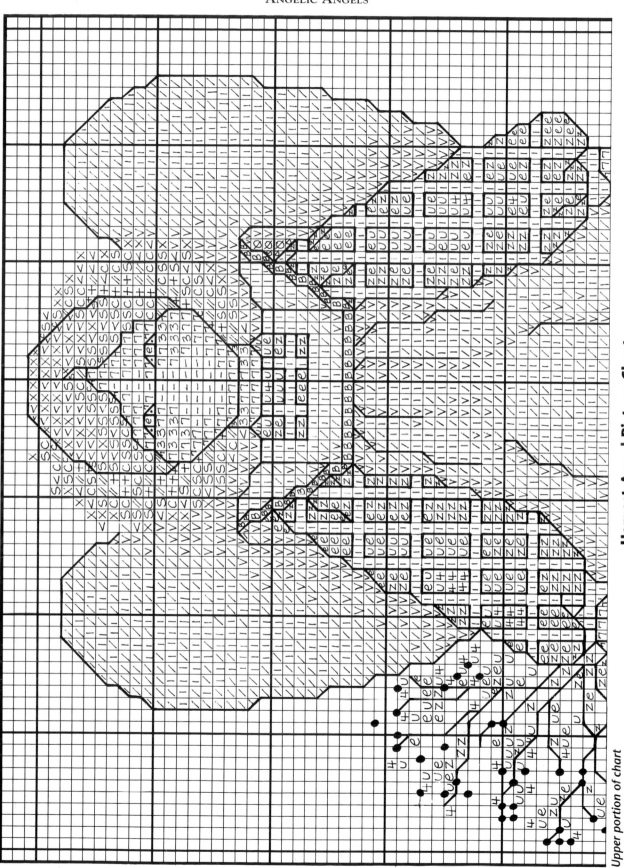

**Harvest Angel Picture Chart**

*Upper portion of chart*

## COLOR KEY

| | DMC | Anchor | J. & P. Coats | Color | | DMC | Anchor | J. & P. Coats | Color |
|---|---|---|---|---|---|---|---|---|---|
| • | White | 2 | 1001 | White | ⊘ | 640 | 903 | 5393 | Vy. Dk. Beige-Gray |
| B | 221 | 897 | 3243 | Vy. Dk. Shell Pink | V | 642 | 392 | 5832 | Dk. Beige-Gray |
| 2 | 223 | 895 | 3240 | Med. Shell Pink | ╱ | 644 | 830 | 5830 | Med. Beige-Gray |
| 3 | 353 | 6 | 3006 | Peach | 7 | 754 | 1012 | 2331 | Lt. Peach |
| X | 402 | 1047 | — | Vy. Lt. Mahogany | I | 822 | 390 | 5933 | Lt. Beige-Gray |
| | 433 | 358 | 5471 | Med. Brown | | 839 | 360 | 5360 | Dk. Beige-Brown |
| \\ | 434 | 310 | 5000 | Lt. Brown | > | 902 | 897 | 3083 | Vy. Dk. Garnet |
| ∧ | 435 | 1046 | 5371 | Vy. Lt. Brown | + | 918 | 341 | 3340 | Dk. Red-Copper |
| 6 | 436 | 1045 | 5943 | Tan | // | 919 | 340 | 2326 | Red-Copper |
| L | 437 | 362 | 5942 | Lt. Tan | C | 920 | 1004 | 3337 | Med. Copper |
| 5 | 500 | 683 | 6880 | Vy. Dk. Blue-Green | S | 921 | 1003 | — | Copper |
| Z | 501 | 878 | 6878 | Dk. Blue-Green | < | 922 | 1003 | 3336 | Lt. Copper |
| e | 502 | 877 | 6876 | Blue-Green | — | 948 | 1011 | 2331 | Vy. Lt. Peach |
| U | 503 | 876 | 6879 | Med. Blue-Green | | 3371 | 382 | 5382 | Black-Brown |
| 4 | 504 | 1042 | 6875 | Lt. Blue-Green | | | | | |

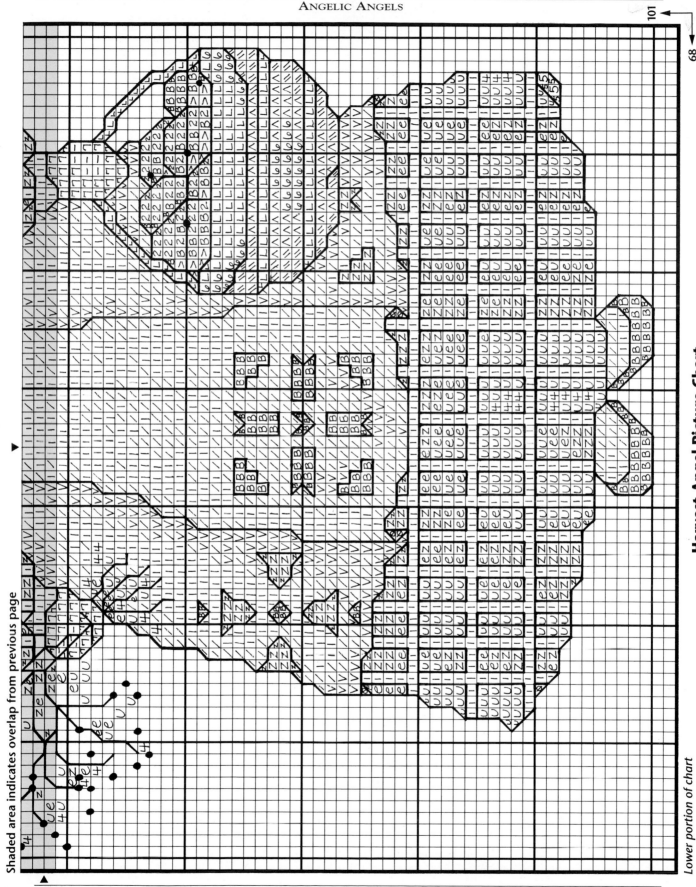

101

68

**Harvest Angel Picture Chart**

*Lower portion of chart*

Shaded area indicates overlap from previous page

# CHRISTMAS IS A-COMING

Oh, boy! I can hardly wait 'til Santa comes swooping down the chimney. Christmas is my favorite time of year. If you're like me, you love to decorate every inch of your home and you spend months getting ready for the holidays.

This chapter will help you with your hugging, hanging, wearing, and accenting plans. Discover Santas in all shapes—tall and thin, round and roly-poly, and itty-bitty, too! So hurry and get stitching because Christmas is just around the corner. And it's never too early to get Santa in the spirit for a little gift giving.

# SIR KRINGLE

*As stately as an English gentleman and as elegant as a nobleman, Sir Kringle regales on tarts and tea at a holiday gathering. His luxurious cloak and tall top hat are simply fit for a king.*

## SIZE

Finished doll is 30" tall

## MATERIALS

★ ⅞ yard of 44"-wide muslin for the body
★ Graphite paper
★ Matching thread
★ Polyester fiberfill
★ Soft-sculpture doll needle
★ Matching buttonhole twist thread
★ ⅝ yard of 44"-wide white solid fabric for the shirt
★ 1⅛ yards of 44"-wide black plaid fabric for the cape lining and trousers
★ ¼ yard of 44"-wide black Ultrasuede for the boots and cummerbund
★ ⅜ yard of 44"-wide teal velveteen for the top hat, mittens, and pouch
★ 1⅛ yards of 44"-wide red velveteen for the cloak and hat band
★ 10" × 12" piece of posterboard for making the top hat
★ 37" square of paper for the cloak pattern
★ 1⅜ yards of 3"-wide white scalloped flat lace for the collar and cuffs
★ 1⅜ yards of ⅝"-wide teal satin ribbon
★ 1¼ yards of metallic gold cording for the boot bows and pouch drawstring

★ Black, razor-point, permanent pen for the outline of the eyes
★ Blue and red colored pencils for the eyes and blush
★ 1 skein of Fur Luxe yarn for the beard and hair*
★ One 6" piece of cardboard
★ Hot-glue gun
★ One small bunch of silk holly for the top hat
★ Wire-rimmed glasses to fit a 2½"–3"-wide doll head

*See "Buyer's Guide" on page 240 for ordering information.

## DIRECTIONS

**Note:** Sir Kringle is for decorative purposes only; his clothing cannot be removed.

1. For instructions on constructing Sir Kringle, see "Cut-and-Sew Method" on page 236. Follow the directions to sew the body, head, legs, and arms, using the patterns on page 109 and the muslin. Using graphite paper, transfer all facial features to the muslin. Leave the neck area of the head open after stuffing. When stuffing the arms and legs, stuff to the dashed line indicated on the patterns, then sew across the arm or leg to form a joint. For the arms, continue stuffing, then whipstitch closed. For the legs, continue stuffing, then flatten the top of each leg so the seams are centered in the front and back. Baste across the upper edge.

2. Using the doll needle and the buttonhole twist, sew the head and legs to the body.

3. Knot a 20" length of buttonhole twist at one end and thread through the doll needle.

Matching the large dots, run the needle from the outside of one arm through to the inside of the arm, then through the body and the other arm. Make several passes through the arms and body to secure. Knot tightly.

**4.** Use the patterns on pages 110 and 111 for Sir Kringle's vestments; sew the vestments using a ¼" seam allowance. From the white solid, cut one shirt. From the black plaid, cut two trousers. From the Ultrasuede, cut four boots and one 2" × 13½" piece for the cummerbund. From the teal velveteen, cut four mittens and two 6½" squares for the pouch. Also cut one 3¾" × 9" piece, one 3¼" circle, and two 5¼" circles for the top hat. From the red velveteen, cut one 2" × 9½" strip for the top hat band. From the posterboard, cut one 3¼" × 8½" piece, one 2¾" circle, and two 4¾" circles for the top hat.

**5.** For Sir Kringle's cloak pattern, fold the 37" paper square into quarters, using the **Cloak Diagram** as a size guide. Draw one-quarter of a 36"-diameter circle, then one-quarter of a 2½"-diameter circle inside the larger one; refer to "Country Tips from Alma Lynne" on the opposite page for directions. Cut through all four layers of the paper on both drawn arcs. Unfold the paper. Cut along one fold line and label the cut edges for the center front.

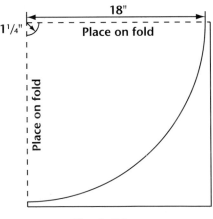

**Cloak Diagram**

**6.** Matching the lines on the **Armhole Guide** with the marked center front and the fold lines on the paper cloak pattern, transfer the armhole curves and dots to the front half of the cloak pattern. Placing the center front edges of the pattern on the lengthwise grain of the fabrics, cut one cloak each from the red velveteen and the black plaid.

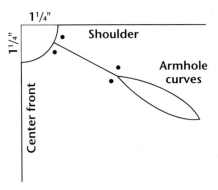

**Armhole Guide**

**7.** With right sides together, sew the shirt front and back together at the underarm seams. Turn under ¼" along the waist edge of the shirt and press; hem. Turn under ½" around each wrist edge and press; hem. Turn the shirt to the right side. Run a gathering thread around the neck edge. Place the shirt on Sir Kringle and pull up the threads to fit; secure the thread.

**8.** Cut a 22" length of lace for the collar. Turn under ¼" on each raw end and whip-stitch in place. Run a gathering thread along the bound edge and place the collar around Sir Kringle's neck, having the turned-under edges in back. Pull up the gathers to fit and secure the thread.

**9.** With right sides together, sew pairs of mittens together, leaving the top edge open. Turn under ¼" along the top edge and press lightly; hem. Carefully place one mitten on each hand. It will be difficult to slide the velveteen onto the muslin, but do so slowly so as not to fray the velveteen or rip the seams.

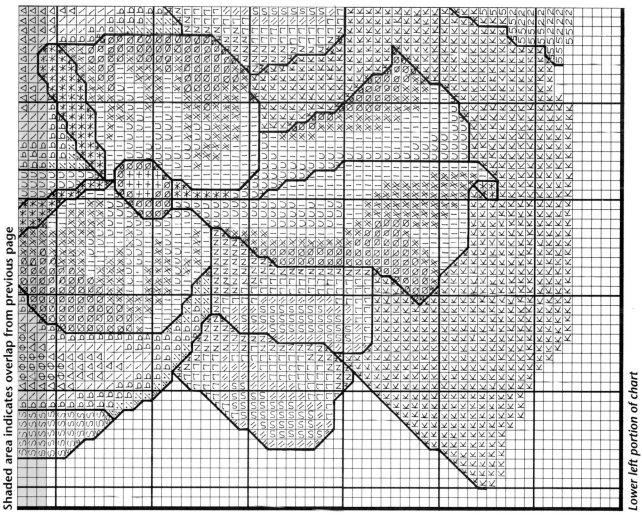

*Shaded area indicates overlap from previous page*

*Lower left portion of chart*

## The Christmas Kiss Picture Chart
### COLOR KEY

| | DMC | Anchor | J. & P. Coats | Color |
|---|---|---|---|---|
| 7 | 729 | 890 | 2875 | Med. Old Gold |
| V | 754 | 1012 | 2331 | Lt. Peach |
| O | 758 | 882 | 2337 | Lt. Terra Cotta |
| ∧ | 760 | 1022 | 3069 | Salmon |
| Z | 761 | 1021 | 3068 | Lt. Salmon |
| Φ | 762 | 234 | 8510 | Vy. Lt. Pearl Gray |
| I | 814 | 45 | 3044 | Dk. Garnet |
| U | 815 | 43 | 3000 | Med. Garnet |
| ✳ | 816 | 1005 | 3021 | Garnet |
| 8 | 838 | 380 | 5478 | Vy. Dk. Beige-Brown |
| 3 | 839 | 360 | 5360 | Dk. Beige-Brown |

| | DMC | Anchor | J. & P. Coats | Color |
|---|---|---|---|---|
| < | 840 | 379 | 5379 | Med. Beige-Brown |
| ⊃ | 841 | 378 | 5376 | Lt. Beige-Brown |
| 6 | 842 | 388 | 5933 | Vy. Lt. Beige-Brown |
| | 898 | 360 | 5476 | Vy. Dk. Coffee Brown |
| ✳ | 902 | 897 | 3083 | Vy. Dk. Garnet |
| Ø | 924 | 851 | 6008 | Vy. Dk. Slate Green |
| 9 | 926 | 850 | 6007 | Slate Green |
| / | 927 | 848 | 6006 | Med. Slate Green |
| C | 928 | 274 | 6005 | Lt. Slate Green |
| // | 948 | 1011 | 2331 | Vy. Lt. Peach |

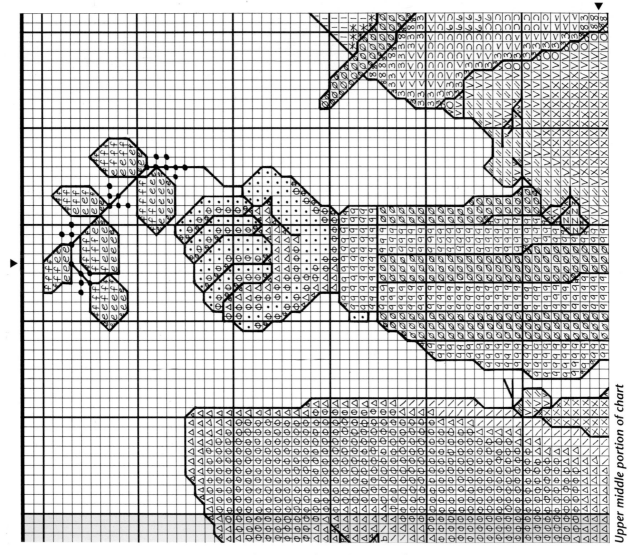

*Upper middle portion of chart*

## The Christmas Kiss Picture Chart
### COLOR KEY

| | DMC | Anchor | J. & P. Coats | Color |
|---|---|---|---|---|
| • | White | 2 | 1001 | White |
| — | Ecru | 387 | 5387 | Ecru |
| ● | 310 | 403 | 8403 | Black |
| ∴ | 317 | 400 | 8512 | Pewter Gray |
| \ | 318 | 399 | 8511 | Lt. Steel Gray |
| | 319 | 228 | 6246 | Vy. Dk. Pistachio Green |
| e | 320 | 215 | 6017 | Med. Pistachio Green |
| + | 321 | 9046 | 3500 | Christmas Red |
| × | 353 | 6 | 3006 | Peach |
| f | 368 | 214 | 6016 | Lt. Pistachio Green |
| S | 413 | 401 | 8514 | Dk. Pewter Gray |

| | DMC | Anchor | J. & P. Coats | Color |
|---|---|---|---|---|
| b | 414 | 235 | 8513 | Dk. Steel Gray |
| △ | 415 | 398 | 8398 | Pearl Gray |
| ⊘ | 498 | 1005 | 3000 | Dk. Christmas Red |
| K | 500 | 683 | 6880 | Vy. Dk. Blue-Green |
| 5 | 501 | 878 | 6878 | Dk. Blue-Green |
| 2 | 502 | 877 | 6876 | Blue-Green |
| > | 503 | 876 | 6879 | Med. Blue-Green |
| P | 504 | 1042 | 6875 | Lt. Blue-Green |
| \\ | 676 | 891 | — | Lt. Old Gold |
| ∽ | 677 | 886 | 5372 | Vy. Lt. Old Gold |
| N | 680 | 901 | 2876 | Dk. Old Gold |

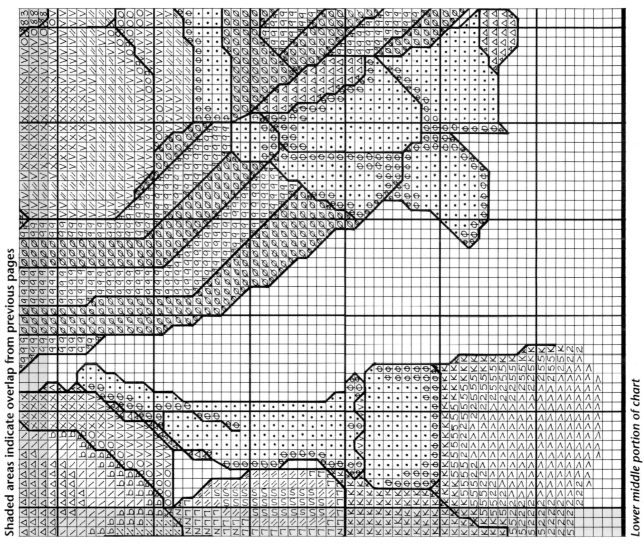

*Shaded areas indicate overlap from previous pages*

*Lower middle portion of chart*

## The Christmas Kiss Picture Chart
### COLOR KEY

| | DMC | Anchor | J. & P. Coats | Color |
|---|---|---|---|---|
| 7 | 729 | 890 | 2875 | Med. Old Gold |
| V | 754 | 1012 | 2331 | Lt. Peach |
| O | 758 | 882 | 2337 | Lt. Terra Cotta |
| ^ | 760 | 1022 | 3069 | Salmon |
| Z | 761 | 1021 | 3068 | Lt. Salmon |
| Φ | 762 | 234 | 8510 | Vy. Lt. Pearl Gray |
| I | 814 | 45 | 3044 | Dk. Garnet |
| U | 815 | 43 | 3000 | Med. Garnet |
| ✗ | 816 | 1005 | 3021 | Garnet |
| 8 | 838 | 380 | 5478 | Vy. Dk. Beige-Brown |
| 3 | 839 | 360 | 5360 | Dk. Beige-Brown |

| | DMC | Anchor | J. & P. Coats | Color |
|---|---|---|---|---|
| < | 840 | 379 | 5379 | Med. Beige-Brown |
| ⊃ | 841 | 378 | 5376 | Lt. Beige-Brown |
| 6 | 842 | 388 | 5933 | Vy. Lt. Beige-Brown |
| | 898 | 360 | 5476 | Vy. Dk. Coffee Brown |
| ✱ | 902 | 897 | 3083 | Vy. Dk. Garnet |
| Ø | 924 | 851 | 6008 | Vy. Dk. Slate Green |
| 9 | 926 | 850 | 6007 | Slate Green |
| / | 927 | 848 | 6006 | Med. Slate Green |
| C | 928 | 274 | 6005 | Lt. Slate Green |
| // | 948 | 1011 | 2331 | Vy. Lt. Peach |

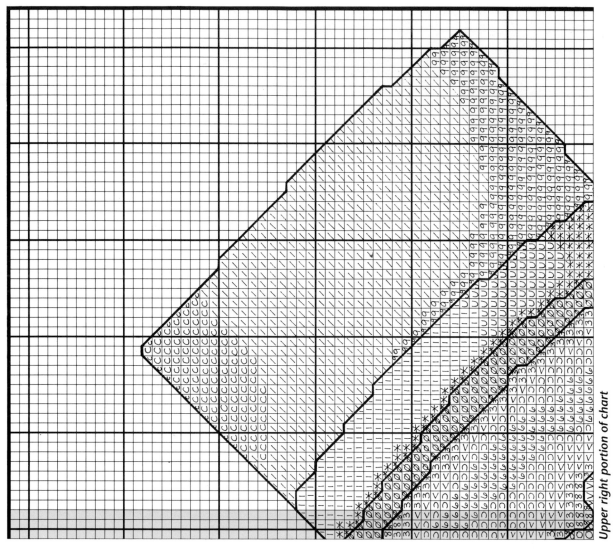

*Upper right portion of chart*

## The Christmas Kiss Picture Chart
### COLOR KEY

| | DMC | Anchor | J. & P. Coats | Color |
|---|---|---|---|---|
| • | White | 2 | 1001 | White |
| — | Ecru | 387 | 5387 | Ecru |
| ● | 310 | 403 | 8403 | Black |
| ∠ | 317 | 400 | 8512 | Pewter Gray |
| \ | 318 | 399 | 8511 | Lt. Steel Gray |
| | 319 | 228 | 6246 | Vy. Dk. Pistachio Green |
| e | 320 | 215 | 6017 | Med. Pistachio Green |
| + | 321 | 9046 | 3500 | Christmas Red |
| × | 353 | 6 | 3006 | Peach |
| f | 368 | 214 | 6016 | Lt. Pistachio Green |
| S | 413 | 401 | 8514 | Dk. Pewter Gray |

| | DMC | Anchor | J. & P. Coats | Color |
|---|---|---|---|---|
| b | 414 | 235 | 8513 | Dk. Steel Gray |
| △ | 415 | 398 | 8398 | Pearl Gray |
| ⊘ | 498 | 1005 | 3000 | Dk. Christmas Red |
| K | 500 | 683 | 6880 | Vy. Dk. Blue-Green |
| 5 | 501 | 878 | 6878 | Dk. Blue-Green |
| 2 | 502 | 877 | 6876 | Blue-Green |
| > | 503 | 876 | 6879 | Med. Blue-Green |
| P | 504 | 1042 | 6875 | Lt. Blue-Green |
| \\ | 676 | 891 | — | Lt. Old Gold |
| ∽ | 677 | 886 | 5372 | Vy. Lt. Old Gold |
| N | 680 | 901 | 2876 | Dk. Old Gold |

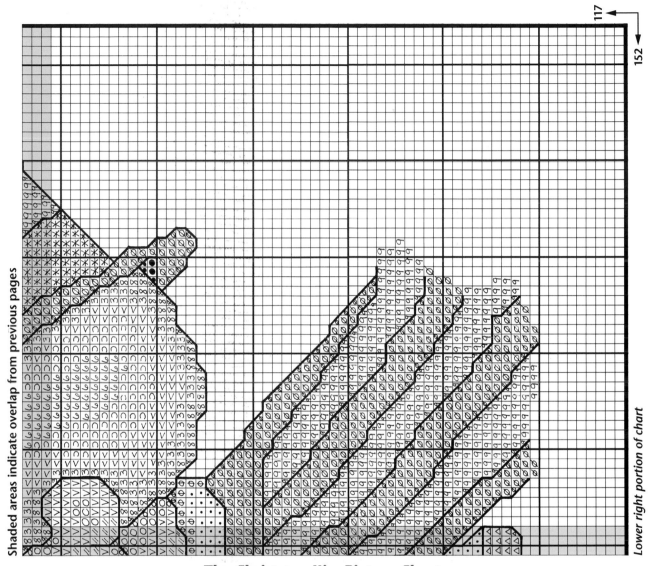

## The Christmas Kiss Picture Chart
### COLOR KEY

| | DMC | Anchor | J. & P. Coats | Color | | DMC | Anchor | J. & P. Coats | Color |
|---|---|---|---|---|---|---|---|---|---|
| 7 | 729 | 890 | 2875 | Med. Old Gold | < | 840 | 379 | 5379 | Med. Beige-Brown |
| V | 754 | 1012 | 2331 | Lt. Peach | ⊃ | 841 | 378 | 5376 | Lt. Beige-Brown |
| O | 758 | 882 | 2337 | Lt. Terra Cotta | 6 | 842 | 388 | 5933 | Vy. Lt. Beige-Brown |
| ∧ | 760 | 1022 | 3069 | Salmon | | 898 | 360 | 5476 | Vy. Dk. Coffee Brown |
| Z | 761 | 1021 | 3068 | Lt. Salmon | ✳ | 902 | 897 | 3083 | Vy. Dk. Garnet |
| Φ | 762 | 234 | 8510 | Vy. Lt. Pearl Gray | Ø | 924 | 851 | 6008 | Vy. Dk. Slate Green |
| I | 814 | 45 | 3044 | Dk. Garnet | 9 | 926 | 850 | 6007 | Slate Green |
| U | 815 | 43 | 3000 | Med. Garnet | / | 927 | 848 | 6006 | Med. Slate Green |
| ✕ | 816 | 1005 | 3021 | Garnet | C | 928 | 274 | 6005 | Lt. Slate Green |
| 8 | 838 | 380 | 5478 | Vy. Dk. Beige-Brown | // | 948 | 1011 | 2331 | Vy. Lt. Peach |
| 3 | 839 | 360 | 5360 | Dk. Beige-Brown | | | | | |

# SANTA'S ON HIS WAY SWEATSHIRT

*Reach into your scrap bag for bits of country fabrics to make this charming Santa appliqué. He's on his pre-Christmas visit, checking to see if the decorations are up, the stockings hung, and the fireplaces free of soot.*

## SIZE

Santa motif is 13½" tall

## MATERIALS

* ¼ yard of dark red solid fabric for the coat, sleeve, hat, and heart
* One 5" × 13" piece of cream solid fabric for the beard, hat trim, sleeve trim, and coat trim
* One 5" × 6" piece of khaki solid fabric for the sack and mitten
* Scrap of dark green print fabric for the tree
* Scrap of black solid fabric for the front and back boots
* Scrap of pink solid fabric for the face
* Scrap of dark red, green, and cream stripe fabric for the front and back pant legs and sleeve cuff
* ¾ yard of fusible webbing
* One adult's dark green sweatshirt
* 8" × 13" piece of tear-away stabilizer
* Matching thread
* One ¼"-diameter light blue button for Santa's eye
* One ¾"-diameter white pom-pom for Santa's hat
* Five ⅝"-diameter flat gold metallic stars for the tree
* 5 clear seed beads for the tree

* 3 yards of 1"-wide dark red grosgrain ribbon for the froufrou
* 3 yards of ¾"-wide dark red and green stripe grosgrain ribbon for the froufrou
* 3 yards of ⅝"-wide cream grosgrain ribbon for the froufrou
* 4 yards of ¼"-wide metallic gold ribbon for the froufrou
* Eight ⅝"-diameter gold jingle bells for the froufrou
* 8" length of ¾"-wide white Velcro strip for the froufrou

## DIRECTIONS

**Note:** Wash, dry, and press your sweatshirt and fabrics before beginning this project.

**1.** Prepare all pattern pieces as directed in "Preparing Patterns" on page 236, using the patterns on page 123.

**2.** Fuse the fusible webbing to each fabric piece as directed in "Fusible Webbing" on page 235.

**3.** Refer to "Machine Appliqué" on page 235 for directions on marking and cutting appliqué pieces. From the dark red solid, mark and cut one coat, one sleeve, one hat, and one heart. From the cream solid, mark and cut one beard, one hat trim, one sleeve trim, and one coat trim. From the khaki solid, mark and cut one sack and one mitten. From the dark green print, mark and cut one tree. From the black solid, mark and cut one front boot and one back boot. From the pink solid, mark and cut one face. From the stripe, mark and cut one front pant leg, one back pant leg, and one sleeve cuff. Remove the paper backing from the appliqués.

## COUNTRY TIPS
### *from Alma Lynne*

The simplicity of this Santa appliqué allows you to adapt it for other purposes. Reduce the patterns on a copy machine, then machine appliqué the Santas marching around the perimeter of a tree skirt. Or reduce the pattern to three or four different sizes and machine appliqué one on a stocking for each member of the family—Dad, of course, gets the largest Santa; Mom, the second largest; the oldest child, the third largest; and so on.

It would be fun to make a stuffed Santa mobile for over the kitchen table. Reduce the pattern about 60 percent and make six Santas; use muslin as the base fabric. Then, flip the pattern over and make six more Santas in the same manner. With wrong sides together, sew one Santa and one flipped Santa together, leaving a small opening. Lightly stuff each one, then whipstitch the openings closed. Attach the Santas to purchased mobile arms with pretty ribbons, then tie a tiny bell on each ribbon end for embellishment.

**4.** Arrange the appliqué pieces on the sweatshirt front, having the top of Santa's hat 2½" from the center front neckline; refer to the **Appliqué Placement Diagram** to layer the pieces as indicated by the dashed lines. Fuse in place as directed in "Fusible Webbing" on page 235.

**5.** Center and pin the tear-away stabilizer to the back of the sweatshirt front. Using matching threads, machine appliqué around all edges. Machine appliqué along the dotted lines to define Santa's moustache and the tree branches.

**6.** Sew the button eye to Santa's face and the pom-pom to the tip of Santa's hat. Sew a star and a bead to the top of the tree and to each branch.

**7.** Cut the ribbons into ½-yard pieces. Using the ribbons, bells, and Velcro, add the froufrou to the shoulders as directed in "Froufrou" on page 239.

**Appliqué Placement Diagram**

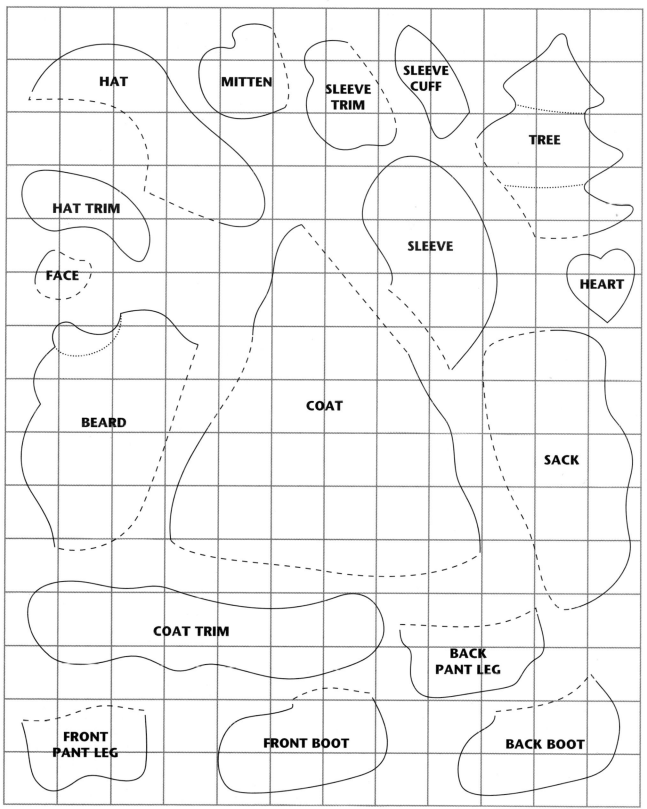

Enlarge 181%

**Santa's on His Way Appliqué Patterns**

1 square = 1"

# TOY SOLDIER AND BACKYARD SNOWMAN ORNAMENTS

*Pressed for time? Whip up these cute ornaments in just one evening! The stoic soldier stands guard at the palace while the always-lovable lumpy snowman waits for his carrot nose and warm muffler.*

## SIZE

Soldier design area is ¾" × 2⅛" (over two threads) on 28-count linen

Snowman design area is 2⅛" square (over two threads) on 28-count linen

## MATERIALS

* ★ Two 7" squares of 28-count periwinkle pastel linen
* ★ One skein of embroidery floss for each color listed in **Color Key**
* ★ Size 24 or 26 tapestry needle
* ★ Compass
* ★ 5" × 10" piece of white posterboard
* ★ Two 4" squares of print fabric for backing
* ★ White tacky glue
* ★ Hot-glue gun
* ★ Two 4½"-diameter grapevine wreaths
* ★ One small bunch of dried baby's-breath
* ★ 10" of red paper ribbon
* ★ 10" of jute twine for hangers

## DIRECTIONS

**1.** Prepare the edges of the linen as directed in "Preparing Fabric Edges" on page 232. Find the center of the linen and mark it with a pin. Find the centers of the **Toy Soldier Chart** and the **Backyard Snowman Chart** by connecting the arrows.

**2.** Matching the centers of the chart and the linen, and using two strands of floss, begin stitching at the center points, working each cross-stitch over two threads. Work outward until the entire design is complete.

**3.** Backstitch the designs with one strand of black-brown. Work the French knots for the snowman eyes with two strands of dark pewter gray.

**4.** Wash and press the completed cross-stitch pieces as directed in "Washing and Pressing" on page 233.

**5.** Using the compass, draw two 3¾" circles on the posterboard. Then draw another two 3⅝" circles on the print fabric. Set the print fabric aside.

**6.** Center one cross-stitch piece, right side up, over the posterboard circle. Trim the linen to ½" beyond the posterboard edge. Begin to pull the raw edges of the linen to the back of the posterboard, taking care to smooth any wrinkles and cutting away excess linen as necessary. Use tacky glue to secure the linen to the posterboard. Repeat for the second cross-stitch design.

7. Use the tacky glue to glue the print fabric circle, right side up, to the back of the cross-stitch mounting.

8. With the design centered and using hot glue, glue the cross-stitch mounting to the back of one grapevine wreath.

9. Repeat Steps 6 through 8 for the remaining cross-stitch piece.

10. Hot-glue two or three stems of baby's-breath to each wreath as desired, fanning out to the left and right from the eight o'clock position.

11. Unravel the paper ribbon and cut it in half lengthwise. Make a bow with each length. Hot-glue one bow over each baby's-breath grouping.

12. Cut the twine in half. To make each hanger, tie the twine around one grapevine stem at the top of the wreath; glue the knot close to the wreath base.

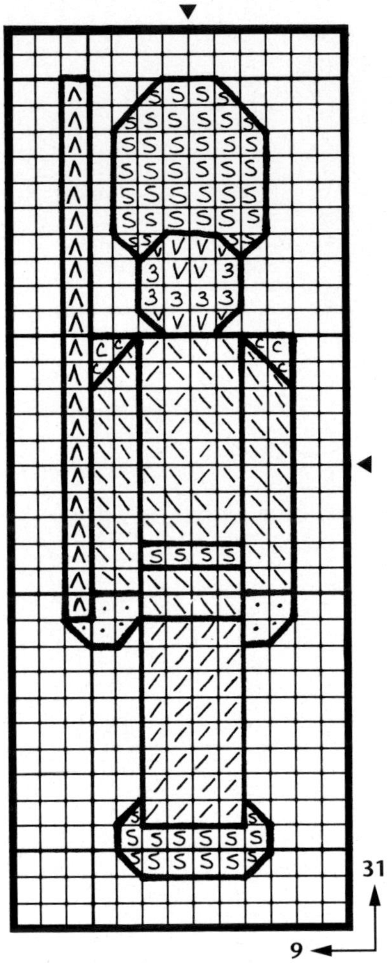


## Toy Soldier

### DESIGN OPTIONS

| Fabric Count | Design Area | Cutting Dimensions |
|---|---|---|
| 22 | ⅜" x 1⅜" | 6⅜" x 7⅜" |
| 18 | ½" x 1¾" | 6½" x 7¾" |
| 14 | ⅝" x 2¼" | 6⅝" x 8¼" |
| 11 | ⅞" x 2¾" | 6⅞" x 8¾" |

## Toy Soldier Chart

### COLOR KEY

| | DMC | Anchor | J. & P. Coats | Color |
|---|---|---|---|---|
| • | White | 2 | 1001 | White |
| / | Ecru | 387 | 5387 | Ecru |
| \ | 223 | 895 | 3240 | Med. Shell Pink |
| S | 310 | 403 | 8403 | Black |
| 3 | 353 | 6 | 3006 | Peach |
| C | 833 | 907 | — | Lt. Olive Green |
| ∧ | 840 | 379 | 5379 | Med. Beige-Brown |
| V | 948 | 1011 | 2331 | Vy. Lt. Peach |
| | 3371 | 382 | 5382 | Black-Brown |

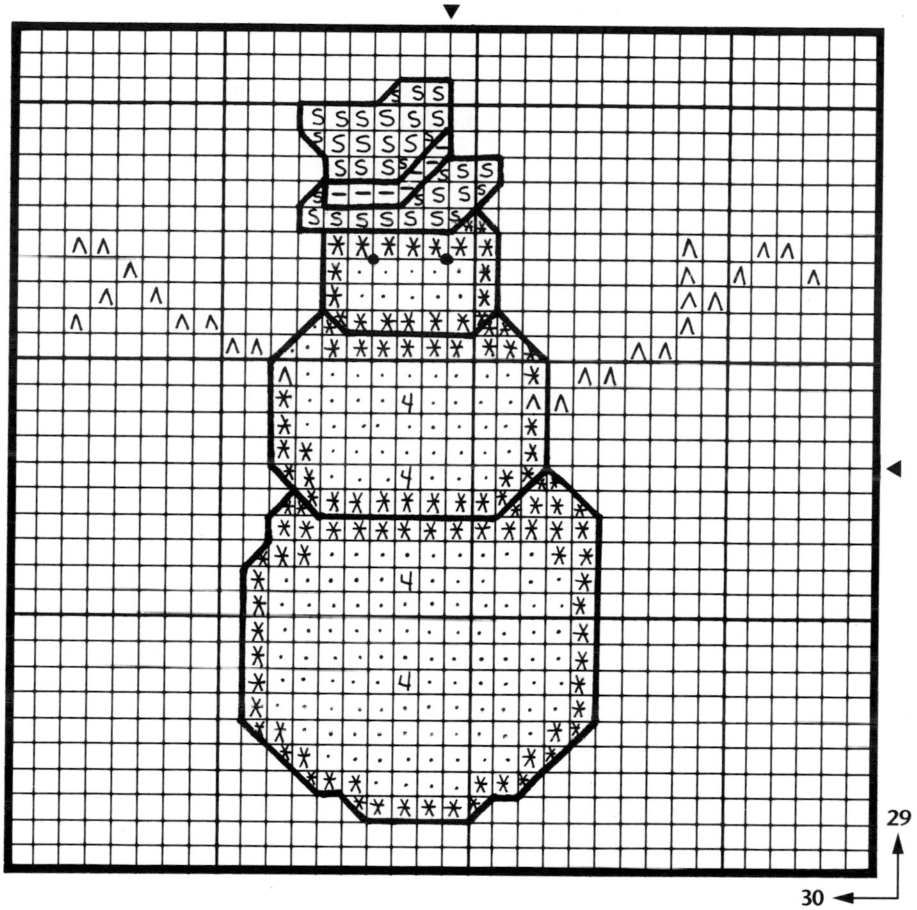


## Backyard Snowman

### DESIGN OPTIONS

| Fabric Count | Design Area | Cutting Dimensions |
|---|---|---|
| 22 | 1⅜" x 1⅜" | 7⅜" x 7⅜" |
| 18 | 1⅝" x 1⅝" | 7⅝" x 7⅝" |
| 14 | 2⅛" x 2⅛" | 8⅛" x 8⅛" |
| 11 | 2¾" x 2⅝" | 8¾" x 8⅝" |

## Backyard Snowman Chart

### COLOR KEY

| | DMC | Anchor | J. & P. Coats | Color |
|---|---|---|---|---|
| • | White | 2 | 1001 | White |
| S | 310 | 403 | 8403 | Black |
| 4 | 413 | 401 | 8514 | Dk. Pewter Gray |
| * | 762 | 234 | 8510 | Vy. Lt. Pearl Gray |
| ∧ | 840 | 379 | 5379 | Med. Beige-Brown |
| — | 902 | 897 | 3083 | Vy. Dk. Garnet |
| | 3371 | 382 | 5382 | Black-Brown |

# NEEDLE LITTLE CHRISTMAS TREE-O

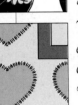

*Dressed in rag-bag clothes and laden with bundles, this charitable Santa travels about bringing hope to folks who "needle" little Christmas spirit. The pint-size stuffed Santa is easy to sew from leftover country plaids. Then accent with a striped satchel and vine wreath. Or machine appliqué coordinating scraps of fabric for the tiny tree skirt and mini quilt.*

## NEEDLE LITTLE CHRISTMAS SANTA

### SIZE

Finished doll is 15" tall

### MATERIALS

* ⅛ yard of 44"-wide tea-dyed small red check fabric for the body*
* ¼ yard of 44"-wide tea-dyed green stripe fabric for the legs, satchel, and boot ties*
* Scrap of unbleached muslin for the head
* Matching thread
* Polyester fiberfill
* Soft-sculpture doll needle
* Matching buttonhole twist thread
* Six ½"-diameter clear buttons
* ⅛ yard of 44"-wide dark green chintz fabric for the knickers
* ⅛ yard of 44"-wide tea-dyed large red check fabric for the boots and wreath ribbon*

* ¼ yard of 44"-wide green stripe fabric for the bag and boot ties
* ⅛ yard of 44"-wide red knit fabric for the mittens, cap, and arms*
* Two blue seed beads for the eyes
* Powdered blusher
* One package natural curly crepe wool hair
* Hot-glue gun
* One ⅝"-diameter bell for the cap
* Two ⅜"-diameter bells for the boots
* One 4½"-diameter grapevine wreath

*See page 239 for directions on tea dyeing.

### DIRECTIONS

**Note:** Needle Little Christmas Santa is for decorative purposes only; his clothing cannot be removed.

1. For instructions on constructing Needle Little Christmas Santa, see "Draw-and-Sew Method" on page 236. Follow the directions to make Santa, using the patterns on page 131 and the following fabrics: small red check for the body and arms, green stripe for the legs, and muslin for the head. Stuff each lightly. Flatten the top of the legs so the seams are centered in the front and back. Baste across the upper edge.

2. Using the doll needle and the buttonhole twist, hand sew the legs and head to the body. Knot a 20" length of buttonhole twist at one end and thread it through the doll needle. Matching the large dots, run the needle from the outside of one arm through to the inside of the arm, then through the body and the other arm. Run the needle up through a hole of one button and down through the other hole, then back through the front arm, the

body, and the other arm. Thread another button onto the buttonhole twist and pass the needle back through the arms and body several times to secure. Knot tightly.

**3.** Use the patterns on the opposite page for Santa's hand-me-down clothing; sew the clothing using a ¼" seam allowance. From the dark green chintz, cut the knickers and two 1" × 6" strips for the suspenders. From the large red check, cut four boots, then tear two 1" × 12" strips for the wreath ribbon. From the green stripe, cut one 4" × 8½" piece for the satchel and one 1" × 5" strip for the satchel strap, then tear two 1" × 9" strips for the boot ties. From the red knit, cut four mittens and one cap, referring to the **Cap Cutting Diagram.**

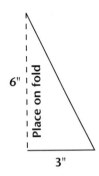

6"

Place on fold

3"

**Cap Cutting Diagram**

**4.** With right sides together, sew the side seam of the knickers. Press under ¼" on the waist and leg openings; turn right side out. Run gathering threads around the openings. Place the knickers on Santa and gather to fit; secure the threads.

**5.** Fold each suspender in half lengthwise with right sides together and sew along the long edge. Turn each to the right side and press. Slip each suspender inside Santa's knickers in the front and hand sew in place, adding a button to the knickers where the suspender joins. Bring one suspender over each shoulder, crossing them in back. Slip each suspender inside Santa's knickers in the back, adding the buttons.

**6.** With right sides together, sew the boots together in pairs, leaving the top edges open. Turn to the right side. Place the boots on Santa. Wrap one boot tie around each ankle and knot, leaving the ends free.

**7.** With right sides together, sew up the long side of the cap. Turn to the right side. Turn under 1" around the opening, then fold ½" back to the right side and hand tack in place. Lightly press. Set the cap aside. With right sides together, sew pairs of mittens together, leaving the wrist edge open. Turn to the right side. Place one mitten on each hand.

**8.** Fold the satchel in half crosswise with right sides together to form a 4" × 4¼" piece. Sew the side seams. Turn under ½" along the top edge and press. Hand sew the hem. Fold the satchel strap in half lengthwise with right sides together and sew along the long edge. Turn to the right side and press. Hand tack one end of the strap inside the satchel at one side seam. Place the strap over Santa's right shoulder and hand tack it to the center of the right suspender. Bend Santa's right elbow and hand tack his hand to the satchel strap and suspender.

**9.** Sew the bead eyes to Santa's face where indicated on the pattern. Blush the cheeks.

**10.** Unravel several inches of the hair and cut it into 3" lengths. Hot-glue the hair to Santa's head and around his face, forming a beard. Groom if necessary.

**11.** Place the cap on Santa's head and hand tack it in place. Bring the cap end to the right side of Santa's face and hand tack it in place. Sew the ⅝" bell to the cap tip.

**12.** Sew one ⅜" bell to each boot tip.

**13.** Wrap one wreath ribbon strip around the wreath and hot-glue the ends to the wreath bottom. Tie the remaining strip in a bow and hot-glue it to the wreath. Place the wreath on Santa's left arm, bending the elbow. Hand tack his left hand to the left suspender.

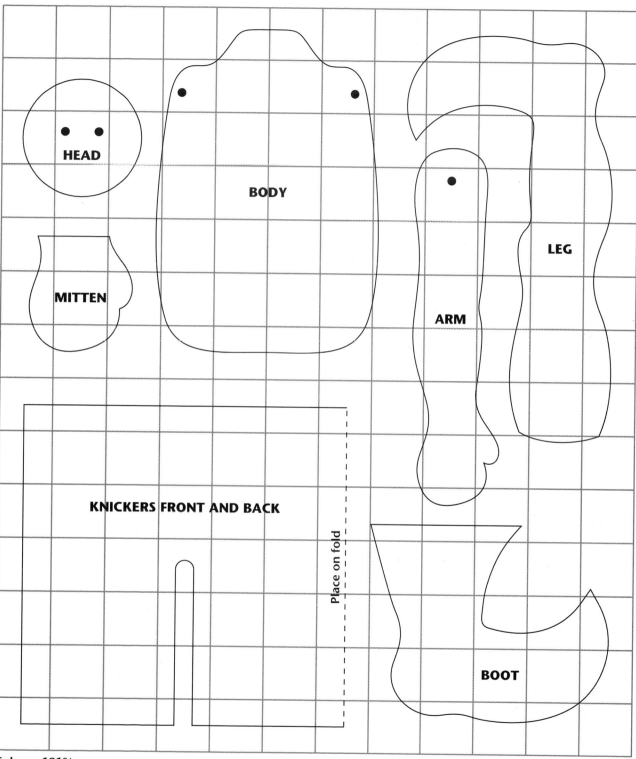

HEAD

BODY

LEG

MITTEN

ARM

KNICKERS FRONT AND BACK

Place on fold

BOOT

Enlarge 181%

**Hand-Me-Down Clothes Patterns**

1 square = 1"

# NEEDLE LITTLE CHRISTMAS TREE SKIRT

## SIZE

Finished tree skirt is 15" square

## MATERIALS

* ½ yard of 44"-wide khaki solid fabric for the tree skirt
* ⅜ yard of 44"-wide tea-dyed green check fabric for the piping*
* ½ yard of fleece
* ¾ yard of fusible webbing
* Scrap of tea-dyed red check fabric for the shirt and boots*
* Scrap of dark green chintz fabric for the knickers and package
* Scrap of white solid fabric for the hair and beard
* Scrap of peach solid fabric for the face
* Scrap of maroon solid fabric for the cap and package
* Scrap of natural burlap for the satchel
* Scrap of black solid fabric for the mittens
* Scrap of tea-dyed green stripe fabric for the leggings*
* Scrap of dark green print fabric for the trees
* Scrap of brown solid fabric for the tree trunks
* Scrap of cream solid fabric for the hat trim
* 9" square of tear-away stabilizer
* Matching thread
* ¾ yard of ⅛"-wide green satin ribbon
* Three 4 mm round gold beads for the hats
* Three ¼"-diameter gold jingle bells for the shoes
* Three blue seed beads for the eyes
* 1⅛ yards of ⅜"-diameter cording
* ¾ yards of 1"-wide dark red grosgrain ribbon

*See page 239 for directions on tea dyeing.

## DIRECTIONS

**Note:** Wash, dry, and press all your fabrics before beginning this project. All seam allowances are ½".

1. Prepare all pattern pieces as directed in "Preparing Patterns" on page 236, using the patterns on page 137.

2. From the khaki, cut two 16" squares for the tree skirt. From the green check, cut one 2" × 66" bias strip for the piping. From the fleece, cut one 16" square.

3. Place the two khaki squares with right sides together. Fold them in half from top to bottom, then fold in half again from side to side. Using a compass, measure and mark a 1" quarter-circle, referring to the **Cutting Diagram.** Cut on the line through all thicknesses to form the opening for the tree trunk.

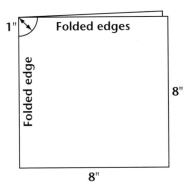

**Cutting Diagram**

4. Cut the fleece to match the khaki squares. Unfold the khaki squares and the fleece. Place the fabrics on top of the fleece. Using a ruler, draw a line from one corner to the center opening. Cut on the line through all thicknesses to form the back opening. Set one square and the fleece aside.

**5.** Fuse the fusible webbing to the remaining fabrics, as directed in "Fusible Webbing" on page 235.

**6.** Refer to "Machine Appliqué" on page 235 for directions on marking and cutting appliqué pieces. From the red check, cut three left sleeves, three right sleeves, three shirts, and three boots. From the dark green chintz, cut three knickers and three large packages. From the white solid, cut three beards. From the peach solid, cut three faces. From the maroon solid, cut three hats and three small packages. From the burlap, cut three satchels. From the black solid, cut three left mittens and three right mittens. From the green stripe, cut three leggings. From the green print, cut three trees. From the brown solid, cut three trunks. From the cream solid, cut three hat trims. Remove the paper backing from the appliqué pieces.

**7.** Referring to the **Tree Skirt Diagram,** arrange the appliqué pieces on the tree skirt; see the **Appliqué Placement Diagram** on

**Tree Skirt Diagram**

page 135 to layer the pieces as indicated by the dashed lines. Fuse in place as directed in "Fusible Webbing" on page 235.

**8.** Center and pin the tear-away stabilizer to the back of the tree skirt. Machine appliqué all edges of the Santa (except the shirt back) and trees using matching threads. Machine appliqué Santa's moustache line with white thread as indicated by the thin line on the beard pattern. Machine appliqué the suspender lines (the shirt back and the thin line on the shirt pattern) and the cuff (the thin line on the knickers) with green thread.

**9.** Cut the green ribbon into three equal lengths. Tie each length in a bow and clip the ribbon ends diagonally. Hand tack one to each satchel. Sew one gold bead to the tip of each cap and one bell to the tip of each boot. Sew one seed bead eye to each face.

**10.** Make 66" of corded piping as directed in "Making Corded Piping" on page 238. Sew the piping to the tree skirt front. Do not trim the seam allowance.

**11.** Layer the fleece, the tree skirt right side up, then the backing wrong side up. Pin the layers together. Sew around all four sides and around the back and center openings, leaving a 6" opening along one side. Grade the seam allowances. Turn the tree skirt to the right side and whipstitch closed.

**12.** Cut the grosgrain ribbon in half. Tie each length in a bow and hand tack one to the top left side and one to the bottom left side of the opening.

# NEEDLE LITTLE CHRISTMAS MINI QUILT

## SIZE

Finished quilt is 15" square

## MATERIALS

* ⅜ yard of 44"-wide khaki solid fabric for the center panel
* ⅛ yard of 44"-wide dark green solid fabric for the inner border strips
* ⅛ yard of 44"-wide dark red solid fabric for the middle border strips
* ½ yard of 44"-wide green check fabric for the outer border strips and backing
* ½ yard of fleece
* ½ yard of fusible webbing
* Scrap of tea-dyed red check fabric for the shirt and boots*
* Scrap of dark green chintz fabric for the knickers and package
* Scrap of white solid fabric for the hair and beard
* Scrap of peach solid fabric for the face
* Scrap of maroon solid fabric for the cap and package
* Scrap of natural burlap for the satchel
* Scrap of black solid fabric for the mittens
* Scrap of tea-dyed green stripe fabric for the leggings*
* Scrap of dark green print fabric for the trees
* Scrap of brown solid fabric for the tree trunks
* Scrap of cream solid fabric for the hat trim
* 9" square of tear-away stabilizer
* Matching thread
* ¼ yard of ⅛"-wide green satin ribbon
* Two 4 mm round gold beads for the shoe and hat
* One blue seed bead for the eye
* 1½ yards of 1"-wide dark red grosgrain ribbon

*See page 239 for directions on tea dyeing.

## DIRECTIONS

**Note:** Wash, dry, and press fabrics before beginning this project. All seam allowances are ¼".

**1.** Prepare all pattern pieces as directed in "Preparing Patterns" on page 236, using the patterns on page 137.

**2.** From the khaki solid, cut a 9½" square for the center panel. From the dark green solid, cut two 1" × 9½" inner border strips and two 1" × 10½" inner border strips. From the dark red solid, cut two 1½" × 10½" middle border

---

## COUNTRY THOUGHTS
### *from Alma Lynne*

The holiday season always brings out the best in people. In my local area, we have many organizations to assist those less fortunate during the holidays and year-round. Along with clothing drives, we have programs that collect toys for children, groceries for seniors, and donations for homeless centers.

I encourage you to become involved in your community's programs, especially around the holidays. Nursing homes and rehabilitation centers welcome your holiday visits. Bring along a basket full of greeting cards, and hand one to each resident. Or gather a few friends and a pile of scrap fabrics, and lead a crafting session with the residents. Instead of exchanging gifts with your extended family, pool your resources and "adopt" a needy family through your local social service agency. When you go to buy your tree this year, buy two and deliver the second one to a shelter. Organize a canned food drive at your place of employment or your church, then deliver the collections to a local soup kitchen.

Every little bit counts when it comes to helping others. Let the holiday spirit inspire you to become involved.

**Appliqué Placement Diagram**

strips and two 1½" × 12½" middle border strips. From the green check, cut two 2" × 12½" outer border strips, two 2" × 15½" outer border strips, and one 15½" square for the backing. From the fleece, cut a 15½" square.

**3.** Fuse the fusible webbing to the remaining fabrics, as directed in "Fusible Webbing" on page 235.

**4.** Refer to "Machine Appliqué" on page 235 for directions on marking and cutting appliqué pieces. Using the patterns on page 137, cut out the pieces as follows: From the red check, cut one left arm, one right arm, one shirt, and one boot. From the chintz, cut one knickers and one large package. From the white solid, cut one beard. From the peach solid, cut one face. From the maroon solid, cut one hat and one small package. From the

burlap, cut one satchel. From the black solid, cut one left mitten and one right mitten. From the green stripe, cut one leggings. From the green print, cut three trees. From the brown solid, cut three trunks. From the cream solid, cut one hat trim. Remove the paper backing from the appliqué pieces.

**5.** Arrange the appliqué pieces on the center panel, referring to the **Appliqué Placement Diagram,** and layering as indicated by the dashed lines. Fuse in place as directed in "Fusible Webbing" on page 235.

**6.** Center and pin the tear-away stabilizer to the back of the center panel. Machine appliqué all edges of the Santa (except the shirt back) and trees using matching threads. Machine appliqué Santa's moustache line with white thread, as indicated by the thin line on the beard pattern. Machine appliqué the suspender lines (the shirt back and the thin line on the shirt pattern) and the cuff (the thin line on the knickers) with green thread.

**7.** With right sides together and raw edges even, sew one 1" × 9½" inner border strip to each side of the center panel, as shown in **Diagram 1.** Press the seams toward the borders. Sew one 1" × 10½" inner border strip to the top and bottom of the center panel in the same manner; see **Diagram 2.** Press the seams toward the borders.

**8.** Repeat Step 7 for the dark red middle border strips and the green check outer border strips.

**9.** Tie a bow with the green ribbon and clip the ends diagonally. Hand tack it to Santa's satchel. Sew one gold bead to the tip of Santa's hat and one to the tip of his boot. Sew the seed bead eye to Santa's face.

**10.** Layer the fleece, the mini quilt top right side up, then the backing wrong side up. Pin all three layers together. Sew around the outer edge, leaving a 6" opening along the bottom edge. Grade the seam allowance to reduce bulk. Turn the mini quilt right side out and whipstitch the opening closed.

**11.** Cut the grosgrain ribbon into four equal lengths. Tie each in a bow and hand tack one to each corner of the mini quilt just inside the outer border.

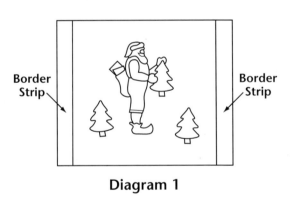

**Diagram 1**

**Diagram 2**

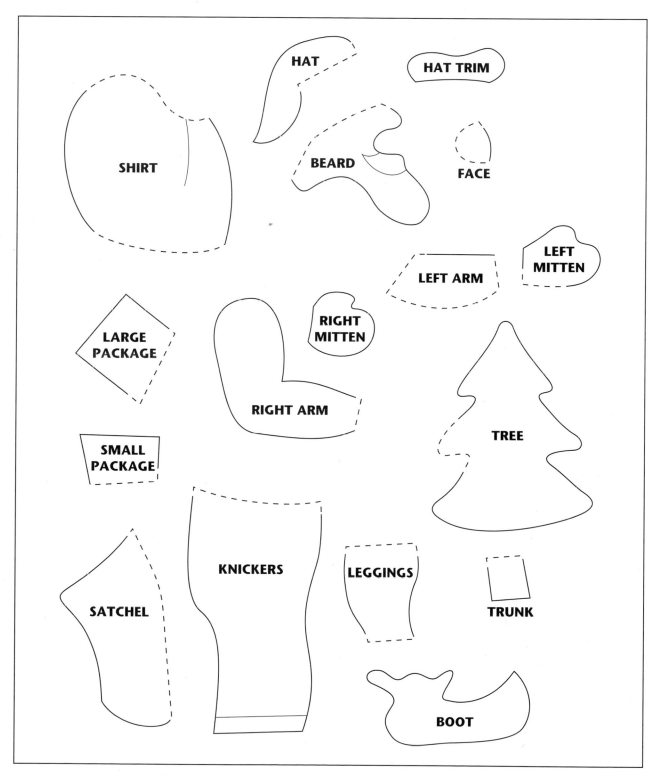

**Full-Size Needle Little Christmas Appliqué Patterns**

# MERRY LITTLE CHRISTMAS PILLOW

*Santa collectors will adore this replica of an old-time Kris Kringle. His beard has lightened gracefully and his eye is still a-twinkle. While his sentiment is simple, it certainly comes from the heart.*

## SIZE

Design area is 4⅞" × 5⅞" (over two threads) on 19-count Cork linen

Finished size is 13½" × 14½", including ruffle

## MATERIALS

- ★ One 10⅞" × 11⅞" piece of 19-count antique white Cork linen
- ★ One skein of embroidery floss for each color listed in **Color Key**
- ★ Size 24 or 26 tapestry needle
- ★ 1 yard of ⅜"-diameter prefinished maroon piping
- ★ 8" × 9" square of fleece
- ★ ¾ yard of 44"-wide red-and-green check fabric
- ★ Matching thread
- ★ 8" × 9" piece of fusible interfacing
- ★ ¼ yard of 44"-wide muslin
- ★ Polyester fiberfill
- ★ 1 yard of ⅝"-wide maroon grosgrain ribbon

## DIRECTIONS

**Note:** All seam allowances are ½".

**1.** Prepare the edges of the linen as directed in "Preparing Fabric Edges" on page 232. Find the center of the linen and mark it with a pin.

Find the center of the **Merry Little Christmas Pillow Chart** by connecting the arrows.

**2.** Matching the centers of the chart and the linen, and using two strands of floss, begin stitching at the center point, working each stitch over two threads. Work outward until the entire design is complete.

**3.** Using one strand of floss, backstitch the flower stems with very dark blue-green, the lettering with medium garnet, the heart with very dark garnet, and Santa with black-brown. Work French knots for the berries with two strands of garnet.

**4.** Wash and press the completed cross-stitch piece as directed in "Washing and Pressing" on page 233.

**5.** With the design centered, trim the linen to 8" × 9".

**6.** Sew the piping to the pillow front as directed in "Sewing On the Piping" on page 238. Do *not* trim the seam allowance. Sew the 8" × 9" piece of fleece to the wrong side of the pillow top along all four edges. Do *not* trim the seam allowance.

**7.** From the check, cut two 7½" × 33" strips for the ruffle and one 8" × 9" piece for the backing. With right sides together and raw edges even, sew the short ends of the two 7½" × 33" ruffle strips together to form one continuous ruffle; see **Diagram 1** on the opposite page. Press the seams open. Turn the strip right side out, fold it in half lengthwise with wrong sides together, and press. Sew a line of gathering stitches ⅜" from the

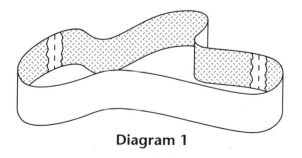

**Diagram 1**

raw edges through both layers of the ruffle. Fold the ruffle in half to find the midpoints, and place a pin at these points. Match the midpoints of the ruffle and mark the quarter-points with pins; see **Diagram 2** on page 140.

**8.** Sew the ruffle to the pillow top as directed in "Ruffles" on page 239.

**9.** Iron an 8" × 9" piece of fusible interfacing onto the wrong side of the pillow backing.

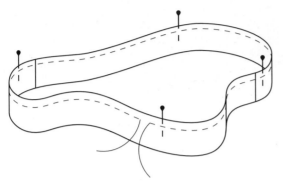

**Diagram 2**

**10.** Make a 6½" × 7½" covered pillow form and assemble the pillow, as directed in "Covered Pillow Forms" and "Assembling a Pillow" on page 239.

**11.** Cut the ribbon in half. Tie a bow with each length and hand tack one to the upper right corner and one to the lower left corner of the pillow top.

### DESIGN OPTIONS

| Fabric Count | Design Area | Cutting Dimensions |
|---|---|---|
| 22 | 2⅛" × 2½" | 12⅛" × 12½" |
| 18 | 2⅝" × 3⅛" | 12⅝" × 13⅛" |
| 14 | 3⅜" × 4" | 13⅜" × 14" |
| 11 | 4¼" × 5⅛" | 14¼" × 15⅛" |

## COUNTRY TIPS
*from Alma Lynne*

Since I'm such a Santa nut, I'm always drawn back to this design when I need a quick gift. I've stitched it as a pillow many times, but I have great ideas for variations on the theme.

If you want a more Victorian look, stitch the lettering, heart, and berries with very dark garnet; change the eye color to a darker blue. Then, back the pillow with a maroon velvet, omitting the piping, ruffle, and bows. It will make a truly elegant statement.

For a more traditional look, stitch the design on white or cream Aida, then pipe the pillow with a brighter red. You could use a candy-cane stripe fabric or a holly-pattern fabric for the backing and ruffle. Add a jingle bell on his hat for a pom-pom and a ceramic button for the heart motif.

Try making a small sachet for a friend or neighbor—it would be a great addition to a holiday gift basket. Stitch the design over one thread on 18- or 22-count fabric, omitting the holly and heart motifs at the bottom. Trim the fabric to within ½" of the design, then cut a same-size piece of fabric for the backing. Place right sides together and sew around the perimeter, leaving an opening for turning. Turn to the right side and stuff with pine-scented potpourri. Whipstitch the opening closed. Hand tack a pretty ribbon hanger to the upper edge so the recipient can hang the sachet from a cupboard door or a doorknob.

**Merry Little Christmas Pillow Chart**
COLOR KEY

| | DMC | Anchor | J. & P. Coats | Color | | DMC | Anchor | J. & P. Coats | Color |
|---|---|---|---|---|---|---|---|---|---|
| • | White | 2 | 1001 | White | O | 775 | 128 | 7031 | Vy. Lt. Baby Blue |
| 3 | 353 | 6 | 3006 | Peach | ■ | 798 | 131 | 7022 | Dk. Delft |
| I | 498 | 1005 | 3000 | Dk. Christmas Red | V | 815 | 43 | 3000 | Med. Garnet |
| | 500 | 683 | 6880 | Vy. Dk. Blue-Green | C | 816 | 1005 | 3021 | Garnet |
| ∧ | 501 | 878 | 6878 | Dk. Blue-Green | \ | 822 | 390 | 5933 | Lt. Beige-Gray |
| L | 502 | 877 | 6876 | Blue-Green | \\ | 902 | 897 | 3083 | Vy. Dk. Garnet |
| ⊃ | 503 | 876 | 6879 | Med. Blue-Green | — | 948 | 1011 | 2331 | Vy. Lt. Peach |
| ✕ | 644 | 830 | 5830 | Med. Beige-Gray | | 3371 | 382 | 5382 | Black-Brown |
| ╱ | 754 | 1012 | 2331 | Lt. Peach | | | | | |

# ROLY-POLY SANTA SWEATER

*He teeters and he totters and he doesn't fall down! It seems that jolly ol' Santa ate too many of Mrs. Claus's cookies before his big trip this year. Not to worry, though—he still manages to deliver Christmas cheer year after year despite his expanding belly!*

## SIZE

Design area is 7½" × 9⅞" on 6 × 8 gauge

## MATERIALS

* One 6 × 8-gauge adult's stockinette stitch white pullover sweater
* One skein of embroidery floss for each color listed in **Color Key** (unless otherwise indicated)
* One skein of angora floss for each color listed in **Color Key***
* Size 22 tapestry needle
* One ¾"-diameter white pom-pom
* One ⅝"-wide flat gold metallic star
* One 5 mm gold bead
* Matching thread
* 1 yard of 1"-wide garnet grosgrain ribbon for the cuff bows
* 2 yards of ⅜"-wide blue grosgrain ribbon for the froufrou
* 2 yards of 1"-wide white grosgrain ribbon for the froufrou
* 2 yards of ⅝"-wide garnet grosgrain ribbon for the froufrou
* ¼ yard *each* of 44"-wide green plaid and green print fabrics for the froufrou
* Pinking shears

* Six ¾"-diameter gold jingle bells
* One 8" length of 1"-wide Velcro for the froufrou

*See "Buyer's Guide" on page 240 for ordering information.

## DIRECTIONS

**1.** Plan the placement of the Roly Poly Santa design on your sweater. You will need at least 105 vertical stitches down the sweater front. On the model, I had 148 verti-

## COUNTRY THOUGHTS
*from Alma Lynne*

I started collecting Santa Clauses many years ago. I have a few Santas from my childhood, and I absolutely treasure them. My first purchased Santa, from a quaint little gift store in town, was named "Mr. Knicker-Britches." It wasn't long before I headed right to the Santa section of any shop—even if it was August. My favorite Santa is one that a friend made for me. He's very tall and very thin, and he's dressed in striped pants, a burlap coat, and a tiny hand-knitted cap. He's propped against his big sack of miniature toys.

I display my Santas in our family dining room so we can enjoy them year-round. During the holidays, I "sprinkle" Santas all over the house. In fact, if you visited us at Christmastime, you'd probably find a Santa around every corner. To say I love Santas is an understatement. Collecting all kinds, shapes, and sizes of the cute little guy is one of my great passions. Perhaps you've noticed that in my needlework designs!

cal stitches. I counted down 53 knit stitches from the center front neckline and marked it with a pin; this was the center stitch of my design. For your sweater, you may follow the directions above, or you can center the design vertically on the sweater front by counting the total number of vertical stitches and dividing that number by two; mark the center stitch with a pin. Find the center of the **Roly-Poly Santa Sweater Chart** by connecting the arrows.

**2.** Read the duplicate stitch basics in "The Stitches" on page 235. Matching the center of the chart with the marked center stitch on the sweater, duplicate stitch the design using six strands of embroidery floss. Use only one strand of angora floss.

**3.** Wash and press the completed duplicate stitch design as directed in "Washing and Pressing" on page 235.

**4.** Sew the pom-pom to the tip of Santa's hat. Sew the star, then the bead, to the top of the Christmas tree.

**5.** Cut the 1"-wide ribbon in half. Tie each length into a bow and sew one to the top of each sleeve cuff.

**6.** Cut the remaining ribbons into ½-yard lengths. Using pinking shears, cut the fabrics into 1½" × 36" strips, then cut each strip into two 18" lengths. Using the ribbons, fabric strips, bells, and Velcro, add the froufrou to the shoulders as directed in "Froufrou" on page 239.

### COLOR KEY

| | DMC | Anchor | J. & P. Coats | Color |
|---|---|---|---|---|
| • | White | 2 | 1001 | White |
| e | 310 | 403 | 8403 | Black |
| 7 | 347 | 1025 | 3013 | Vy. Dk. Salmon |
| 3 | 353 | 6 | 3006 | Peach |
| ∧ | 501 | 878 | 6878 | Dk. Blue-Green |
| ⊃ | 503 | 876 | 6879 | Med. Blue-Green |
| / | 739 | 387 | 5369 | Ultra Vy. Lt. Tan |
| V | 754 | 1012 | 2331 | Lt. Peach |
| × | 775 | 128 | 7031 | Vy. Lt. Baby Blue |
| — | 797 | 132 | 7143 | Royal Blue |
| ✳ | 814 | 45 | 3044 | Dk. Garnet |
| C | 816 | 1005 | 3021 | Garnet (2 skeins) |
| S | 930 | 1035 | 7052 | Dk. Antique Blue |
| I | 931 | 1034 | 7051 | Med. Antique Blue |
| L | 932 | 1033 | 7050 | Lt. Antique Blue |
| ＼ | 948 | 1011 | 2331 | Vy. Lt. Peach |
| Ø | Rainbow Gallery Angora Floss SB-1 | | | |

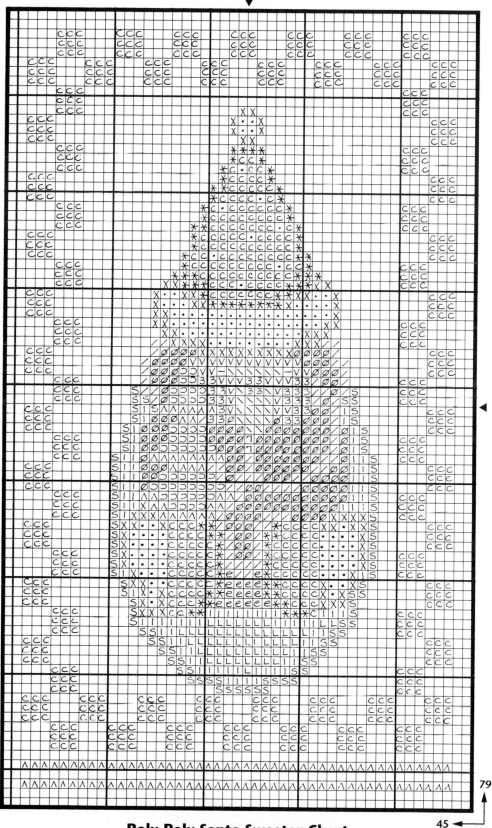

**Roly-Poly Santa Sweater Chart**

79

45

# DAYS
## TO CELEBRATE

If it were up to me, I'd host a party every day of the year and I'd invite every one of you! I have so much fun decorating my home for each holiday—big and little alike— that I just had to share some of my favorite projects with you.

Whether it's rejoicing at the start of warm weather, enjoying a much-deserved day off, or spooking the neighborhood trick-or-treaters, you'll be inspired to stitch your way through the year with these great ideas. Even though each project celebrates a specific occasion or holiday, you can enjoy them all year just as I do!

# FIRST DAY OF SPRING SWEATER

*Celebrate Mother Earth's awakening by duplicate stitching this cheery sweater for a sweet little girl. The first day of spring always promises the song of robins and the bloom of flowers—and puts a bounce in your step.*

## SIZE

Design area for a single tulip is $3\frac{3}{8}$" × $8\frac{3}{8}$" on 6 × 8 gauge

## MATERIALS

* One 6 × 8-gauge child's stockinette stitch white pullover sweater
* One skein of embroidery floss for each color listed in **Color Key** (unless otherwise indicated)
* Size 22 tapestry needle
* 1½ yards *each* of 1"-wide yellow, white, green, and gold satin ribbons
* Two 1" rustproof safety pins

## DIRECTIONS

**1.** Plan the placement of the tulip motifs on your sweater. You will need room for at least 62 horizontal stitches near the ribbing to allow for two tulip motifs. On the model, I had 88 horizontal stitches. I marked the center stitch with a pin. I counted 16 horizontal stitches to the right of the center stitch and 36 vertical stitches from the top of the ribbing and placed

another pin. The second pin was the center stitch of the first tulip motif. I counted 16 stitches in the opposite direction from the first pin to start the second tulip motif. For your sweater, you may follow the directions above, or you can center the two tulips by counting the total number of vertical stitches and dividing by two; mark the center stitch with a pin. You will still need to count 16 horizontal stitches to the right and left of the center pin for the centers of the tulip motifs. Find the center of the **First Day of Spring Sweater Chart** by connecting the arrows.

**2.** Read the duplicate stitch basics in "The Stitches" on page 235. Matching the center of the **First Day of Spring Sweater Chart** and the marked center stitch (indicated by the second pin), duplicate stitch the first tulip motif using six strands of floss. Follow the directions above to center and duplicate stitch the second tulip motif.

**3.** Wash and press the completed duplicate stitch design as directed in "Washing and Pressing" on page 235.

**4.** Cut the ribbon lengths in half. Holding one length each of yellow, white, green, and gold ribbon together as if they were one, tie them into a bow and clip the ribbon ends diagonally.

**5.** Working from inside the sweater, pin each bow in place through the bow's knot. Remove the bows before laundering the garment.

# COUNTRY THOUGHTS
### *from Alma Lynne*

As soon as the gentle spring weather appears, I don my favorite gardening gloves, grab my shovel, and head into our courtyard. The tulips look so beautiful dotted around the flower beds. Thank goodness I have them to look at while I'm arranging my bedding plants. All that fall planting was worth it!

Tulips are easy to grow—the difficult part is choosing from the hundred or so varieties! Tulips come in every color except true blue. The most common shades are white, pink, red, and yellow. How can you choose? First, decide whether you want the tulips to bloom throughout the season, or just for a big show for a few weeks in mid to late spring. Here are some popular types listed by bloom season.

### Early Blooming Tulips

★ Single early: Fragrant 2"–4" flowers with 12"–14" stems
★ Double early: 3"–4" flowers with many petals; 12"–14" stems
★ Greigii: 3"-long flowers; 6"–12" stems with purple-striped foliage
★ Kaufmanniana: 3" flowers with 4"–8" stems; often called waterlily tulips
★ Fosteriana: 4" flowers with 12" stems

### Mid-Season Tulips

★ Darwin hybrid: 3"–4" flowers with 36" stems
★ Triumph: 2"–4" flowers with 15"–18" stems

### Late-Season Tulips

★ Lily-flowered: 2"–4" flowers with curved, spreading petals and 20" stems
★ Single late: 3"–4" long, egg-shaped flowers with 18"–24" stems
★ Parrot: 6"-wide feather-edged flowers, often with contrasting colors; 20" stems
★ Double late: 6"-wide, peonylike flowers with 20" stems; the last tulips to bloom

Plant the bulbs in the fall before the ground freezes, in a sunny spot in well-drained

*In my first flower garden*

soil. Bury new bulbs at a depth of 8" from the soil surface to the bottom of the bulb. If you are planting tulips for a bedding display, be sure to plant them all at the same depth or they will bloom unevenly. Space the bulbs 2"–6" apart, depending on the size of the plants.

You may need to water the tulips you've planted if the spring rains amount to less than 1" or so per week. Do not remove the foliage until it is fully yellow since each year's flower production depends on the previous year's foliage.

Mice, squirrels, and chipmunks will eat your bulbs with gusto. You can discourage them by laying a piece of wire mesh 1" over the bulbs. Rabbits may nibble the leaves and flowers, and deer can eat the planting to the ground overnight. Scatter lime about the area to repel these unwanted visitors to your tulip bed.

Tulips look spectacular against an evergreen hedge and in groups at the edge of your patio. Combine your tulips with a sprinkling of phlox, pansies, irises, azaleas, or lilacs. Smaller species are perfect for rock gardens, and many are wonderful when forced in pots.

When spring arrives, meander through your yard during the morning when the dew is still on the tulip petals. There isn't a lovelier sight anywhere! I was so inspired when my yellow tulips peeked above the ground this year. And this pretty tulip sweater was the first design off my drawing board when Mother Nature awoke and blessed us with a new spring.

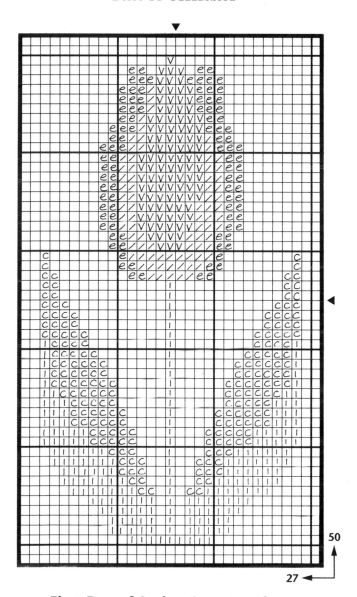

## First Day of Spring Sweater Chart
### COLOR KEY

|   | DMC | Anchor | J. & P. Coats | Color |
|---|-----|--------|---------------|-------|
| I | 501 | 878 | 6878 | Dk. Blue-Green |
| c | 502 | 877 | 6876 | Blue-Green |
| e | 743 | 302 | 2294 | Med. Yellow |
| / | 744 | 301 | 2293 | Pale Yellow |
| V | 745 | 300 | 2296 | Lt. Pale Yellow |

# "It's My Birthday" Chair Tie-On

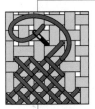

*Tie this pretty decoration to the back of the celebrant's chair. Then blow out the candles and enjoy the chocolate frosting and yummy cake!*

## Size

Design area is 6⅜" square on 14-count Aida

Finished size is 15½" square

## Materials

- ★ One 12⅜" square of 14-count white Aida
- ★ One skein of embroidery floss for each color listed in **Color Key**
- ★ Size 22 or 24 tapestry needle
- ★ ¼ yard of 44"-wide blue solid fabric for the inner borders and piping
- ★ ⅛ yard of 44"-wide pink solid fabric for the middle borders
- ★ ¾ yard of 44"-wide yellow print fabric for the outer borders and backing
- ★ Matching thread
- ★ 2 yards of ⅜"-diameter cording
- ★ 16½" square of fleece
- ★ 16½" square of fusible interfacing
- ★ 4 yards each of 1"-wide yellow and white satin ribbons
- ★ 2 yards each of ⅜"-wide blue satin and ½"-wide pink grosgrain ribbon

## Directions

**Note:** All seam allowances are ¼" unless otherwise indicated.

**1.** Prepare the edges of the Aida as directed in "Preparing Fabric Edges" on page 232. Find the center of the Aida and mark it with a pin. Find the center of the **"It's My Birthday" Chair Tie-On Chart** by connecting the arrows.

**2.** Matching the centers of the chart and the Aida, and using two strands of floss, begin stitching at the center point, working outward until the entire design is complete.

**3.** Using one strand of floss, backstitch the lettering with dark antique blue and the remaining areas with black.

**4.** Wash and press the completed cross-stitch piece as directed in "Washing and Pressing" on page 233.

**5.** With the design centered, trim the Aida to a 7½" square.

**6.** From the blue, cut two 1½" × 7½" inner border strips, two 1½" × 9½" inner border strips, and one 2" × 68" bias strip for the piping. From the pink, cut two 1½" × 9½" middle border strips and two 1½" × 11½" middle border strips. From the yellow, cut two 3" × 11½" outer border strips, two 3" × 16½" outer border strips, and one 16½" square for the backing.

**7.** With right sides together and raw edges even, sew the 1½" × 7½" blue border strips to the top and bottom of the completed cross-

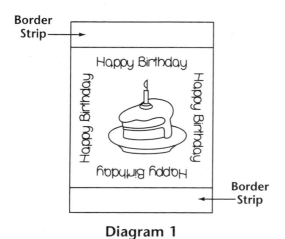

**Diagram 1**

stitch, as shown in **Diagram 1.** Press the seams toward the borders. Sew the 1½" × 9½" blue border strips to the sides of the cross-stitch piece in the same manner; see **Diagram 2** on page 154. Press the seams toward the borders.

**8.** Repeat Step 7 for the pink middle border strips and the yellow outer border strips.

**9.** Make 68" of corded piping and sew the piping to the tie-on front, using a ½" seam allowance; refer to "Making Corded Piping" and "Sewing On the Piping" on page 238. Do *not* trim the seam allowance.

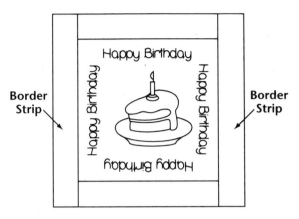

**Diagram 2**

**10.** Sew the 16½" square of fleece to the wrong side of the tie-on along all four edges.

**11.** Iron a 16½" square of fusible interfacing onto the wrong side of the tie-on backing.

**12.** Place the tie-on top and the tie-on backing right sides together and sew around the outer edge, leaving a 5" opening along the bottom edge. Grade the seam allowances to reduce bulk. Turn right side out and whipstitch the opening closed.

**13.** From the yellow and white ribbons, cut two 1-yard lengths each. Cut the blue ribbon in half. Hold one yellow, one white, and one blue ribbon together as if they were one and fold in half. Hand tack the fold to the upper back corner of the chair tie-on. Repeat for the remaining upper back corner. Trim the ribbon ends diagonally.

**14.** Cut the remaining ribbon lengths in half. Holding one yellow, one white, and one pink ribbon together as if they were one, tie a bow and hand tack the knot to the upper front corner of the chair tie-on. Repeat for the remaining upper front corner. Trim the ribbon ends diagonally.

## COUNTRY TIPS
### *from Alma Lynne*

When I was growing up, there was quite a bit of hoopla when it came to birthdays. I designed this chair tie-on to add even more fun to birthday celebrations. Before the birthday girl or boy wakes up, sneak into the kitchen to tie this on the chair. Serve a favorite breakfast and give an inexpensive gift to start the day off right.

If your chairs aren't the right shape for a tie-on, make a place mat. You only need to make a few easy changes. Sew on the blue and pink borders, then sew one 3" × 11½" yellow border to each side of the place mat to give it a rectangular shape. Finish with piping, following the instructions in "Making Corded Piping" and "Sewing On the Piping" on page 238. You'll want to leave off the ribbons as well because they will be difficult to launder.

### DESIGN OPTIONS

| Fabric Count | Design Area | Cutting Dimensions |
|---|---|---|
| 22 | 4⅛" × 4⅛" | 14⅛" × 14⅛" |
| 18 | 5" × 5" | 15" × 15" |
| 14 | 6⅜" × 6⅜" | 16⅜" × 16⅜" |
| 11 | 8⅛" × 8⅛" | 18⅛" × 18⅛" |

**"It's My Birthday" Chair Tie-On Chart**
COLOR KEY

| | DMC | Anchor | J. & P. Coats | Color | | DMC | Anchor | J. & P. Coats | Color |
|---|---|---|---|---|---|---|---|---|---|
| ╱ | White | 2 | 1001 | White | V | 762 | 234 | 8510 | Vy. Lt. Pearl Gray |
| | 310 | 403 | 8403 | Black | ∧ | 814 | 45 | 3044 | Dk. Garnet |
| S | 498 | 1005 | 3000 | Dk. Christmas Red | Z | 838 | 380 | 5478 | Vy. Dk. Beige-Brown |
| ✕ | 725 | 305 | 2294 | Topaz | O | 839 | 360 | 5360 | Dk. Beige-Brown |
| C | 726 | 295 | 2295 | Lt. Topaz | — | 840 | 379 | 5379 | Med. Beige-Brown |
| • | 727 | 293 | 2289 | Vy. Lt. Topaz | | 930 | 1035 | 7052 | Dk. Antique Blue |
| 7 | 743 | 302 | 2294 | Med. Yellow | 9 | 932 | 1033 | 7050 | Lt. Antique Blue |

155

# JULIANNE AND JONATHAN JELLYBEAN

*As silly as colored jellybeans, Julianne and Jonathan have dressed in their bunny best to celebrate Eastertime. Then they're off with a hippity-hop to the Rabbit Egg Hunt to find the prize-winning egg!*

## JULIANNE JELLYBEAN

### SIZE

Finished doll is 22" tall

### MATERIALS

* ¾ yard of 44"-wide unbleached muslin for the body
* ⅛ yard of fusible interfacing
* Black, razor-point, permanent pen for the eyes
* Blue colored pencil for the eyes
* Powdered blusher
* Matching thread
* Polyester fiberfill
* Matching buttonhole twist thread
* Soft-sculpture doll needle
* ½ yard of 44"-wide green-and-white stripe fabric for the bloomers
* ⅜ yard of 44"-wide dark green floral fabric for the skirt
* ⅜ yard of 44"-wide mint green print fabric for the jacket
* ⅜ yard of 44"-wide rose pindot fabric for the jacket lining
* 1 yard of ½"-wide rose satin ribbon for the ankle bows
* ⅜ yard of 1"-wide pregathered cream lace for the jacket ruffle
* ½ yard of ¾"-wide pregathered cream lace for the sleeve trim
* Two ½"-diameter dark rose ribbon roses
* ½ yard of 6"-wide flat double-scalloped cream lace for the apron
* One yard of ¾"-wide rose satin ribbon for the apron strings
* One yard *each* of ⅜"-wide pink and white satin ribbons for the head accent
* Five small dark rose silk roses for the head accent
* Hot-glue gun

### DIRECTIONS

**Note:** Julianne Jellybean is for decorative purposes only; her clothing cannot be removed. All seam allowances are ¼".

1. Prepare all patterns as directed in "Preparing Patterns" on page 236, using the patterns on pages 162 and 163.

2. Use the **Julianne and Jonathan Jellybean Patterns** for the body. Referring to "Cut-and-Sew Method" on page 236, from the muslin, mark and cut two bodies, two heads, four arms, four legs, and two 4½" × 20" pieces for the ears. From the fusible interfacing, cut one 4½" × 20" piece.

3. Using the razor-point pen and the pattern as a guide, draw the eyes, eyebrows, and eyelashes. Color the eye's irises with blue pencil. Fill in the pupils with black, leaving the "gleam" uncolored. Blush the nose and the underside of the ears. Thread a needle with two lengths of cream thread and insert the needle into a whisker dot on one side of the mouth, pass it behind the muslin, and out at the corresponding dot on the other side of

her mouth, leaving 2"-long tails on each side. Repeat for the remaining four whiskers.

**4.** With right sides together, sew the body front and back together, leaving an opening for turning. Trim the seam allowance and clip the curves. Turn to the right side and press. Stuff to desired firmness. Whipstitch the opening closed.

**5.** Repeat Step 3 for the head, leaving an opening along the neck edge. Turn, press, and stuff, but do not whipstitch closed.

**6.** Repeat Step 3 for each arm and leg.

**7.** Hand sew the head to the body at the neck edge.

**8.** Knot a 20" length of buttonhole twist at one end and thread through the doll needle. Matching the large dots, run the needle from the outside of one arm through to the inside of the arm, then through the body and the other arm. Pass the needle back through the arm, the body, and the other arm. Pass back through the arms and body several times to secure. Knot tightly to secure.

**9.** Repeat Step 8 to attach the legs.

**10.** Fuse the fusible interfacing to the wrong side of one muslin ear piece, as directed in "Fusible Webbing" on page 235. Mark and cut two ears, one from the unfused muslin ear piece and one from the fused muslin ear piece. Place the right sides together and sew, leaving a 1" opening. Clip the curves, then turn to the right side and press. Do not stuff. Whipstitch the opening closed. Referring to **Diagram 1,** tie the center of the

**Diagram 1**

ears in a half-knot and hand tack them to the top of the head.

**11.** Use the **Julianne and Jonathan Wardrobe Patterns** for her clothing. From the green-and-white stripe, cut two bloomers with the stripes running lengthwise. From the dark green floral, cut one 11" × 36" piece for the skirt. From the mint green print, cut two jacket fronts and one jacket back. From the pindot, cut two jacket fronts and one jacket back for the jacket lining.

**12.** With right sides together, sew the bloomers front and back together at the side seams and inseam. Turn under ½" around the waist edge and press. Run a gathering thread around the waist. Turn under ¼" around each ankle edge and press; hem. Run a gathering thread around each ankle, about 1" above the ankle hem. Place the bloomers on Julianne and pull up gathers at the waist and ankles to fit; secure the threads.

**13.** Cut the ½"-wide rose ribbon in half. Wrap one length around each ankle to cover the gathering threads and tie in a bow; clip the ribbon ends diagonally.

**14.** With right sides together, sew the short ends of the skirt piece together to form a loop. Turn under ¼", then another ¼", along one long edge and press; hem. This is the lower edge of the skirt. Turn under ½" around the waist edge and press. Run a gathering thread around the waist. Place the skirt on Julianne over the bloomers and pull up the gathers to fit. Secure the thread.

**15.** With right sides together, sew each jacket front to the jacket back at the underarm seams and the shoulder seams. Turn under ¼" on each wrist edge and press. Fold the 1"-wide lace in half. With right sides together and matching the raw edge of one jacket front with the bound edge of the doubled-over lace piece, baste the lace to the jacket front to form the jacket ruffle; see **Diagram 2**.

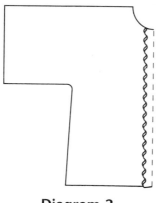

**Diagram 2**

**16.** With right sides together, sew each jacket lining front to the jacket lining back at the underarm seams and the shoulder seams, leaving a 5" opening along one shoulder seam; sew at least 1" of the seam at each end of this shoulder seam for ease in turning.

**17.** With right sides together, sew the jacket and jacket lining together, leaving the wrist edges open. Trim the seam allowances and clip the underarm curves. Carefully turn the jacket right side out, but do not place the sleeve linings inside the sleeves yet. Whipstitch the shoulder seam opening closed.

**18.** Cut the ¾"-wide lace length in half. With right sides together and matching the raw edge of each sleeve lining with the bound edge of each lace piece, sew the lace to the sleeve linings, overlapping the lace edges ½". Slip the sleeve linings into the sleeves, then whipstitch the wrist edges together. Place the jacket on Julianne and overlap the front edges, having the lace-trimmed edge on the top. Sew the two ribbon rose buttons to the lace, sewing through the other jacket front. Fold the cuffs up to expose the lining and lace.

**19.** For the apron, cut the 6"-wide lace length in half. Layer one length on top of the other, having the bottom layer's top edge 2" below the top layer's top edge; see **Diagram 3**. Baste the layers together. Run a gathering thread about 1" from the top edge of the apron. Pull up the gathers to about 6".

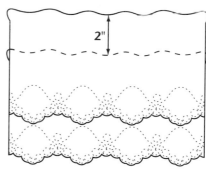

**Diagram 3**

**20.** Find the center of the ¾"-wide rose ribbon and mark it with a pin. To make the apron strings, place the ribbon over the apron's gathering thread and hand tack it in place; see **Diagram 4**. Place the apron on Julianne and tie a bow in the back. Clip the ribbon ends diagonally.

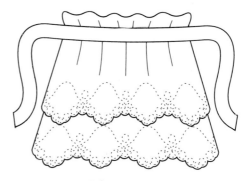

**Diagram 4**

**21.** Cut the ⅜"-wide pink and white ribbons in half. Holding the four ribbons as if they were one, tie them in a bow. Hand tack the bow to the center of Julianne's ears.

**22.** Bunch the silk roses together and fold up the stems. Hot-glue the stem grouping together. Hand tack or hot-glue the flowers over the ribbons on the ears.

# JONATHAN JELLYBEAN

## SIZE

Finished doll is 22" tall

## MATERIALS

* ¾ yard of 44"-wide unbleached muslin for the body
* ⅛ yard of fusible interfacing
* Black, razor-point, permanent pen for the eyes
* Blue colored pencil for the eyes
* Powdered blusher
* Matching thread
* Polyester fiberfill
* Matching buttonhole twist thread
* Soft-sculpture doll needle
* ½ yard of 44"-wide green-and-white stripe fabric for the pants
* ¼ yard of 44"-wide mint green print fabric for the shirt
* ½ yard of 44"-wide dark green floral fabric for the jacket
* ½ yard of 44"-wide rose pindot fabric for the jacket lining
* ⅞ yard of ¾"-wide rose satin ribbon for the ankle accents and bow tie
* ⅜ yard of mint green double-fold bias tape
* Two snaps
* ½ yard of ¾"-wide pregathered cream lace for the sleeve trim
* Two ⅝"-diameter pearl shank buttons for the lapels
* ¼ yard of 6"-wide flat double-scalloped cream lace for the jabot
* Pink straw doll hat to fit a 3" doll head

## DIRECTIONS

**Note:** Jonathan Jellybean is for decorative purposes only; his clothing cannot be removed. All seam allowances are ¼".

**1.** Repeat Steps 1 through 10 of Julianne Jellybean, beginning on page 156, to make Jonathan's body.

**2.** Use **Julianne and Jonathan's Wardrobe Patterns** for his clothing. From the green-and-white stripe, cut two pants with stripes running lengthwise. From the mint green print, cut one shirt front and two shirt backs. From the dark green floral, cut two jacket fronts and two jacket backs. From the pindot, cut two jacket fronts and two jacket backs for the jacket lining.

**3.** With right sides together, sew the pants front and back together at the side seams and inseam. Turn under ½" around the waist edge and press. Run a gathering thread around the waist. Turn under ¼" around each ankle edge and press; hem. Run a gathering thread around each ankle, about 1" above the ankle hem. Place the pants on Jonathan, but do not pull up the waist gathers yet. Pull up the gathers at the ankles to fit and secure the thread.

**4.** From the ¾"-wide rose ribbon, cut two 6" lengths. Wrap one length around each ankle to cover the gathering threads and whipstitch the ends in place.

**5.** With right sides together, sew each shirt back to the shirt front at the shoulder and underarm seams. Clip the underarm seams. Turn under ¼", then another ¼", at the center back edge of each shirt back to form the plackets and press; hem. Turn under ¼", then another ¼", around the waist edge and press; hem. Following the directions in "Bias Tape" on page 237, bind the raw neck edge with bias tape, turning the ends in ¼".

**6.** Turn the shirt to the right side and press. Sew two snaps to the shirt to overlap the plackets. Place the shirt on Jonathan and snap it closed. Tuck the shirt inside the pants. Pull up the gathers at the waist to fit and secure the thread.

## COUNTRY TIPS
*from Alma Lynne*

Easter is another of my favorite holidays, especially since the preferred colors are pastels and the "mascots" are bunnies! Can Easter egg popularity be far behind?

I must admit to you that I have highly developed Easter egg–coloring skills. I don't readily share my secret techniques, but I suppose I can make an exception for a fellow needle-crafter. If you're looking for an easy (and fast) way to color eggs, add red onion skins to your boiling water for about 30 minutes; you'll be pleasantly surprised with a light purple color. Or add frozen blueberries for a gray-blue hue, paprika for a red-brown look, or beets for a raspberry color. Red cabbage dyes eggs a blue color, instant coffee a dark brown, and the spice turmeric yields a warm yellow shade. You can dip cooked eggs in the dye bath or you can simmer your uncooked eggs for a deeper shade.

Remember, most of these colors will lighten as they dry, so judge your steeping time accordingly. If your eggs don't seem to take the color, try this nifty trick: Mix 1 tablespoon of vinegar and 1 cup of water, then rub the eggs with a clean cloth that has been saturated with this solution.

Instead of the usual swabbed-on designs, try these:

• Wind rubberbands around your eggs in all different directions. Dip the egg in the dye, then blot it dry with a paper towel. Remove the rubberbands and you'll have tiny white lines crisscrossing your egg.

• For a spiral design, dip your egg in a very light color and blot it dry. Wind cellophane tape around the entire egg, pleating it as necessary. Then dip the egg in a darker dye. Blot it dry and remove the tape.

• To create an artsy look, dip your egg in a light color and blot it dry. Place ¾" lengths of cellophane tape on the eggs, either randomly or moving in a woven pattern around the egg. Dye the egg a darker color the second time and blot it dry. Repeat the taping process in a different direction and dye the egg with a darker color. Blot it dry, then remove the tape.

• For a marbled effect, wrap the egg in onion skins, then tie a small piece of cheesecloth or nylon netting around it to keep the skins or leaves in place. Boil the eggs as usual, but turn them frequently for even coloring. Happy Egging!

---

**7.** With right sides together, sew the center back seam of the jacket backs. Sew each jacket front to the jacket back at the underarm seams, ending the seam at the dot. Sew the jacket front to the jacket back at the shoulder seams. Turn under ¼" on each wrist edge and press.

**8.** With right sides together, sew the center back seam of the jacket lining. With right sides together, sew each jacket lining front to the jacket lining back at the underarm seams and at the shoulder seams, leaving a 5" opening along one shoulder seam; sew at least 1" of the seam at each end of this shoulder seam for ease in turning.

**9.** With right sides together, sew the jacket and jacket lining together, leaving wrist edges open. Trim the seam allowances and clip the underarm curves. Carefully turn the jacket right side out, but do not place the sleeve linings inside the sleeves yet. Whipstitch the shoulder seam opening closed.

**10.** Cut the ¾"-wide lace length in half for the sleeve trim. With right sides together and matching the raw edge of each sleeve lining with the bound edge of each lace piece, sew the lace to the sleeve linings, overlapping the lace edges ½". Slip the sleeve linings into the sleeves, then whipstitch the wrist edges together. Place the jacket on Jonathan. Fold the cuffs up to expose the lining and lace. Turn back the upper edge of the jacket to form the lapels. Sew one button to the lower part of each lapel, sewing through the shirt to secure them in place.

**11.** Turn under the raw ends of the jabot lace. Run a gathering thread about ¾" from the top edge and pull up the gathers to about 3". Hand tack the jabot to the top of Jonathan's shirt. Tie a bow with the remaining ribbon and hand tack it to the center top of the jabot. Clip the ribbon ends diagonally.

**12.** Cut a slit in the top of the hat for the ears. Place the hat on Jonathan's head and pull the ears through the top of the hat.

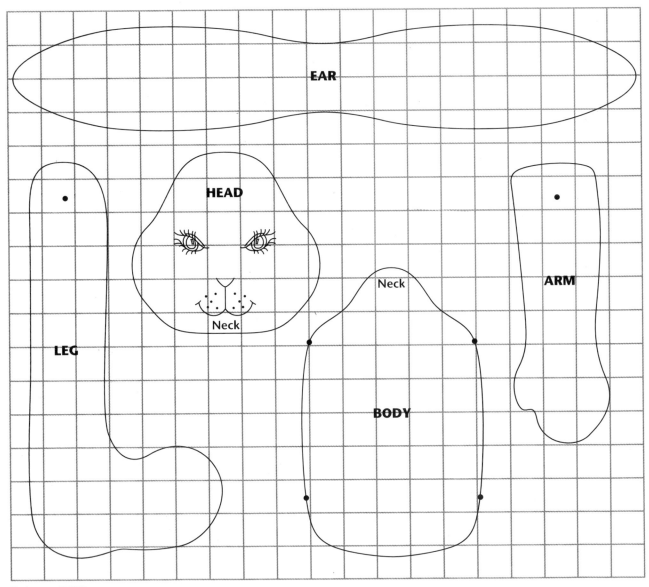

Enlarge 288%

**Julianne and Jonathan Jellybean Patterns**

1 square = 1"

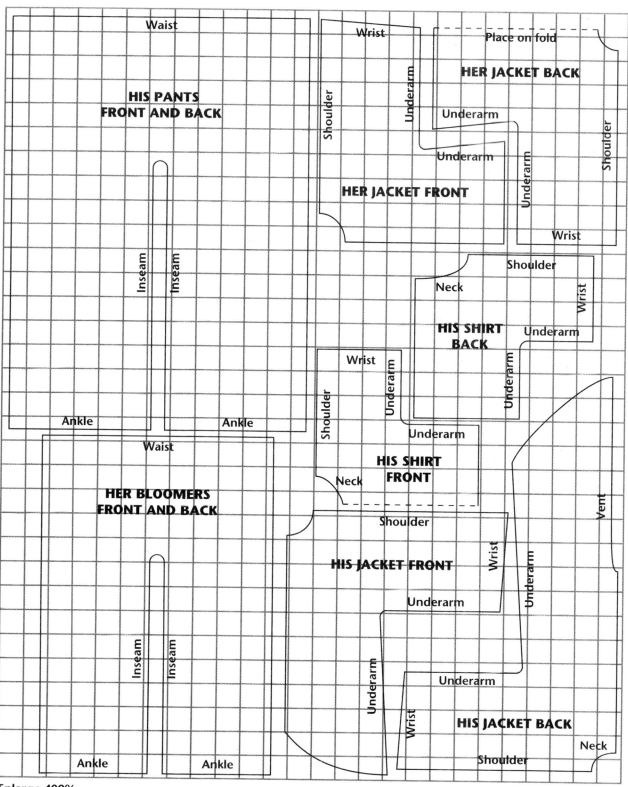

Enlarge 400%

**Julianne and Jonathan Wardrobe Patterns**

1 square = 1"

# "A Day Off from Work" Sweaters

*Indulge on your day off with your favorite hobbies! Spend a carefree day stitching and relaxing. You can choose the "I Love Cross-Stitch" or the "I Love Sewing" design or, if you have a whole week off, make both!*

## "I Love Cross-Stitch" Sweater

### Sizes

**Note:** Designs are stitched on 6 × 8 gauge
"I Love Cross-Stitch" design area is
7⅝" × 9"
Scissors design area is 2" × 6⅜"
Tape Measure design area is 6⅜" × 11⅛"
Needle Case design area is 1⅞" × 3⅝"
Needle and Floss design area is 3½" × 4⅞"
Tulip design area is 1⅝" × 7⅜"

### Materials

* One 6 × 8-gauge adult's stockinette stitch white pullover sweater
* One skein of embroidery floss for each color listed in **Color Key** (unless otherwise indicated)
* Size 22 tapestry needle
* One spool of ribbon floss for each color listed in **Color Key**
* Five ⅝"-diameter pink heart buttons
* 2 yards of ⅜"-wide green satin ribbon for the froufrou
* 2 yards *each* of ⅝"-wide blue and pink satin ribbon for the froufrou
* ¼ yard *each* of 44"-wide green, blue, and pink solid fabrics for the froufrou

* Two skeins *each* of green, blue, and pink embroidery floss for the froufrou
* Pinking shears
* One 8" length of 1"-wide Velcro strip for the froufrou

### Directions

**1.** Plan the placement of the designs on your sweater. On the model, I counted down 57 rows from the center front neckline and marked it with a pin; this was the center stitch for the "I Love Cross-Stitch" motif. I placed the scissors, tape measure, needle case, and needle and floss motifs randomly on the sweater front; refer to the **Cross-Stitch Motifs Placement Diagram** for ideas. For your sweater, you may follow the directions above or you may center the "I Love Cross-Stitch" motif by counting the total vertical stitches (from the center front neckline to the top of the ribbing) and dividing by two. Randomly place the remaining cross-stitch motifs. Find the center of each chart by connecting the arrows.

**2.** Lay the sweater sleeves flat so the underarm seams are at the lower edges.

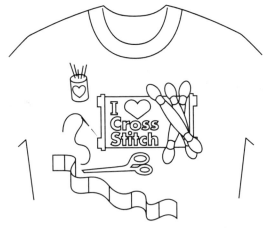

**Cross-Stitch Motifs Placement Diagram**

Finger-press folds at the opposite edges to find the sleeve centers. Measure 3" up from the top of the cuff ribbing along the sleeve center folds and mark them with pins. Find the center of the **Tulip Chart** by connecting the arrows.

**3.** Read the duplicate stitch basics in "The Stitches" on page 235. Matching the center of the **"I Love Cross-Stitch" Chart** with the marked stitch on the sweater, duplicate stitch the design using six strands of floss or one strand of ribbon. Duplicate stitch the remaining sweater front motifs (except the needle and floss) using the **Scissors Chart,** the **Tape Measure Chart,** and the **Needle Case Chart.** Duplicate stitch the sleeve design using the **Tulip Chart.**

**4.** Cut a 9½" length of medium antique blue floss. Lay the sweater flat and arrange the floss length in a curving line, using the **Needle and Floss Chart** for reference. Couch the floss in place, referring to "The Stitches"

on page 235 for stitch details. Make a long straight stitch for the needle with silver ribbon.

**5.** Backstitch the horizontal lines on the needlework frame with two strands of very light pearl gray and the lines on the tape measure with two strands of black. Make long straight stitches for the needles in the needle case with silver ribbon.

**6.** Wash and press the completed duplicate stitch design as directed in "Washing and Pressing" on page 235.

**7.** Sew the buttons to the neckband, evenly spacing them around the front edge.

**8.** Cut the ribbons into ½-yard pieces, then knot each end of the ribbon lengths. Using pinking shears, cut the fabrics into 1½" × 36" strips, then cut each strip into two 18" lengths. Using the ribbons, fabric strips, floss skeins, and Velcro, add the froufrou to the shoulders as directed in "Froufrou" on page 239.

## "I Love Cross-Stitch" Sweater Charts
### COLOR KEY

| | DMC | Anchor | J. & P. Coats | Color |
|---|---|---|---|---|
| Ø | 310 | 403 | 8403 | Black (6 skeins) |
| ⊃ | 434 | 310 | 5000 | Lt. Brown |
| C | 502 | 877 | 6876 | Blue-Green |
| V | 503 | 876 | 6879 | Med. Blue-Green |
| 4 | 725 | 305 | 2294 | Topaz (3 skeins) |
| | 762 | 234 | 8510 | Vy. Lt. Pearl Gray |
| O | 783 | 307 | 5307 | Christmas Gold (3 skeins) |
| \ | 801 | 359 | 5472 | Dk. Coffee Brown |
| ‡ | 899 | 52 | 3282 | Med. Rose |
| × | 930 | 1035 | 7052 | Dk. Antique Blue |
| ∩ | 931 | 1034 | 7051 | Med. Antique Blue (2 skeins) |
| ‖ | 3326 | 36 | 3126 | Lt. Rose |
| H | Kreinik Balger ⅟₁₆" Flat Silver Ribbon #001 HL | | | |
| 2 | Kreinik Balger ⅟₁₆" Flat Gold Ribbon #002 HL | | | |

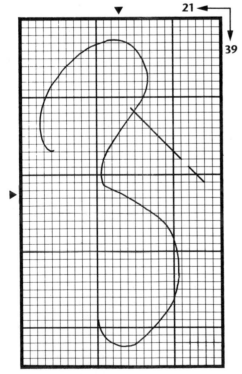

**Needle and Floss Chart**

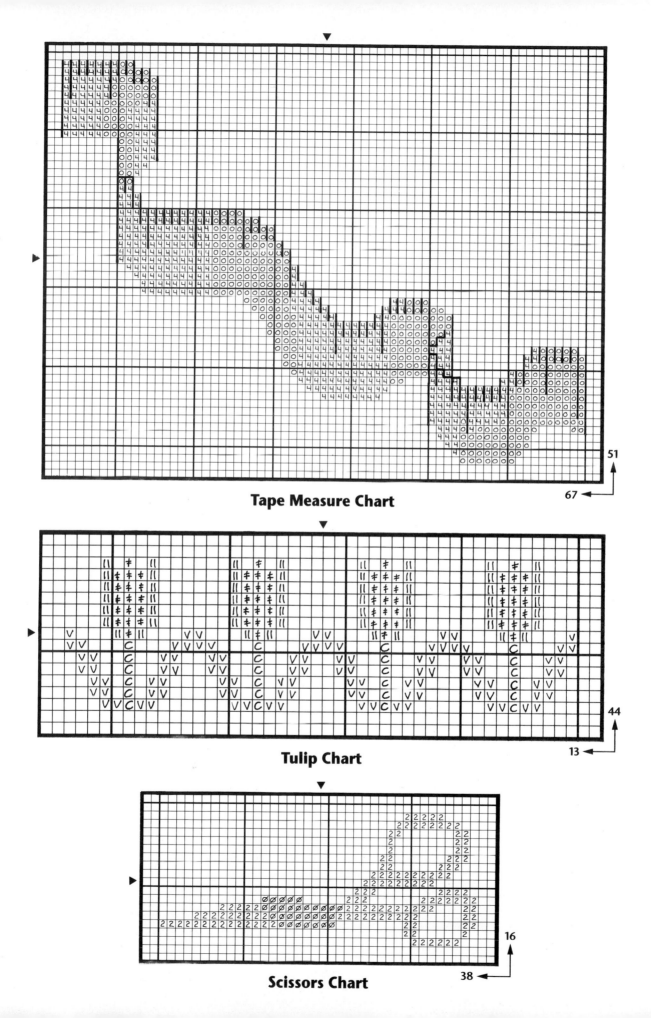

**Tape Measure Chart**

51

67 ◄

**Tulip Chart**

44

13 ◄

**Scissors Chart**

16

38 ◄

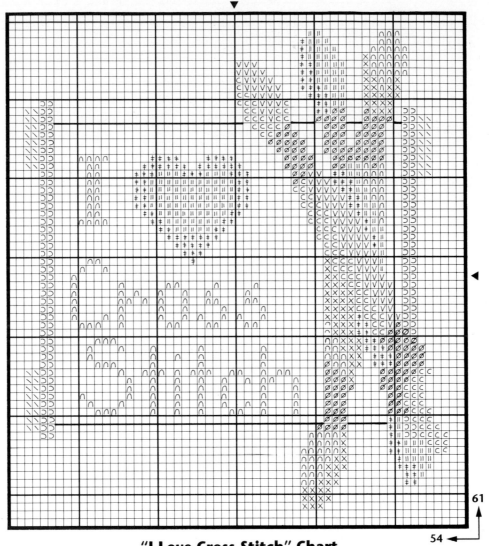

**"I Love Cross-Stitch" Chart**

61
54

## "I Love Cross-Stitch" Sweater Charts
### COLOR KEY

| | DMC | Anchor | J. & P. Coats | Color |
|---|---|---|---|---|
| Ø | 310 | 403 | 8403 | Black (6 skeins) |
| ⊃ | 434 | 310 | 5000 | Lt. Brown |
| C | 502 | 877 | 6876 | Blue-Green |
| V | 503 | 876 | 6879 | Med. Blue-Green |
| ‡ | 725 | 305 | 2294 | Topaz (3 skeins) |
| | 762 | 234 | 8510 | Vy. Lt. Pearl Gray |
| O | 783 | 307 | 5307 | Christmas Gold (3 skeins) |
| \ | 801 | 359 | 5472 | Dk. Coffee Brown |
| ‡ | 899 | 52 | 3282 | Med. Rose |
| × | 930 | 1035 | 7052 | Dk. Antique Blue |
| ∩ | 931 | 1034 | 7051 | Med. Antique Blue (2 skeins) |
| ‖ | 3326 | 36 | 3126 | Lt. Rose |
| H | Kreinik ⅟₁₆" Flat Silver Ribbon #001 HL | | | |
| 2 | Kreinik ⅟₁₆" Flat Gold Ribbon #002 HL | | | |

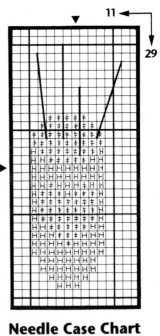

11
29

**Needle Case Chart**

# I Love Sewing Sewater

## Sizes

**Note:** Designs are stitched on 6 × 8 gauge
"I Love Sewing" design area is 3⅝" × 5⅛"
Sewing Machine design area is 7½" square
Scissors design area is 2" × 6⅜"
Thimble design area is 1⅛" × 1¼"
Pincushion design area is 4⅜" × 6"
Row of Spools design area is 1½" × 2⅛"
Tape Measure design area is 6⅜" × 11⅛"

## Materials

★ One 6 × 8-gauge adult's stockinette stitch white pullover sweater
★ One skein of embroidery floss for each color listed in **Color Keys** (unless otherwise indicated)
★ Size 22 tapestry needle
★ One spool of ribbon floss for each color listed in **Color Key**
★ Three black glass pebble beads
★ Scraps of black check, green print, and maroon solid fabrics
★ Two ¾" brass safety pins
★ Five rustproof safety pins in assorted sizes
★ Approximately 70 buttons in assorted shapes, sizes, and styles
★ ½ yard of 1"-wide white lace trim with pearls
★ ½ yard of ½"-wide white upholstery braid
★ 1⅜ yards of ½"-wide tape measure–look ribbon
★ 1" length of ½"-wide Velcro

## Directions

**1.** Plan the placement of the designs on your sweater. On the model, I counted down 31 rows from the center front neckline and marked it with a pin; this was the center stitch for the "I Love Sewing" motif. For the sewing machine motif, I counted down 90 rows in the same manner and marked it with a pin for the center stitch. I placed the scissors, single spool, and thimble motifs random-

ly on the sweater front; refer to the **Sweater Front Placement Diagram** for ideas. For your sweater, you may follow the directions above or you may randomly place the sewing motifs on the front. Find the center of each chart by connecting the arrows.

**Sweater Front Placement Diagram**

**2.** Lay the sweater sleeves flat so the underarm seams are at the lower edges. Finger press folds at the opposite edges to find the sleeve centers. On the right sleeve, count up 24 rows from the top of the cuff ribbing along the sleeve center fold and mark it with a pin; this is the center stitch for the pincushion motif. Count up 120 rows in the same manner and mark it with a pin; this is the center stitch for the row of spools motif. On the left sleeve, count up 15 rows and mark it with a pin; this is the center stitch for the row of spools motif. Count up 96 rows and mark it with a pin; this is the center stitch for the tape measure motif. Refer to the **Sleeve Placement Diagrams** on page 170 for ideas. For your sweater, you may follow the directions above or you may randomly place the sewing motifs on the sleeves. Find the center of each chart by connecting the arrows.

**3.** Read the duplicate stitch basics in "The Stitches" on page 235. Matching the centers

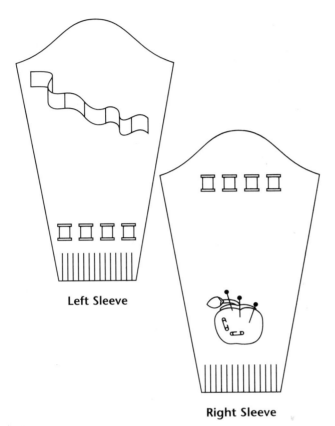

**Left Sleeve**

**Right Sleeve**

## Sleeve Placement Diagrams

machine needle with silver ribbon. Make long straight stitches for the needle in the upper left spool and for the pins on the pincushion with silver ribbon. Use silver ribbon to sew the glass beads to the top of the pins. Cut a 6" and a 12" length of garnet floss. Knot the 6" length, then pass it through the wrong side of the sweater and out at the left side of the spool near the left shoulder. Run the 12" length from the spool

of the charts with the marked center stitches, duplicate stitch the design using six strands of floss or one strand of ribbon; for the sweater front, use the **"I Love Sewing" Chart,** the **Sewing Machine Chart,** the **Scissors Chart** (on page 167), the **Thimble Chart,** and one spool from the **Row of Spools Chart.** Duplicate stitch the single spool with light tan, dark Christmas red, and dark garnet. For the sleeves, use the **Tape Measure Chart** (on page 167), the **Pincushion Chart,** and the **Row of Spools Chart.** For the row of spools motif, use the **Row of Spools Chart Color Key** and duplicate stitch one spool in each color grouping. For the thimble motif, use one strand of silver ribbon.

**4.** Backstitch the tape measure lines with two strands of black and the sewing

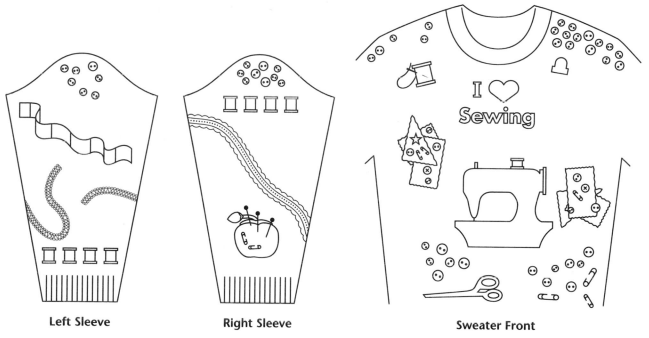

**Left Sleeve**     **Right Sleeve**          **Sweater Front**

**Embellishment Diagrams**

to the sewing machine needle as if it were threaded in the machine.

**5.** Wash and press the completed duplicate stitch design as directed in "Washing and Pressing" on page 235.

**6.** Use pinking shears to cut two 2" × 3" pieces from the black check, two 2" × 4" pieces from the green print, and one 3" square from the maroon solid. Cut the 3" square in half diagonally to form two triangles.

**7.** Using the **Embellishment Diagrams** as a guide, add fabric swatches, safety pins, buttons, lace, and braid to the sweater as follows: Arrange three fabric pieces on each side of the sewing machine motif, then secure them in place by sewing on three buttons. Pin the two brass pins to the swatches on the left and one rustproof pin to the

swatches on the right. Scatter and sew the remaining buttons on the sweater front and sleeves. Pin the remaining rustproof pins to the pincushion and the lower right corner of the sweater front. Hand tack the lace trim on the left sleeve and the braid on the right sleeve. Sew the loop side of the Velcro to the sweater at the center back neck and the hook side to the middle of the ribbon. Clip the ribbon ends diagonally.

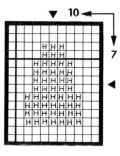

**Thimble Chart**

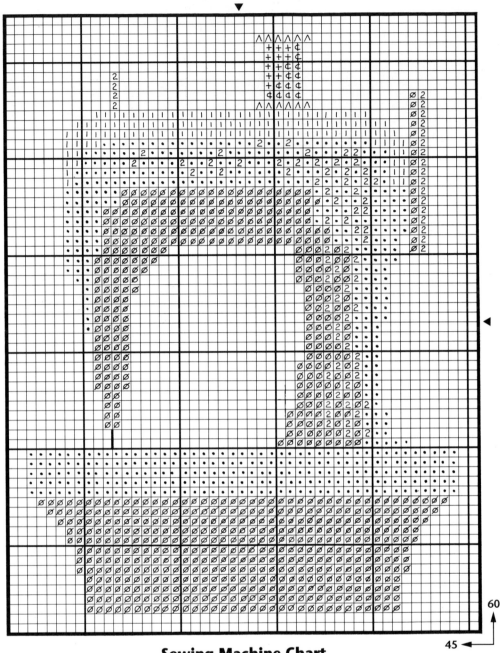

60

45

**Sewing Machine Chart**

**"I Love Sewing" Sweater Charts**
**COLOR KEY**

| | DMC | Anchor | J. & P. Coats | Color | | DMC | Anchor | J. & P. Coats | Color |
|---|---|---|---|---|---|---|---|---|---|
| Ø | 310 | 403 | 8403 | Black (6 skeins) | O | 783 | 307 | 5307 | Christmas Gold (3 skeins) |
| ∧ | 437 | 362 | 5942 | Lt. Tan | ¢ | 814 | 45 | 3044 | Dk. Garnet (2 skeins) |
| L | 498 | 1005 | 3000 | Dk. Christmas Red (2 skeins) | Ɛ | 815 | 43 | 3000 | Med. Garnet |
| U | 500 | 683 | 6880 | Vy. Dk. Blue-Green | + | 816 | 1005 | 3021 | Garnet (2 skeins) |
| ∕ | 501 | 878 | 6878 | Dk. Blue-Green | • | 3799 | 236 | 8999 | Vy. Dk. Pewter Gray (2 skeins) |
| I | 535 | — | 8400 | Vy. Lt. Ash Gray | H | Kreinik Balger ¹⁄₁₆" Flat Silver Ribbon #001 HL | | | |
| Ϥ | 725 | 305 | 2294 | Topaz (3 skeins) | 2 | Kreinik Balger ¹⁄₁₆" Flat Gold Ribbon #002 HL | | | |

172

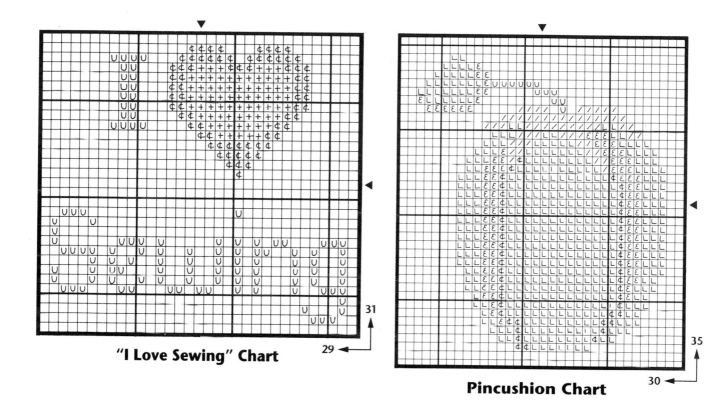

**"I Love Sewing" Chart**

29 ◄     31

**Pincushion Chart**

30 ◄     35

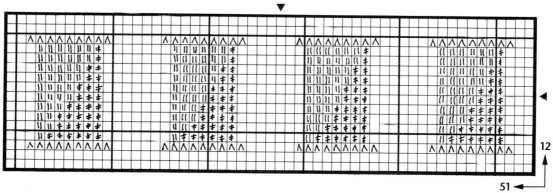

**Row of Spools Chart**
**COLOR KEY**

| | DMC | Anchor | J. & P. Coats | Color | | DMC | Anchor | J. & P. Coats | Color |
|---|---|---|---|---|---|---|---|---|---|
| ∧ | 437 | 5942 | 362 | Lt. Tan | ∧ | 437 | 5942 | 362 | Lt. Tan |
| ‡ | 798 | 7022 | 131 | Dk. Delft | ‡ | 498 | 3410 | 43 | Dk. Christmas Red |
| ‖ | 799 | 7030 | 136 | Med. Delft | ‖ | 814 | 3044 | 45 | Dk. Garnet |
| ∧ | 437 | 5942 | 362 | Lt. Tan | ∧ | 437 | 5942 | 362 | Lt. Tan |
| ‡ | 743 | 2302 | 302 | Med. Yellow | ‡ | 500 | 6880 | 879 | Vy. Dk. Blue-Green |
| ‖ | 744 | 2293 | 301 | Pale Yellow | ‖ | 501 | 6878 | 878 | Dk. Blue-Green |

# ROCKY THE ROCKING HORSE BABY BIB

*Celebrate baby's arrival with a rocking horse to call his very own! Cross-stitch this little pony with his saddle and stirrups, then accent with a western-style checker border and sunset-red hearts.*

## SIZE

Design area is 3⅝" × 7⅞" on 14-count prefinished baby bib

## MATERIALS

- One "Tidy Tot" blue eyelet 14-count prefinished baby bib*
- One skein of embroidery floss for each color listed in **Color Key**
- Size 22 or 24 tapestry needle
- ⅞ yard of 1"-wide light blue satin ribbon

*See "Buyer's Guide" on page 240 for ordering information.

## DIRECTIONS

**1.** Measure 3¾" up from the bottom center of the bib and 5½" in from the side and mark with a pin; this is where you will place your center stitch. Find the center of the **Rocky the Rocking Horse Baby Bib Chart** by connecting the arrows.

**2.** Matching the centers of the chart and the marked center stitch on the bib, and using two strands of floss, begin stitching at the center point, working outward until the entire design is complete.

**3.** Backstitch the design with one strand of black-brown.

**4.** Wash and press the completed cross-stitch bib as directed in "Washing and Pressing" on page 233.

**5.** Cut the ribbon in half and tie each length into a bow. Clip the ribbon ends diagonally. Tack one bow to each bottom corner of the cross-stitch design.

**DESIGN OPTIONS**

| Fabric Count | Design Area | Cutting Dimension |
|---|---|---|
| 22 | 2¼" x 4⅞" | 12¼" x 14⅞" |
| 18 | 2¾" x 6" | 12¾" x 16" |
| 14 | 3½" x 7¾" | 13½" x 17¾" |
| 11 | 4½" x 9¾" | 14½" x 19¾" |

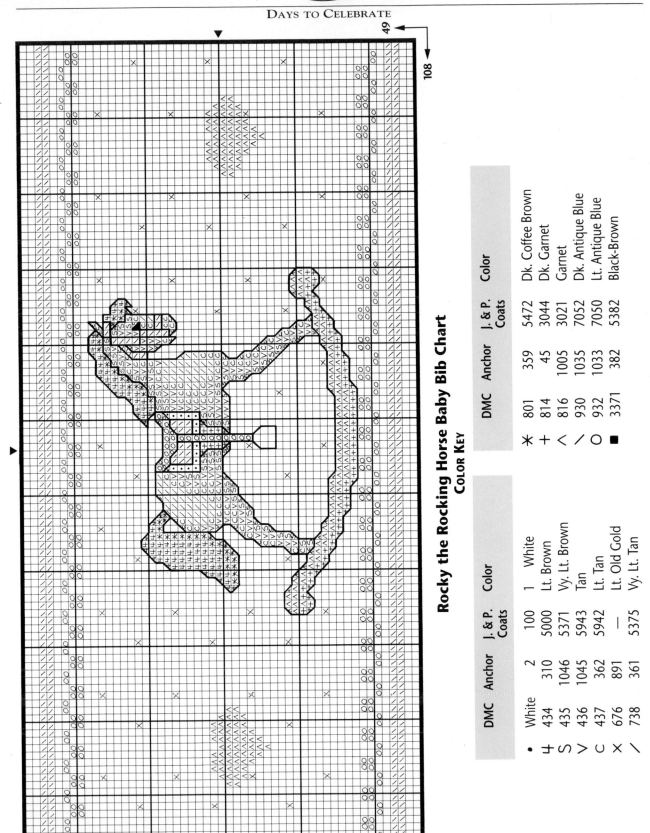

## Rocky the Rocking Horse Baby Bib Chart
### Color Key

| | DMC | Anchor | J. & P. Coats | Color |
|---|---|---|---|---|
| • | White | 2 | 100 | White |
| + | 434 | 310 | 5000 | Lt. Brown |
| S | 435 | 1046 | 5371 | Vy. Lt. Brown |
| V | 436 | 1045 | 5943 | Tan |
| C | 437 | 362 | 5942 | Lt. Tan |
| X | 676 | 891 | — | Lt. Old Gold |
| / | 738 | 361 | 5375 | Vy. Lt. Tan |

| | DMC | Anchor | J. & P. Coats | Color |
|---|---|---|---|---|
| ✳ | 801 | 359 | 5472 | Dk. Coffee Brown |
| + | 814 | 45 | 3044 | Dk. Garnet |
| < | 816 | 1005 | 3021 | Garnet |
| / | 930 | 1035 | 7052 | Dk. Antique Blue |
| O | 932 | 1033 | 7050 | Lt. Antique Blue |
| ■ | 3371 | 382 | 5382 | Black-Brown |

# COUNTRY TIPS
### *from Alma Lynne*

Rocky the Rocking Horse would look just as cute as Calliope the Carousel Horse—so I've recharted the design to resemble a merry-go-round horse. I've added a peppermint-striped pole, a feathery plume, and a pretty scalloped saddle. Use the new chart to cross-stitch the carousel horse, then refer back to the original chart for the hearts and dots, using the new colors there as well. Stitch the upper border as positioned on the original chart, just break it two stitches before and two stitches after the outer edge of Calliope the Carousel Horse to allow for the plume and pole; remember to use the new colors for the border.

## COLOR KEY

| | DMC | Anchor | J. & P. Coats | Color |
|---|---|---|---|---|
| • | White | 2 | 1001 | White |
| 4 | 317 | 400 | 8510 | Pewter Gray |
| V | 318 | 399 | 8511 | Lt. Steel Gray |
| * | 413 | 401 | 8514 | Dk. Pewter Gray |
| S | 414 | 235 | 8513 | Dk. Steel Gray |
| C | 415 | 398 | 8398 | Pearl Gray |
| / | 762 | 234 | 8510 | Vy. Lt. Pearl Gray |
| + | 899 | 52 | 3282 | Med. Rose |
| \ | 958 | 187 | 6186 | Dk. Sea Green |
| O | 959 | 186 | 6185 | Med. Sea Green |
| ∧ | 3326 | 36 | 3126 | Lt. Rose |
| ■ | 3371 | 382 | 5382 | Black-Brown |

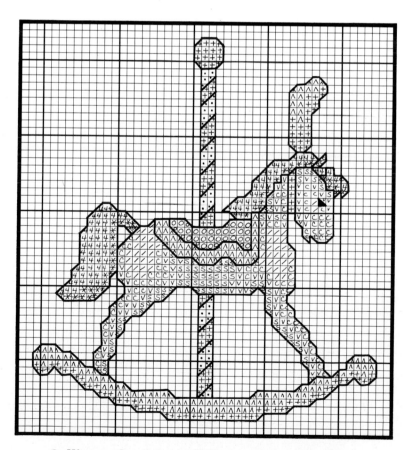

## Calliope the Carousel Horse Baby Bib Chart

# WITCH CHARMING
# WALLHANGING

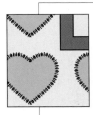

*Which witch is charming? This beguiling one, of course. Ms. Charming and her trusty kitty look downright spooky—perfect for a Halloween celebration.*

## SIZE

Finished wallhanging is 36" × 44"

## MATERIALS

★ ⅝ yard of 44"-wide khaki solid fabric for the center panel
★ 2¼ yards of 44"-wide dark green plaid fabric for the first and fourth border, backing, and bows*
★ ⅜ yard of 44"-wide burnt orange print fabric for the second border, blouse, and lower ruffle
★ ⅝ yard of 44"-wide unbleached muslin for the third border, witch's hands, face, and apron
★ ¼ yard of 44"-wide black solid fabric for the shoes, hat, and cats
★ Scrap of black plaid for the stockings
★ 1¼ yards of tear-away stabilizer
★ 1½ yards of fusible webbing
★ Matching thread
★ 36½" × 44½" piece of fleece
★ One 4" square of stencil Mylar
★ 5" square of glass with filed or masked edges
★ Craft knife with extra blades
★ Masking tape
★ Saucer or palette
★ Dark green acrylic paint
★ Stencil brush
★ Paper towels

★ Black, razor-point, permanent pen
★ Tan and cream hand-quilting thread
★ 13¼ yards of jute twine for the hair
★ One 6½" and one 4" piece of cardboard
★ 2 yards of ¼"-wide black satin ribbon
★ 7 yards of cream cotton yarn for the broom
★ 9" length of ¼"-diameter dowel for the broomstick

*If using a print or solid fabric instead of a plaid, you need to purchase only 2 yards.

## DIRECTIONS

**Note:** Wash, dry, and press all your fabrics before beginning this project. All seam allowances are ¼".

**1.** Prepare all patterns as directed in "Preparing Patterns" on page 236, using the patterns on page 183.

**2.** From the khaki, cut a 20" × 28" piece for the center panel. From the green, cut two 1½" × 20" first border strips, two 1½" × 30" first border strips, two 1¾" × 34" fourth border strips, two 1¾" × 44½" fourth border strips, and one 36½" × 44½" piece for the backing. Also tear four 4" × 23" strips for the rag bows. From the orange, cut two 2½" × 22" second border strips and two 2½" × 34" second border strips. From the muslin, cut two 4½ × 26" third border strips and two 4½" × 42" third border strips. From the tear-away stabilizer, cut one 20" × 28" piece for the center panel and twelve 4" × 5" pieces for the border cats.

**3.** Fuse the fusible webbing to the remaining pieces of orange, black, and muslin fabrics as directed in "Fusible Webbing" on page

235. Also fuse the fusible webbing to the black plaid fabric.

**4.** Refer to "Machine Appliqué" on page 235 for directions on marking and cutting appliqué pieces. From the orange, cut one blouse and one lower ruffle. From the muslin, cut one apron, one face, one right hand, and one left hand. From the black solid, cut one hat, one right shoe, one left shoe, one little kitty, and twelve full-size border cats. From the black plaid, cut one right stocking and one left stocking. Remove the paper backing from the appliqués.

**5.** Center the appliqué pieces on the center panel, referring to the **Appliqué Placement Diagram** and layering as indicat-

ed by the dashed lines. Fuse in place as directed in "Fusible Webbing" on page 235.

**6.** Pin the 20" × 28" piece of tear-away stabilizer to the back of the center panel. Machine appliqué all edges of Witch Charming using matching threads.

**7.** With right sides together and raw edges even, sew one 1½" × 20" first border strip to the top and bottom of the center panel, as shown in **Diagram 1.** Press the seams toward the borders. Sew one 1½" × 30" first border strip to each side of the center panel in the same manner; see **Diagram 2.** Press the seams toward the borders.

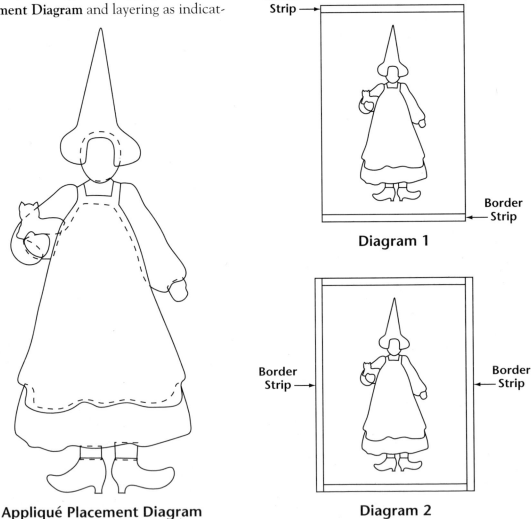

**Appliqué Placement Diagram**

**Diagram 1**

**Diagram 2**

**8.** Repeat Step 7 for the second, third, and fourth border strips.

**9.** Arrange the border cats on the third border, referring to the **Cat Placement Diagram.** Fuse in place as directed in "Fusible Webbing" on page 235. Pin one 4" × 5" piece of tear-away stabilizer to the back of each border cat. Machine appliqué around each cat using matching thread.

**Cat Placement Diagram**

**10.** Place the wallhanging top and backing right sides together, then place them on top of the fleece and pin them together. Sew around the outer edge, leaving an 8" opening along the bottom edge. Grade the seam allowance. Turn the wallhanging right side out and whipstitch the opening closed.

**11.** Tie each torn rag strip in a bow and hand tack one to each corner of the center panel, with the bow facing toward the center.

**12.** Trace the **Full-Size Stencil Pattern,** omitting the leg and whisker lines and the eye dots, onto the Mylar. To cut the stencil, place the Mylar on the glass and tape it to secure. Holding the craft knife like a pencil, carefully cut out the design on the tracing line. Cut toward you, turning the glass as you

cut. If your knife should slip, mend both sides of the cut with masking tape. Position the stencil along the bottom edge of the apron, leaving enough room for three cats; tape in

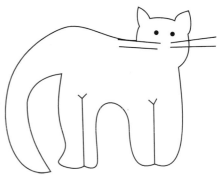

**Full-Size Stencil Pattern**

place. Place 2 tablespoons of paint on the saucer or palette. Dip the tip of the stencil brush into the paint, then pounce on the paper towels until the brush is almost dry. Holding the brush perpendicular to the surface, brush over the cutout areas with a circular motion, working over the stencil edges. Allow the paint to dry on one cat before moving to the second and third. After stenciling, wash the brushes and saucer with soap and water.

**13.** Using the razor-point pen, draw thin lines to define the cat's legs, then dot each eye. Using the tan thread, make two small stitches on the cat's face for whiskers, leaving long tails at both ends.

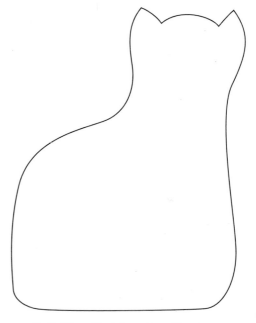

**Full-Size Border Cat Pattern**

# COUNTRY TIPS
*from Alma Lynne*

Transform Witch Charming into Witchy Poo with a twist of the wand, a snap of the fingers, and a dose of magical needlecrafting dust!

Use bright orange and yellow fabrics instead of the somber ones I've used here. Find a fabric with pumpkins for the first and fourth borders and the backing to get you into the trick-or-treating spirit. Purchase nubby black yarn for rough-textured hair. Add green French knot eyes

to the little kitty and rename him "scratchy cat."

Instead of black cat appliqués, use the **Border Patterns** below to cut out 12 orange jack-o'-lanterns and 12 green stems. Machine appliqué in place around the third border. Stencil three boiling cauldrons on Witchy Poo's skirt, using the **Full-Size Stencil Patterns;** use black paint for the cauldron and green paint for the bubbling potion.

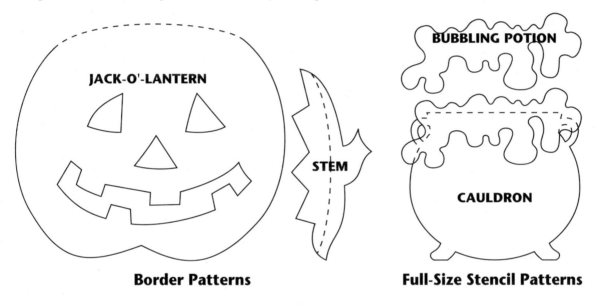

**JACK-O'-LANTERN**

**STEM**

**BUBBLING POTION**

**CAULDRON**

**Border Patterns**

**Full-Size Stencil Patterns**

**14.** For the hair, wrap the twine around the 6½" piece of cardboard 16 times. Cut through the twine along one end of the cardboard. Bunch and center the twine on Witch Charming's head, then hand tack it to the bottom center of the hat. Cut the black ribbon into four ½-yard pieces. Bunch one side of the hair into a ponytail and tie a bow with the black ribbon. Repeat for the other side. Wrap the twine around the cardboard 20 times in the same manner. Cut, bunch, and hand tack the twine in the same manner, then tie each side into a bow with the black ribbon.

**15.** Hand tack the dowel to Witch Charming's left hand. Wrap the yarn around the 4" piece of cardboard 30 times. Cut

through the yarn along one end of the cardboard. Keeping the fold at the center of the yarn bunch, place the yarn over the bottom end of the broomstick to form bristles. Cut an 8" length of yarn and wrap it around the bristles about ¾" from the top; knot it at the back of the bristles. Hand tack the bristles to the wallhanging.

**16.** Using the tan thread, hand quilt ⅛" around the outside of Witch Charming. Using the cream thread, hand quilt ⅛" around the outside of each border cat.

**17.** Using the cream thread, make three small stitches on each appliquéd cat's face, including the little kitty's face, for whiskers; leave long tails on both ends.

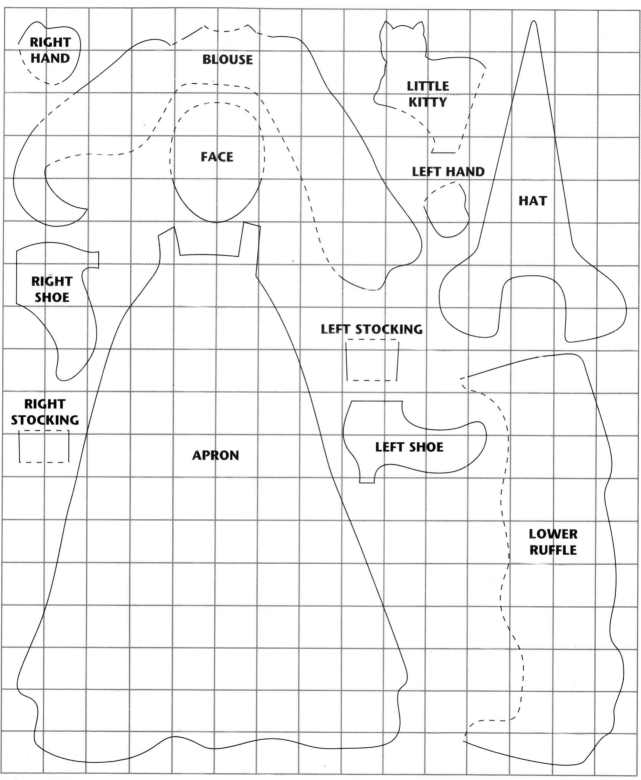

Enlarge 226%

**Witch Charming Wallhanging Patterns**

1 square = 1"

# COUNTRY CLAUS

*Christmas comes just once a year, but this rustic Claus is reason to celebrate all year long. His humble attire is reminiscent of the manger setting where the tradition of gift giving began.*

## SIZE

Finished Claus is 20" tall

## MATERIALS

* 1 yard of 44"-wide tea-dyed muslin for the body*
* ⅝ yard of 44"-wide teal striped wool fabric for the robe
* 1¼ yard of 44"-wide burgundy wool fabric for the coat
* Scrap of cream solid fabric for the toy bunny
* Scrap of cream print fabric for the toy bunny's dress
* ⅛ yard of natural burlap for the goodie sack
* Matching thread
* Polyester fiberfill
* Matching buttonhole twist thread
* Soft-sculpture doll needle
* Two skeins of cream cotton slubby yarn for the hair and beard
* One 10", one 5", and one 3" piece of cardboard
* Hot-glue gun
* 2 yards of jute twine for the goodie sack strap, ornament string, and belt
* One toy alphabet block
* One 2½"-diameter and one 5"-diameter green silk wreath

* Two 2"–4" wooden cutout shapes for the belt ornaments
* One 3"-diameter grapevine wreath
* One small bunch of baby's breath

*See page 239 for directions on tea dyeing.

## DIRECTIONS

**Note:** Country Claus is for decorative purposes only; his clothing cannot be removed. All seam allowances are ¼".

**1.** Prepare all patterns as directed in "Preparing Patterns" on page 236, using the patterns on pages 188 and 189.

**2.** Referring to "Cut-and-Sew Method" on page 236, from the muslin, cut two bodies, two arms, and two legs. From the striped wool, cut two robes and two neck facings. From the solid wool, cut four coats. From the cream solid, cut two toy bunnies. From the cream print, cut two bunny dresses. From the burlap, cut two 4" × 5½" pieces for the goodie sack.

**3.** With right sides together, sew the body pieces together, leaving an opening for turning. Clip the curves. Turn to the right side and stuff firmly. Whipstitch the opening closed.

**4.** Repeat Step 3 for each arm and leg.

**5.** Knot a 20" length of buttonhole twist at one end and thread it through the doll needle. Matching the large dots, run the needle from the outside of one arm through to the inside of the arm, then through the body and the other arm. Make several passes through the arms and body to secure. Knot tightly. Repeat for the legs.

**6.** For Country Claus's hair, wrap the yarn around the largest cardboard piece 125 times. Cut through the yarn along one end of the cardboard. Bunch and center the yarn on his head, forming a part with your stitches. For his beard, wrap the yarn around the medium-size cardboard piece 40 times in the same manner. Cut along one end. Bunch and center the yarn under his "mouth," then hand sew in place. For the moustache, wrap the yarn around the smallest cardboard piece 10

times. Cut along one end. Bunch and center the yarn under Country Claus's "nose," then hand sew in place.

**7.** With right sides together, sew the robe front and back together, leaving the left shoulder open from the large dot to the neckline edge. With right sides together, sew the right shoulder seam of the neck facing. Zigzag stitch the outer edge of the neck facing to prevent fraying. With right sides together, sew the neck facing to the robe from shoulder dot to shoulder dot along the neckline. Trim the seam allowance and clip the curves. Turn the facing to the inside and press. Hand tack together at the inside seams. With right sides together, sew the underarm seams. Clip the curves. Turn under ¼", then another ¼" around each armhole, and press; hem. Turn under ¼", then another ¼" around the lower edge, and press; hem. Turn right side out. Place the robe on Country Claus. Whipstitch the left shoulder closed.

**8.** To make the coat and lining front, cut two of the coats in half along the center front/back line. With right sides together, sew the two coat fronts to one coat back at the shoulder and underarm seams to form the coat shell. For the coat lining, sew the two coat front linings to the remaining coat back, having right sides together and leaving a 6" opening along one shoulder seam; sew at least 1" of the seam at each end of this shoulder seam for ease in turning. Sew the underarm seam.

**9.** With right sides together, sew the coat shell and coat lining together, leaving the wrist edges open. Trim the seam allowances and clip the underarm curves. Carefully turn right side out; do not place the lining sleeves inside the coat sleeves yet. Whipstitch the

## COUNTRY TIPS
### from Alma Lynne

If you're planning a holiday get-together, use Country Claus as a centerpiece. Make a burlap goodie sack for each guest, and fill it with trinkets, candies, or small handmade gifts. Tie a piece of jute around the sack to close the bag up tight.

Buy extra wool fabric to make place mats to match the centerpiece. Cut the fabric into 12½" × 18½" rectangles, then fray about ½" around all four sides. For a table runner, cut a length of burlap to fit your table and fray the edges. Small grapevine wreaths would make great napkin rings. If you have ladderback chairs, buy 6"-diameter green silk wreaths and accent with baby's-breath. Using jute as a hanger, tie one wreath to a post on each chair.

When you plan your party, build in extra time to decorate in a country way. With a rustic Christmas as your theme, serve home-cooked comfort foods in old crocks and antique bowls. Take a quick search through your buffet or china closet for stoneware platters or pottery dishes. Hand-rolled beeswax candles will set the mood. Then, gather your family, light a glowing fire in the fireplace, and have a very rustic Christmas!

shoulder seam of the lining closed. Turn the edges of the shell sleeves and lining sleeves ¼" to the wrong side and press. Slip the linings into the sleeves. Hand sew the lining to the shell at the wrist edge. Turn the cuffs up 1½" and hand tack in place. Place the coat on Country Claus.

10. With right sides together, sew around three sides of the goodie sack. Turn and press. Cut a 27" length of jute. Thread one end through the weave of the burlap at each side seam and tie a knot for the goodie sack strap. Set the sack aside.

11. With right sides together, sew the toy bunny front and back together, leaving an opening along one leg. Clip the curves. Turn to the right side and stuff lightly. Whipstitch the opening closed. With right sides together, sew the bunny dress front and back together at the shoulder and underarm seams. Turn to the right side. Run a gathering thread around the neck edge. Place the dress on the toy bunny and pull up the gathers to fit. Secure the thread. Fray the raw edges of the neckline, sleeves, and lower edge to create a worn country look.

12. Stuff the bottom of the goodie sack with fiberfill. Place the toy bunny and the wooden block in the sack. Hand tack the small silk wreath to the outside of the sack. Place the sack strap diagonally over Country Claus's shoulder.

13. Cut a 9" length of jute. Hot-glue one end to the back of one cutout and the other end to the back of the other cutout for the belt ornaments. Wrap the remaining jute length around Country Claus's waist for a belt and tie one-half of a square knot. Place the belt ornament string in front of the knot and finish tying the knot. Knot the ends of the belt to prevent raveling.

14. Hand sew the grapevine wreath to one of Country Claus's hands.

15. Place several small bunches of baby's-breath in the large silk wreath. Hand sew the wreath to Country Claus's head.

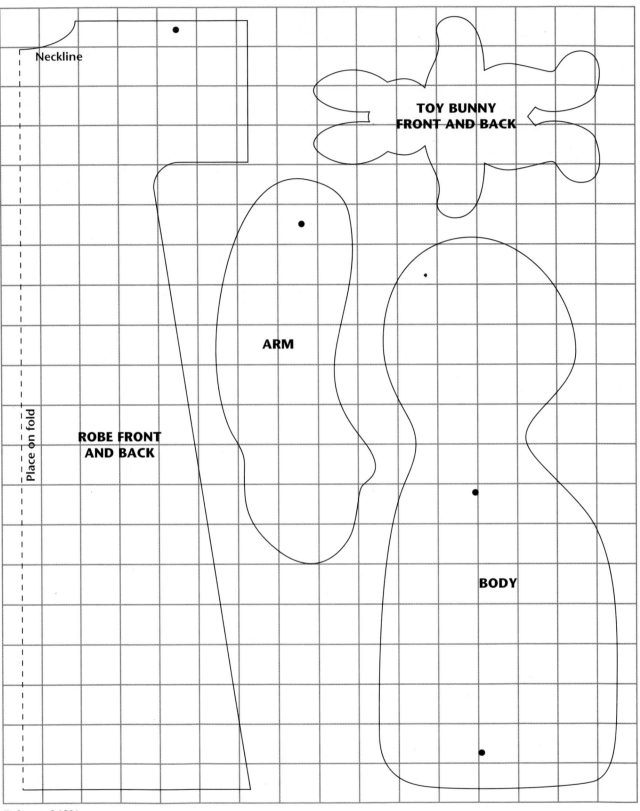

Neckline

Place on fold

TOY BUNNY
FRONT AND BACK

ARM

ROBE FRONT
AND BACK

BODY

Enlarge 242%

## Country Claus Patterns
1 square = 1"

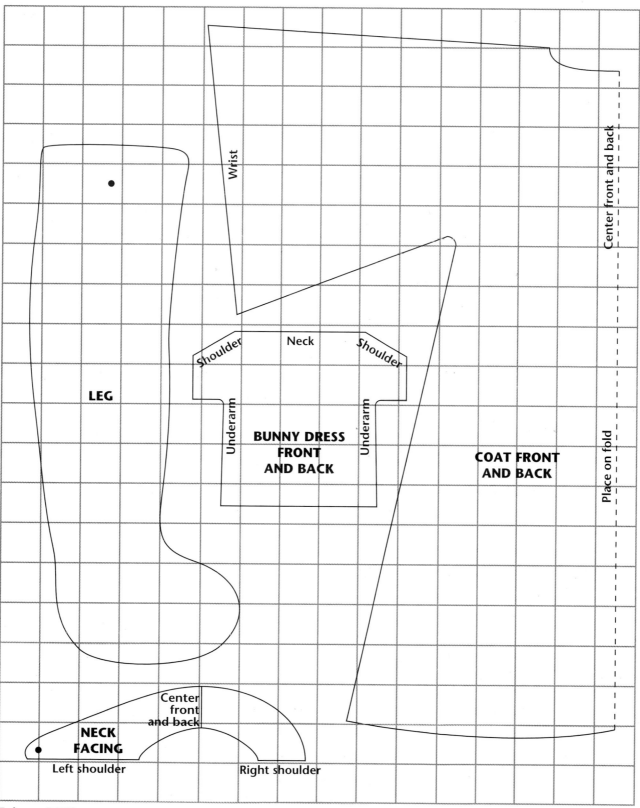

**LEG**

Wrist

Shoulder    Neck    Shoulder

Underarm    Underarm

**BUNNY DRESS FRONT AND BACK**

**COAT FRONT AND BACK**

Center front and back

Place on fold

Center front and back

**NECK FACING**

Left shoulder    Right shoulder

Enlarge 242%

**Country Claus Patterns**

1 square = 1"

# HOME
## SWEET HOME

Home is where you hang your hat and your handiwork. It's a retreat from the bustle of everyday life and a cozy, comfortable place to be. I designed the projects in this chapter to reflect our love affair with "home" and our need to "nest." These decorator accents give our homes their unique personalities. Display the wallhanging on the back of a door, the flag on the front porch, and the hand towels in the guest bath. You'll delight in finding the perfect accessory for that special nook. It's just so easy to decorate your Home Sweet Home with your heart and hands!

# JACK-O'-LANTERN FLAG

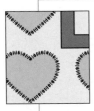

*Hang this colorful outdoor flag for Halloween. With these simple instructions, you'll be finished sewing before the first trick-or-treaters arrive!*

## SIZE

Flag measures 34½" × 57"

## MATERIALS

★ 1⅛ yards of 60"-wide black flag bunting for the background
★ ¾ yard of 60"-wide orange flag bunting for the jack-o'-lantern and sashing strips
★ ½ yard of 60"-wide white flag bunting for the checkerboard
★ ⅜ yard of 60"-wide gold flag bunting for the corner blocks, eyes, nose, and toothy grin
★ ⅛ yard (or scrap) of 60"-wide brown flag bunting for the stem
★ 3 large spools of black thread
★ Black permanent marker for marking the checkerboard
★ Very sharp craft or embroidery scissors

## DIRECTIONS

**Note:** Thread your sewing machine with black thread and set it on a wide satin stitch. Be sure to test your stitching on a scrap of flag bunting. This flag is constructed using two layers of flag bunting. In order to make it reversible, it is necessary to cut out one of the layers to make the first side (this allows the second layer of bunting to show through); the reverse side has the corresponding layer cut away.

1. Prepare all patterns as directed in "Preparing Patterns" on page 236, using the patterns on page 195.

2. From the black, cut one 36" × 57" piece for the background. From the gold, cut four corner blocks, two eyes, one nose, and one toothy grin. From the white, cut the four checkerboard strips. (Even though the strips are referred to as "checkerboard," they will be plain white until you snip away the layers.) From the orange, cut four sashing strips and one jack-o'-lantern. From the brown bunting, cut one stem.

3. For the rod pocket, measure and mark with pins 6" in along one short end of the flag. This will be the right-hand side of your flag as you appliqué. You should not appliqué in this rod pocket area.

4. Using the marker and **Diagram 1** as a guide, draw the checkerboard lines on the white border strips. Draw the 'fraidy cat outlines on the gold corner blocks, having two 'fraidy cats facing in one direction and the remaining two 'fraidy cats facing in the opposite direction.

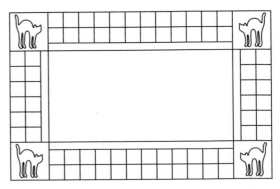

**Diagram 1**

**5.** With the rod pocket on the right-hand side of the flag, place the white border strips, gold corner blocks, and orange sashing strips on the black background and baste them in place.

**6.** Place the pumpkin and stem in place in the center of the background. Using the marker, trace around the portion of the stem that extends into the orange border.

**7.** Machine appliqué the lines on the checkerboards through both layers of fabric, having the line butting the rod pocket be the only outside checkerboard line you appliqué. Machine appliqué the 'fraidy cat outlines and the orange sashing strips, appliquéing only up to the stem outline on the upper sashing strip.

**8.** Place the flag on a flat surface, having the side with the appliquéd pieces facing up.

## COUNTRY THOUGHTS
*from Alma Lynne*

This flag is a biggie; it measures almost 3' × 5'! If you need to make it smaller, you could leave off the checkerboard and the 'fraidy cats, or you could enlarge the patterns until 1 square=¾". For a variation, you could place one very large 'fraidy cat on the center panel and have the jack-o'-lanterns as the small corner motifs.

Referring to **Diagram 2,** insert the tip of the scissors into the top layer of fabric and carefully cut out the gold fabric *inside* the 'fraidy cat appliqué lines to expose the black background. Turn the flag to the other side and cut out the black fabric *outside* the 'fraidy cat appliqué lines to expose the gold corner blocks.

### Diagram 2

**9.** Turn the flag over again. Cut out every other white square checkerboard-fashion to expose the black background. Turn the flag over and cut out the opposite squares to expose the white fabric.

**10.** Turn under ¼", then ½", around three sides of the flag. Press and hem, leaving the short side with the rod pocket unhemmed.

**11.** Turn under ¼" on the rod pocket side and press. Fold the rod pocket in half along the length, bringing the fold of the turned-under edge to the machine-appliquéd line along the outside of the checkerboard; see **Diagram 3.** Stitching as close to the folded edge as possible, sew the rod pocket in place with a straight stitch.

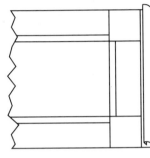

### Diagram 3

**12.** Using the marker and the **Jack-o'-Lantern Flag Patterns** as a guide, draw the eyes, nose, and toothy grin on the orange jack-o'-lantern.

**13.** Place the flag on a flat surface so the appliquéd side is facing up. Place the pumpkin and stem in the center of the background again, matching the traced line on the sashing strip with the stem. Baste in place, then machine appliqué the stem and pumpkin outlines, extending into the top of the pumpkin, as indicated on the pattern.

**14.** Turn the flag over and cut out the black background inside the jack-o'-lantern appliqué lines to expose the orange fabric. Cut out the black background and orange sashing fabric inside the stem appliqué lines to expose the brown fabric.

**15.** Turn the flag over again. Place the eyes, nose, and toothy grin appliqués on the jack-o'-lantern. Baste in place, then machine appliqué around the appliqués. Turn the flag over and cut out the orange fabric inside the appliqué lines to expose the gold fabric.

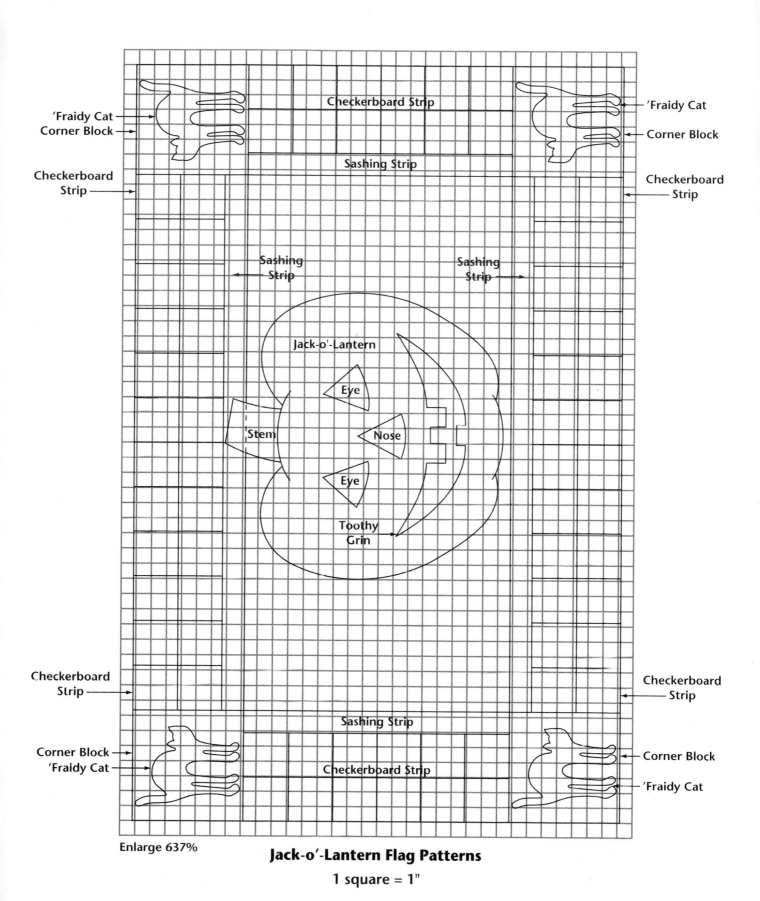

'Fraidy Cat
Corner Block

Checkerboard Strip

'Fraidy Cat

Corner Block

Checkerboard
Strip

Checkerboard
Strip

Sashing Strip

Sashing
Strip

Sashing
Strip

Jack-o'-Lantern

Eye

Stem

Nose

Eye

Toothy
Grin

Checkerboard
Strip

Checkerboard
Strip

Corner Block

Sashing Strip

Corner Block

'Fraidy Cat

Checkerboard Strip

'Fraidy Cat

Enlarge 637%

## Jack-o'-Lantern Flag Patterns

### 1 square = 1"

# PATRIOTIC HEARTS SWEATSHIRT

*Be the hostess with the mostest when you wear this All-American sweatshirt at your Labor Day gathering. As the day draws to a close and the fireworks light up the sky, you'll be reveling in the toasty warmth of this patriotic design.*

## SIZE

Design area is 4½" × 19⅛" on 6 × 8 gauge

## MATERIALS

* ★ One 6 × 8-gauge cream Dupli-Band*
* ★ One skein of embroidery floss for each color listed in **Color Key** (unless otherwise indicated)
* ★ Size 22 tapestry needle
* ★ One adult's navy blue sweatshirt
* ★ One 7" × 22" piece of fusible webbing
* ★ ⅞ yard of 1"-wide navy print pregathered ruffle
* ★ 2¼ yards of ⅝"-wide burgundy print ribbon trim with a crocheted edge
* ★ Matching thread

*See "Buyer's Guide" on page 240 for ordering information.

## DIRECTIONS

**1.** Find the center of the Dupli-Band and mark it with a pin. Find the center of the **Patriotic Hearts Sweatshirt Chart** by connecting the arrows.

**2.** Read the duplicate stitch basics in "The Stitches" on page 235. Matching the center of the chart with the marked center stitch on the Dupli-Band, duplicate stitch the design using six strands of floss.

**3.** Wash and press the completed duplicate stitch design as directed in "Washing and Pressing" on page 235. Wash and dry the sweatshirt.

**4.** Following the manufacturer's directions, apply the fusible webbing to the back of the completed Dupli-Band. Remove the paper backing. Position the Dupli-Band across the chest area of the sweatshirt, turning the upper side edges under, if necessary, to match the raglan sleeve seams. Turn the side edges of the Dupli-Band under ¼" to ½", if necessary, to match the sweatshirt's side seams.

**5.** Pin the ruffle along the lower edge of the Dupli-Band, inserting the raw edge of the ruffle at least ¼" under the Dupli-Band and turning the ruffle ends under ½"; trim the ruffle to length. Fuse the Dupli-Band and ruffle in place.

---

### COUNTRY TIPS
*from Alma Lynne*

This would be an easy design to stitch on a purchased sweater. Since the motifs are quite small, you can randomly place them to cover the entire sweater. You could center the first heart on the sweater front, then stagger the others, leaving about five or six rows between designs. Or you could leave the design to chance and stitch the motifs wherever your heart desires. Either way, your sweater will surely be a hit!

**6.** Measure the top of the Dupli-Band and cut one piece of trim this measurement plus 1". Measure the bottom of the Dupli-Band and cut one piece of trim in the same manner. Pin the trim in place over the top and bottom edges of the Dupli-Band, turning each raw end of the trim under ½".

**7.** Using matching thread and taking a ⅛" seam allowance, sew the trim to the sweatshirt along all four edges of the trim. Using cream thread, sew each side of the Dupli-Band to the sweatshirt.

**8.** With the remaining trim, tie a bow and hand tack the knot to the lower trim at the center front of the sweatshirt. Clip the trim ends diagonally.

### COLOR KEY

| | DMC | Anchor | J. & P. Coats | Color |
|---|---|---|---|---|
| C | 814 | 45 | 3044 | Dk. Garnet (3 skeins) |
| / | 823 | 152 | 7982 | Dk. Navy Blue (4 skeins) |

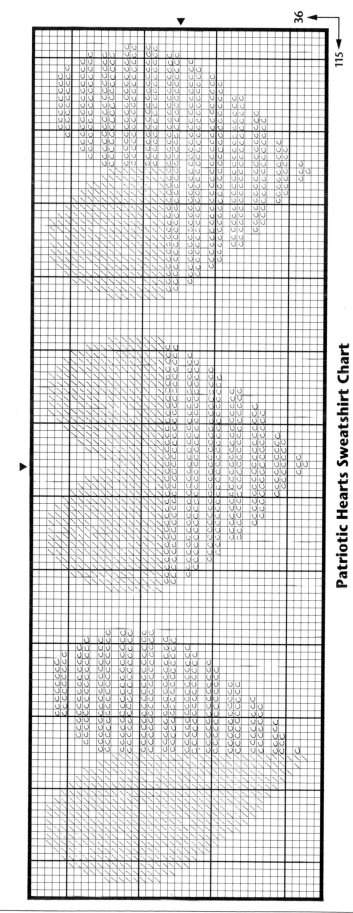

**Patriotic Hearts Sweatshirt Chart**

# THE PREACHER'S KIDS

*These kids are practicing what their daddy is preaching! Victoriana's old-world cloche delicately accents her pretty face, and Victor's tuxedo is the perfect choice for the Sunday School's holiday performance.*

## VICTORIANA, THE PREACHER'S DAUGHTER

### SIZE

Finished doll is 28" tall

### MATERIALS

* 1¼ yards of 44"-wide muslin for the body
* Matching thread
* Polyester fiberfill
* Spray starch (optional)
* Powdered blusher
* Black, razor-point, permanent pen for the eyes, eyebrows, and pupils
* Green colored pencil for the eyes
* Matching buttonhole twist thread
* Soft-sculpture doll needle
* 1⅛ yards of dark blue floral print fabric for the dress and hat bow
* ⅞ yard of dark blue corduroy for the cape and hat lining
* 1⅛ yards of maroon cotton moiré fabric for the cape lining, cloche, and slippers
* ⅜ yard of dark blue double-fold bias tape for the dress
* 2"-wide Battenburg lace collar for the dress
* 1¼ yards of 1½"-wide scalloped flat white lace for the dress hem

* Two snaps
* 3¼ yards of 1"-wide maroon satin ribbon for the shoelaces
* 1-yard strand of ivory pearls for the cloche
* 1½ yards each of ⅛"-wide maroon, dark blue, and cream satin ribbon for the cloche
* Three small maroon silk roses
* Hot-glue gun

### DIRECTIONS

**Note:** Victoriana is for decorative purposes only; her clothing cannot be removed. All seam allowances are ¼", unless otherwise indicated.

**1.** Prepare all patterns as directed in "Preparing Patterns" on page 236, using the patterns on pages 207 and 208.

**2.** Referring to "Cut-and-Sew Method" on page 236, from the muslin, cut two bodies, four ears, four arms, four legs, and two heads.

**3.** With right sides together, sew the two bodies together, leaving the bottom edge open for turning. Clip the curves, turn to the right side, and press. Stuff the body firmly. Whipstitch the opening closed.

**4.** With right sides together, sew the two heads together, leaving the neck edge open for turning. Clip the curves, turn to the right side, and press. Stuff firmly. Whipstitch the neck edge closed.

**5.** With right sides together, sew around the curved edge of two ears, leaving the straight end open. Repeat for the other ear. Clip the curves, turn, and press. Fold ¼" on

the open end to the inside. Whipstitch the opening closed. Spray the ears with starch if extra stiffening is desired. Hand sew the ears to the head where indicated on the pattern.

**6.** Hand sew the head to the body.

**7.** For the nose, sew back and forth through the face, pulling the thread slightly to pucker the nose, using the dot on the pattern as a placement guide. To make whiskers, insert a needle threaded with cream thread into one side of Victoriana's face about 1" above her nose and ½" from the center seam; bring the needle out the other side of her face, leaving long tails on both sides. Make three additional passes. Lightly blush the tip of the nose.

**8.** Using the razor-point pen and the pattern as a placement guide, draw the eyes, eyebrows, and eyelashes. Color the eye's irises with green pencil. Fill in the pupils with black, leaving the "gleam" uncolored.

**9.** With right sides together, sew two legs together, leaving an opening at the upper back. Clip the curves. Turn, press, and stuff firmly. Whipstitch the openings closed. Repeat for the remaining leg and arms.

**10.** Knot a 20" length of buttonhole twist at one end and thread through the doll needle. Matching the large dots, run the needle from the outside of one arm through to the inside of the arm, then through the body and the other arm. Pass back through the arms and body several times to secure. Knot tightly. Repeat for the legs. Set Victoriana aside.

**11.** From the floral print, cut one front bodice, one back bodice and one back bodice reverse, two sleeves, two 15" × 22" pieces for the skirt front and skirt back, and one 8" × 12" piece for the bow on the cloche. From the corduroy, cut one cape, placing the center back on the lengthwise grain of fabric;

also cut one cloche. From the moiré, cut one cape, placing the center back on the lengthwise grain of fabric; also cut one cloche and four 5" × 11" pieces for the slippers. Do not cut out the slippers at this point.

**12.** With right sides together, sew each bodice front to the bodice back at the shoulders.

**13.** Run a gathering thread a scant ¼" from the cap edge of each sleeve. Pull up the thread to gather each sleeve cap. With right sides facing, pin each sleeve into an armhole, matching the dots at the shoulders and leaving ½" smooth at the underarm.

**14.** With right sides together, sew the bodice fronts to the bodice back at the underarm seams. Clip the curves. Turn under ¼", then another ¼", around each wrist edge and press; hem. Run a gathering thread on each sleeve 1" from the wrist edge; do not gather.

**15.** Turn under ¼", then another ¼", at the center back edge of each back bodice and press; hem. Following the directions in "Bias Tape" on page 237, bind the raw neck edge with bias tape, turning the ends in ¼".

**16.** From the lace collar, cut a 10½" length, having one of the collar's finished ends be one end of the cut length. Wrap the lace around Victoriana's neck, overlapping the raw end with the finished end to make a V and having the overlap at the back of the neck, as shown in the **Collar Diagram.**

**Front**

**Collar Diagram**

**17.** With right sides facing, sew the skirt front and skirt back together along one shorter side to form the center front seam. Then sew the skirt front and back together along the remaining shorter side to form the center back seam, using a ½" seam allowance and leaving 4" open at one end for the placket. Press the center back seam open and topstitch the placket edges ¼" from the fold; see **Diagram 1**. Run a gathering thread around the top edge of the skirt (the placket side). Pull the gathers to fit the waist edge of the bodice. With right sides facing, pin and sew the skirt to the bodice to form the dress, matching the placket openings. Press the seam allowance toward the bodice.

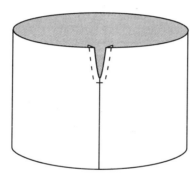

**Diagram 1**

**18.** Turn under ½" around the lower edge of the dress and press; hem. Topstitch the scalloped lace to the dress just above the fold of the hem.

**19.** Turn the dress to the right side and press. Sew two snaps to the dress to overlap the plackets. Place the dress on Victoriana. Pull the wrist gathers to fit and knot the thread.

**20.** For each slipper, place two 5" × 11" moiré pieces together with right sides facing. Transfer the slipper's solid and dashed lines to the fabric. Sew on the sewing (dashed) line from dot to dot, leaving the top open. Cut out the slippers on the cutting (solid) line. Zigzag stitch the raw edges of the slipper opening. Clip the curves, then turn the slippers right side out. Turn under ½" on the opening and press; hand tack the turned-

under edges to the seam allowances. Place one slipper on each foot.

**21.** From the wide maroon ribbon, cut two ½-yard lengths. Tie each length in a bow and hand tack one to the vamp of each slipper. Clip the ends diagonally. Cut the remaining wide maroon ribbon in half. Hand tack the center of each length to the top of the slipper's back seam. Wrap the ribbon around Victoriana's leg, crisscrossing it in the front, then in the back. Bring the ribbon to the front and tie it in a bow, as shown in **Diagram 2**. Clip the ends diagonally.

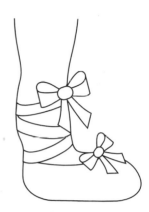

**Diagram 2**

**22.** With right sides together, sew the cape and the cape lining together, leaving the V area on the shoulder open between the small dots. For the arm openings, cut on the solid lines between the large dots as indicated on the pattern; see **Diagram 3**. Trim inside the arm opening holes and around the cape to reduce bulk. Clip and notch the curves. Carefully turn right side out through one shoulder. Working through the shoulder hole and having the right sides of the cape together, sew darts in the cape between the small

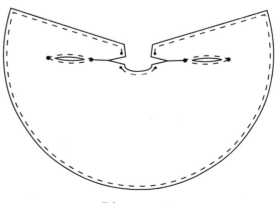

**Diagram 3**

dot and the upper large dot, being careful not to catch the cape lining fabric in the seams. Hand sew the darts in the cape lining to close the opening. Turn under the raw edges on the armholes on the cape and cape lining, using the dashed lines as a guide. Whipstitch the cape and lining together to finish the armholes. Place the cape on Victoriana.

**23.** With right sides together, sew the center back seam of the cloche and the cloche lining from dot to dot. Clip the curves and press the seam open. With right sides together, sew the cloche and the cloche lining together, leaving an opening for turning near the center back seam. Turn to the right side and whipstitch closed. Press carefully.

**24.** With right sides together, fold the cloche bow strip in half lengthwise. Sew along one short edge and the long edge. Trim the seam allowance and turn. Whipstitch closed. Fold the strip so the short edges meet in the back to form a loop. Pinch the center and secure the ends in place by taking several small stitches. Make several loops with the pearl strand, leaving 3"-long tails; pinch and secure the center with a few stitches. Holding the three ⅛" ribbons as if they were one, make several loops and leave 10" tails. Pinch and secure the center of the loops with a few stitches.

**25.** Place the cloche on Victoriana and turn up the brim. Decide on the placement of the cloche accent and mark it with a pin. Remove the cloche. Center the pearl loops over the bow center, then add the looped ribbons; wrap thread around the center area to secure the assembly in place. Hot-glue the rosebuds over the wrapped center. Hand tack the cloche accent to the cloche where marked.

# VICTOR, THE PREACHER'S SON

## SIZE

Finished doll is 28" tall

## MATERIALS

- ★ 1¼ yards of 44"-wide muslin for the body
- ★ Matching thread
- ★ Polyester fiberfill
- ★ Spray starch (optional)
- ★ Powdered blusher
- ★ Black, razor-point, permanent pen for the eyes, eyebrows, and pupils
- ★ Green colored pencil
- ★ Matching buttonhole twist thread
- ★ Soft-sculpture doll needle
- ★ 1 yard of 44"-wide blue corduroy fabric for the tuxedo and trousers
- ★ 1 yard of maroon cotton moiré fabric for the tuxedo lining, shoes, and top hat
- ★ ½ yard of 44"-wide dark blue floral print fabric for the shirt
- ★ 10" × 12" piece of posterboard for making the top hat
- ★ ⅜ yard of dark blue double-fold bias tape for the shirt
- ★ Two snaps
- ★ ½ yard of 2"-wide scalloped white lace for the tuxedo sleeves
- ★ Six ⅝"-diameter pearl shank buttons
- ★ 1 yard of 1"-wide maroon satin ribbon for the shoes
- ★ Hot-glue gun
- ★ ⅜ yard of 1"-wide blue satin ribbon for the top hat
- ★ Two sprigs of eucalyptus for the top hat
- ★ Small sprig of dried red berries for the top hat
- ★ ¼ yard of ⅛"-wide blue satin ribbon for the top hat

## DIRECTIONS

**Note:** Victor is for decorative purposes only; his clothing cannot be removed. All seam allowances are ¼".

**1.** Repeat Steps 2–10 to make Victor's body, using the patterns on page 207.

**2.** Prepare the patterns on page 209 for Victor's clothing. From the corduroy, cut two trousers, two tuxedo fronts, and one tuxedo back, having the corduroy wales running lengthwise for each piece. From the moiré, cut two tuxedo fronts, one tuxedo back, one 4½" × 35" strip for the bow tie, and four 5" × 11" pieces for the shoes. Do not cut out the shoes at this point. Also cut one 3¾" × 9" strip, one 3¼" circle, and two 5¼" circles for the top hat. From the floral print, cut one shirt front and two shirt backs. From the posterboard, cut one 3¼" × 8½" piece, one 2¾" circle, and two 4¾" circles for the top hat; see "Country Tips from Alma Lynne" on page 107 for instructions on drafting circles.

**3.** With right sides together, sew each shirt front to the shirt back at the shoulder seams and the underarm seams. Clip the underarm seams. Turn under ¼", then another ¼", at the center back edge of each back bodice and press; hem. Following the directions in "Bias Tape" on page 237, bind the raw neck edge with bias tape, turning the ends in ¼". Turn under ½" around the lower edge of the shirt and press; hem. Turn to the right side; press. Sew two snaps to the shirt to overlap the plackets. Place the shirt on Victor.

**4.** With right sides together, sew the trousers front and back together along the side seams and inseam. Trim the seam allowances and clip the inseam. Turn right side out and press. Turn under ¼", then another ¼", on each ankle edge and press; hand tack the hem in place. Turn under ½" at the waist edge and press. Run a gathering thread around the waist. Place the trousers on Victor, tucking the shirt inside the trousers, and pull up the gathering threads to fit. Secure the thread.

**5.** With right sides together, sew each jacket front to the jacket back at the shoulder and underarm seams. Turn under ¼" on each wrist edge and press.

**6.** With right sides together, sew each jacket lining front to the jacket lining back at the underarm seams and at the shoulder seams, leaving a 5" opening along one shoulder seam; sew at least 1" of the seam at each end of this shoulder seam for ease in turning.

**7.** With right sides together, sew the jacket and jacket lining together, leaving the wrist edges open. Trim the seam allowances and clip the underarm curves. Carefully turn right side out, but do not place the sleeve linings inside the sleeves yet. Whipstitch the shoulder seam opening closed.

**8.** Cut the 2"-wide lace length in half. With right sides together and matching the raw edge of each sleeve lining with the bound edge of each lace piece, sew the lace to the sleeve linings, overlapping the lace edges ½". Slip the sleeve linings into the sleeves, then whipstitch the wrist edges together. Place the jacket on Victor. Fold the cuffs up to expose the lining and lace. Turn back the lapels. Sew one button to each lapel about ½" above the lower edge; sew through the trousers to secure the jacket in place.

**9.** Sew one button to each cuff at the outside seam and one button to each upper corner of the back vent.

**10.** With right sides together, fold the bow tie strip in half lengthwise. Sew along one short edge, using the **Bow Tie End Diagram** on page 206 as a guide, then along the long raw edge. Trim the seam allowance and turn to the right side. Cut the open end to match the diagonal line on the opposite end, then whipstitch the opening closed. Wrap the bow tie around Victor's neck and tie it in a bow.

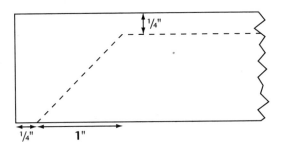

**Bow Tie End Diagram**

**11.** For each shoe, place two 5" × 11" moiré pieces together with right sides facing. Transfer the shoe's solid and dashed lines to the fabric. Sew on the sewing (dashed) line from dot to dot, leaving the top edge open. Cut out the shoes on the cutting (solid) line. Zigzag stitch the raw edges of the shoe opening. Clip the remaining seam allowances, then turn the shoes right side out. Turn under ½" on the zigzag-stitched edges and press; hand tack the turned-under edges to the seam allowances. Place one shoe on each of Victor's feet.

**12.** From the wide maroon ribbon, cut two ½-yard lengths. Tie each length in a bow and hand tack one to the vamp of each shoe. Clip the ribbon ends diagonally.

**13.** Center and cover each posterboard component with its corresponding moiré piece, hot-gluing the raw ends in place. With wrong sides facing, hot-glue the two largest circles together to form the hat's brim. Using the small circle as a size guide, bend the rectangular piece into a cylinder, overlapping the ends until the small circle rests on the outer edges; hot-glue it in place. Hot-glue the small circle to the top of the hat. Hot glue the hat to the brim. Wrap the wide ribbon around the top hat, resting one long edge on the top of the brim and overlapping the edges; whipstitch the ends together. Hot-glue the eucalyptus and dried berries to the hat brim near the bow. Tie the narrow ribbon in a bow and hot-glue it to the hat brim.

## COUNTRY THOUGHTS
*from Alma Lynne*

I set up Victoriana and Victor in a tiny vignette to add real personality to their photograph. I found the church pew and the podium at a used furniture store, then accented the setting with child-size books and a miniature tree.

Keep your eyes peeled at flea markets and yard sales for small pieces of furniture. You can always refinish or paint the odds and ends to match your bunnies' outfits. Or grab a hammer, some nails, a saw, and some wood and adapt a bargain piece for bunny use! Use mini pickle barrels for country stools, and dresser drawers for bunk beds. It's so much fun to dream up a whole houseful of furniture for Victoriana and Victor. There's only one problem—just where will I find room to put it all? Of course, I could always ask my hubby to build an extra "family" room for the bunnies!

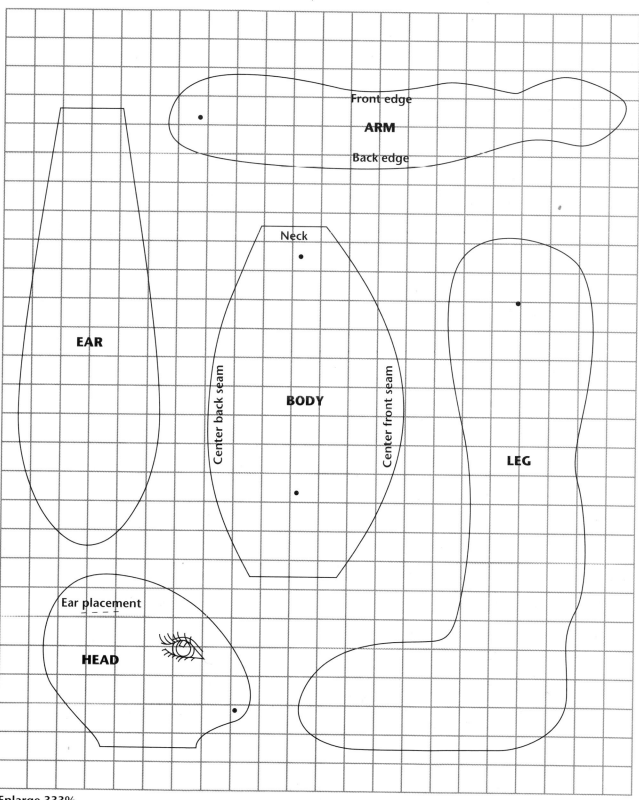

Enlarge 333%

**The Preacher's Kids Patterns**

1 square = 1"

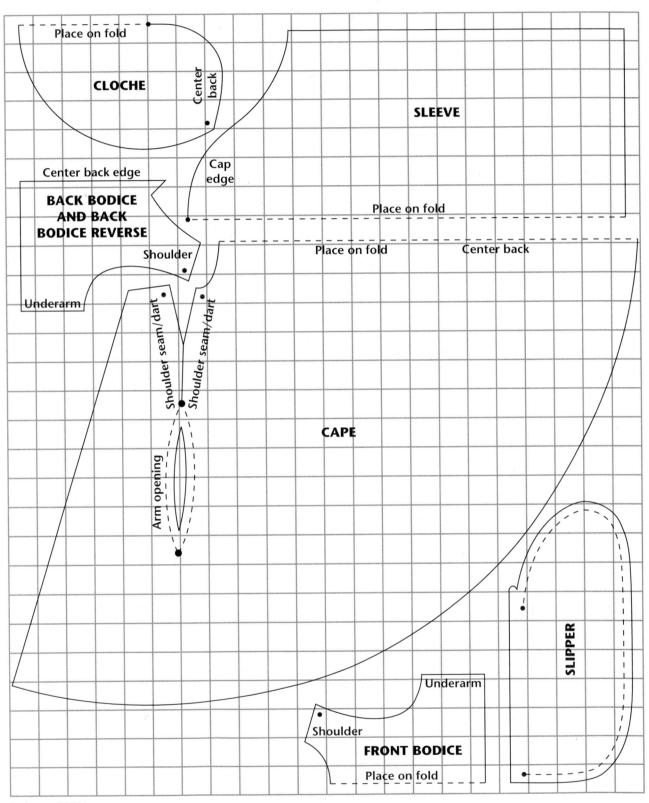

**Victoriana's Wardrobe Patterns**

1 square = 1"

Enlarge 333%

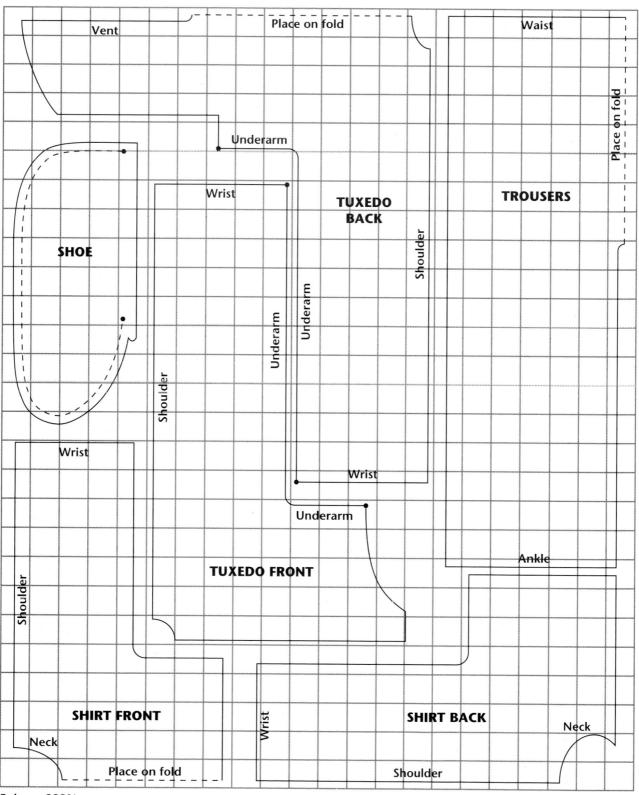

Enlarge 333%

**Victor's Wardrobe Patterns**

1 square = 1"

# WASH DAY PICTURE

*Patriotic Betsy Floss is busy with chores at home. She washes and scrubs and hangs her needlework flags out to dry in the bright morning sun. Capture this glimpse of colonial America in easy cross-stitch.*

## SIZE

Design area is 5⅝" × 5⅞" (over two threads) on 25-count Lugana

## MATERIALS

★ One 11⅝" × 11⅞" piece of 25-count mushroom Lugana
★ One skein of embroidery floss for each color listed in **Color Key**
★ Size 26 tapestry needle

## DIRECTIONS

**1.** Prepare the edges of the Lugana as directed in "Preparing Fabric Edges" on page 232. Find the center of the Lugana and mark it with a pin. Find the center of the **Wash Day Picture Chart** by connecting the arrows.

**2.** Matching the centers of the chart and the Lugana, and using two strands of floss, begin stitching at the center point, working each cross-stitch over two threads. Work outward until the entire design is complete.

**3.** Backstitch the entire design with one strand of black-brown.

**4.** Work the half-stitches for the shadows on the ground with two strands of very dark beige-gray.

**5.** Work the long stitches for the clothesline with two strands of black-brown, passing over the posts and behind the clothespins; allow the floss to hang free from the outside of each post. Work a French knot with two strands of black-brown for the goose's eye. See "The Stitches" on page 233 for instructions on making French knots.

**6.** Wash and press the completed cross-stitch piece as directed in "Washing and Pressing" on page 233.

**7.** Mat and frame as desired.

### DESIGN OPTIONS

| Fabric Count | Design Area | Cutting Dimensions |
| --- | --- | --- |
| 22 | 3¼" × 3⅜" | 13¼" × 13⅜" |
| 18 | 4" × 4⅛" | 14" × 14⅛" |
| 14 | 5⅛" × 5¼" | 15⅛" × 15¼" |
| 11 | 6½" × 6¾" | 16½" × 16¾" |

# COUNTRY TIPS

*from Alma Lynne*

There are cross-stitchers the world over but not many designs featuring the flags of other countries. Well, I'll just have to fix that!

I've recharted the flags on the washline for Canadian, British, and Australian cross-stitchers. Follow the charts below for the flags of those nations. The symbols correspond to the **Color Key,** since the colors remain the same.

To simplify things for yourself when stitching the starred flag in the washtub, just change the light beige-gray stitches to navy blue for the Australian and British flags. For the Canadian flag in the washtub, change very dark navy blue to very dark garnet, dark navy blue to very dark shell pink, and navy blue to medium shell pink.

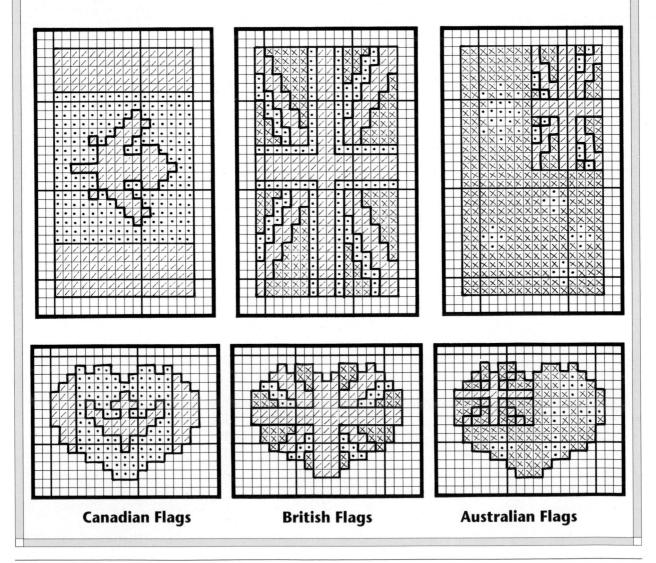

**Canadian Flags**     **British Flags**     **Australian Flags**

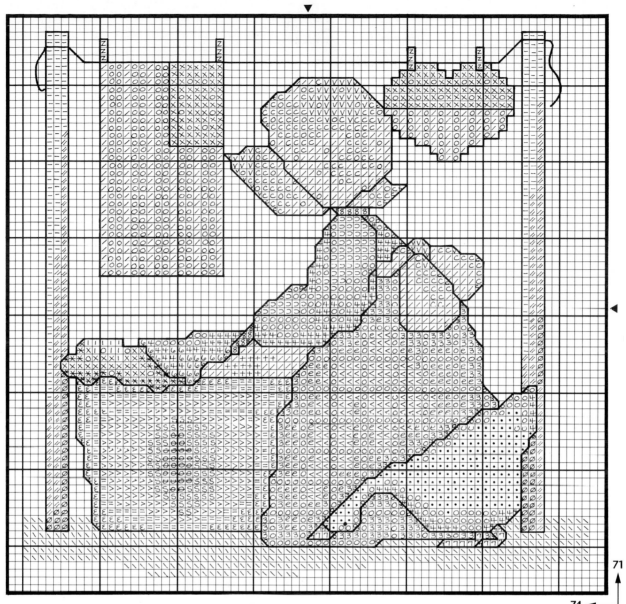

**71**

**74**

## Wash Day Picture Chart
### Color Key

| | DMC | Anchor | J. & P. Coats | Color | | DMC | Anchor | J. & P. Coats | Color |
|---|---|---|---|---|---|---|---|---|---|
| • | White | 2 | 1001 | White | 7 | 783 | 307 | 5307 | Christmas Gold |
| ⊃ | Ecru | 387 | 5387 | Ecru | + | 815 | 43 | 3000 | Med. Garnet |
| c | 221 | 897 | 3243 | Vy. Dk. Shell Pink | O | 822 | 390 | 5933 | Lt. Beige-Gray |
| v | 223 | 895 | 3240 | Med. Shell Pink | × | 823 | 152 | 7982 | Dk. Navy Blue |
| I | 336 | 150 | 7981 | Navy Blue | Ø | 840 | 379 | 5379 | Med. Beige-Brown |
| ε | 433 | 358 | 5471 | Med. Brown | // | 841 | 378 | 5376 | Lt. Beige-Brown |
| = | 434 | 310 | 5000 | Lt. Brown | — | 842 | 388 | 5933 | Vy. Lt. Beige-Brown |
| > | 435 | 1046 | 5371 | Vy. Lt. Brown | / | 902 | 897 | 3083 | Vy. Dk. Garnet |
| S | 436 | 1045 | 5943 | Tan | 3 | 930 | 1035 | 7052 | Dk. Antique Blue |
| Φ | 437 | 362 | 5942 | Lt. Tan | e | 931 | 1034 | 7051 | Med. Antique Blue |
| \ | 640 | 903 | 5393 | Vy. Dk. Beige-Gray | < | 932 | 1033 | 7050 | Lt. Antique Blue |
| 6 | 642 | 392 | 5832 | Dk. Beige-Gray | ✳ | 939 | 152 | 7160 | Vy. Dk. Navy Blue |
| 4 | 644 | 830 | 5830 | Med. Beige-Gray | 8 | 948 | 1011 | 2331 | Vy. Lt. Peach |
| Z | 738 | 361 | 5375 | Vy. Lt. Tan | | 3371 | 382 | 5382 | Black-Brown |

# QUILTER'S CHARM
# WALLHANGING

*Quilters love to be surrounded by the tools of their trade—colorful calicoes, traditional block patterns, and a ready supply of needles and pins. This pretty wallhanging has all this, plus a dose of quilting inspiration.*

## SIZE

Finished wallhanging is 11" × 40½"

## MATERIALS

* ⅝ yard of 44"-wide light blue print fabric for the sashing and border strips, backing, hanging sleeve, and strips for two blocks
* ⅜ yard of 44"-wide rose solid fabric for the background blocks and small hearts
* ⅝ yard of tear-away stabilizer
* 11½" × 41" piece of fleece
* 1½ yards of fusible webbing
* Scrap of light blue solid fabric for two thread spools
* Scrap of mint solid fabric for the pincushion and two thread spools
* One 5" × 10" piece of rose print fabric for the pincushion, emery, and large heart
* One 11" square of dark rose solid fabric for the pincushion, large square, one thread spool, and one small heart
* One 6" × 12" piece of mint print fabric for the triangles and medium and small squares
* Scrap of tan solid fabric for the spools
* One 4" × 8" piece of gold lamé for the scissors
* Matching thread

* Six 1"-diameter ceramic specialty buttons in shapes such as scissors, thimble, spool, sewing machine, tape measure
* Approximately 70 buttons in assorted shapes, colors, and sizes
* Two needles
* Four ball-head straight pins
* Three safety pins in assorted sizes
* Six 4 mm pearl beads
* Hot-glue gun
* 12" bellpull hardware

## DIRECTIONS

**Note:** Wash, dry, and press all your fabrics before beginning this project. All seam allowances are ¼".

**1.** Prepare all patterns as directed in "Preparing Patterns" on page 236, using the patterns on page 219.

**2.** From the light blue print, cut four 2¼" × 8" sashing strips, two 2¼" × 41" border strips, two 2¼" × 11½" border strips, one 11½" × 38" backing piece, and one 2" × 10" strip for the hanging sleeve. From the dark rose solid, cut two 6" × 8" pieces for the background of Blocks A and E and three 8" squares for the background of Blocks B, C, and D. From the tear-away stabilizer, cut three 8" squares and two 6" × 8" pieces. From the fleece, cut one 11½" × 38" piece.

**3.** Fuse the fusible webbing to the remaining pieces of fabric as directed in "Fusible Webbing" on page 235.

**4.** Refer to "Machine Appliqué" on page 235 for directions on marking and cutting appliqué pieces. From the light blue solid, cut

**Block A**

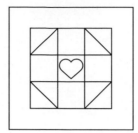

**Block B**

**Block C**

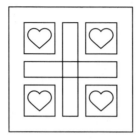

**Block D**

**Block E**

## Appliqué Placement Diagrams

two threads. From the mint solid, cut two threads, one pincushion top, and one emery top. From the rose print, cut one strawberry emery, one tomato middle, and one large heart. From the dark rose solid, cut one tomato, one small heart, one 6" square, and one thread. From the mint print, cut four triangles, one 5" square, and four 2⅛" squares. From the light blue print, cut two 1" × 6" strips and two 1¾" × 5¾" strips. From the tan solid, cut five spools. From the rose solid, cut four small hearts. From the gold lamé, cut one pair of scissors.

**5.** Center the appliqué pieces on the individual blocks, referring to the **Appliqué Placement Diagrams** for each block and to the photograph on page 215, and layering as indicated by the dashed lines. Fuse in place as directed in "Fusible Webbing " on page 235.

**6.** Center and pin the tear-away stabilizer to the back of each block. Machine appliqué all edges of the appliqués using matching thread. Machine appliqué a curving line from the top of the emery to the top of the pincushion.

**7.** With right sides together and raw edges even, sew one 2¼" × 8" sashing strip to the bottom of Block A, as shown in **Diagram 1.** Press the seam toward the sashing strip. Repeat for Blocks B, C, and D.

**8.** With right sides together and raw edges even, sew the bottom of the Block A sashing strip to the top of Block B, referring to **Diagram 2.** Press the seam toward the sashing strip. Repeat for Blocks C, D, and E.

**9.** With right sides together and raw edges even, sew one 2¼" × 41" border strip to each side of the wallhanging, as shown in **Diagram 3.** Press the seams toward the border.

**Sashing Strip**

**Diagram 1**

**Sashing Strip**

**Diagram 2**

**Diagram 3**          **Diagram 4**

Sew the 2¼" × 11½" border strips to the top and bottom of the wallhanging in the same manner; see **Diagram 4.**

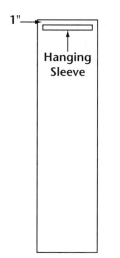

**Diagram 5**

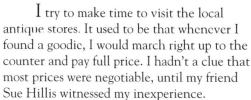

**10.** Press under ¼" on all edges of the hanging sleeve. Place the wrong side of the sleeve on the right side of the backing about 1" below the top edge; see **Diagram 5.** Sew in place along the top and bottom edges of the sleeve, leaving the sides open to insert the hardware.

**11.** Place the wallhanging top and backing right sides together, then place them on top of the fleece. Pin all three layers together. Sew around the outer edge, leaving a 6" opening along the bottom edge. Grade the seam allowance to reduce bulk. Turn the wallhanging right side out and whipstitch the opening closed.

# COUNTRY THOUGHTS
*from Alma Lynne*

I try to make time to visit the local antique stores. It used to be that whenever I found a goodie, I would march right up to the counter and pay full price. I hadn't a clue that most prices were negotiable, until my friend Sue Hillis witnessed my inexperience.

"You could've bought that for half the price you paid," she said, as I loaded my antique lace tablecloth into the car. Was she crazy? The price was clearly marked. I wasn't about to question the shop owner as to whether her price was fair. But Sue convinced me that I had to learn to haggle, so she taught me the finer points of bargaining.

On our next outing, I discovered a lovely coverlet that had certainly seen better days. It was missing some of its patches and many of the seams were ripped, but I wanted it anyway. Sue said it was a good time for me to use my newly acquired negotiating skills.

The coverlet's price tag said $240. Okay, I thought, I'll offer half of that. It would be a good tip-off to the saleslady that I wasn't going to pay too high a price. I figured that I'd go as high as $160 because I really wanted that coverlet. And I hoped the saleslady was ready for the haggling of her life.

I marched right up to the counter and said "I'll give you $120 for this piece here." I waited for the inevitable. She was going to yell. She was going to tell me that I was out of my mind. And then she'd be so mad she wouldn't even let me buy that coverlet.

Well, all of a sudden, she said "SOLD!" What? Was she crazy? Why didn't she haggle? This certainly didn't go as I had planned. I guess my dumbfounded look said it all. She leaned over the counter and glanced around to see who was listening, then said with a smile, "I would've sold you that quilt for $65."

I learned a valuable lesson that day, and I think P. T. Barnum said it best—"There's a sucker born every minute."

**12.** Referring to the **Embellishment Diagram** for ideas, sew the specialty buttons in place on the sashing strips. Sew one button on each corner of the five blocks, then sew the remaining buttons in two graceful curves below Blocks A and E. Place one needle in the blue thread spool in Block E; thread the remaining needle with blue thread and place it in the blue thread spool in Block A. Place the safety pins and straight pins in the pincushion in Block A.

**13.** Hot-glue the pearls among the button clusters.

**14.** Insert the wallhanging hardware in the hanging sleeve, following the manufacturer's directions.

**Embellishment Diagram**

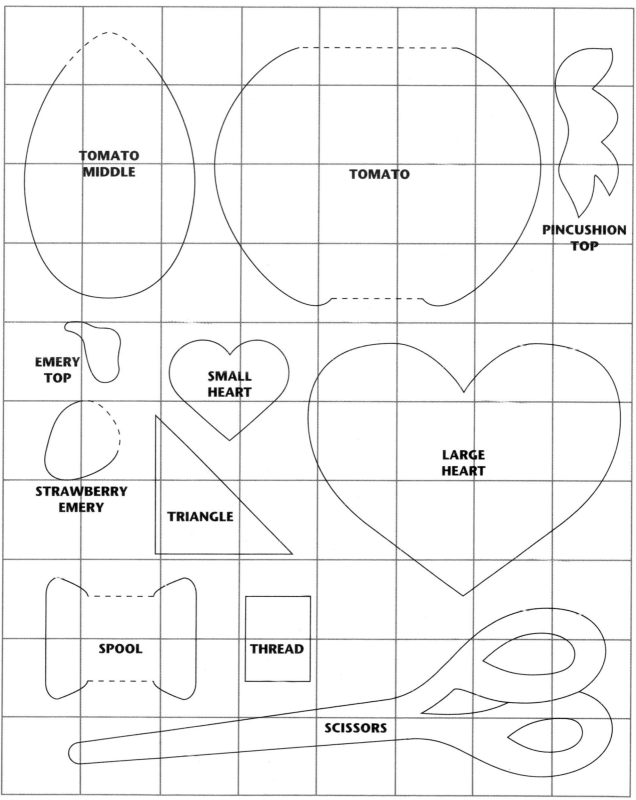

**TOMATO MIDDLE**

**TOMATO**

**PINCUSHION TOP**

**EMERY TOP**

**SMALL HEART**

**LARGE HEART**

**STRAWBERRY EMERY**

**TRIANGLE**

**SPOOL**

**THREAD**

**SCISSORS**

Enlarge 122%

**Appliqué Patterns**

1 square = 1"

# GUESTS OF HONOR
# HAND TOWELS

*Perfect for a guest bath or antique washstand, these cheerful hand towels are the epitome of country elegance. They're quick to stitch and would make delightful hostess gifts when enjoying the hospitality of close friends.*

## BLUEBIRDS OF HAPPINESS HAND TOWEL

### SIZE

Design area is 1½" × 6½" on a 14-count prefinished hand towel

### MATERIALS

★ One Royal Lace light blue 14-count prefinished hand towel*
★ One skein of embroidery floss for each color listed in **Color Key**
★ Size 22 or 24 tapestry needle
★ ½ yard ⅜"-wide blue satin ribbon

*See "Buyer's Guide" on page 240 for ordering information.

### DIRECTIONS

**1.** Find the center of the Aida band on the towel and mark it with a pin. Find the center of the **Bluebirds of Happiness Hand Towel Chart** by connecting the arrows.

**2.** Matching the centers of the chart and the Aida band on the towel and, using two strands of floss, begin stitching at the center point, working outward until the entire design is complete.

**3.** Using one strand of floss, backstitch the birds with light navy blue, the hearts with medium rose, and the floral garland with very dark pistachio green.

**4.** Work the French knots for the eyes with black-brown. Work the French knots for the flowers with medium rose, medium pink, and very light baby blue.

**5.** Wash and press the completed cross-stitch towel as directed in "Washing and Pressing" on page 233.

**6.** Tie the ribbon into a bow, trimming the ribbon ends diagonally. Tack the bow to the center of the band above the garland.

## TULIPS AND POLKA DOTS HAND TOWEL

### SIZE

Design area is 2¼" × 7⅞" on a 14-count prefinished hand towel

### MATERIALS

★ One mint green Cafe Check 14-count prefinished kitchen towel*
★ One skein of embroidery floss for each color listed in **Color Key**
★ Size 22 or 24 tapestry needle

*See "Buyer's Guide" on page 240 for ordering information.

## DIRECTIONS

**1.** Find the center of the Aida band on the towel and mark it with a pin. Find the center of the **Tulips and Polka Dots Hand Towel Chart** by connecting the arrows.

**2.** Matching the centers of the chart and the Aida band on the towel, and using two strands of floss, begin stitching at the center point, working outward until the entire design is complete.

**3.** Using one strand of floss, backstitch the vine with dark blue-green and the remaining areas with black-brown.

**4.** Wash and press the completed cross-stitch towel as directed in "Washing and Pressing" on page 233.

## COUNTRY TIPS
### *from Alma Lynne*

If you're planning an extended visit to a friend's home, you might consider using the towel motifs to cross-stitch a whole hostess set. In addition to prefinished towels, you can purchase pot holders, aprons, totes, makeup bags, and more with Aida bands.

You can easily add to the size of any of these designs by adding more tulip motifs or extending the floral garland. Or, if you wish, choose just one motif for the pot holder or apron and cross-stitch over two or three threads to enlarge the design.

## TULIPS IN THE WIND HAND TOWEL

### SIZE

Design area is 1¾" × 5¾" on a 14-count prefinished hand towel

### MATERIALS

★ One Royal Lace white 14-count prefinished hand towel*
★ One skein of embroidery floss for each color listed in **Color Key**
★ Size 22 or 24 tapestry needle
★ ½ yard ⅜"-wide rose satin ribbon

*See "Buyer's Guide" on page 240 for ordering information.

### DIRECTIONS

**1.** Find the center of the Aida band on the towel and mark it with a pin. Find the center of the **Tulips in the Wind Hand Towel Chart** by connecting the arrows.

**2.** Matching the centers of the chart and the Aida band on the towel, and using two strands of floss, begin stitching at the center point, working outward until the entire design is complete.

**3.** Using one strand of floss, backstitch the pink tulips with deep rose, the lavender tulip with very dark lavender, and the leaves and stems with ultra dark pistachio green.

**4.** Wash and press the completed cross-stitch towel as directed in "Washing and Pressing" on page 233.

**5.** Tie the ribbon into a bow, trimming the ends diagonally. Tack the bow to the center of the Aida band above the lavender tulip.

### Bluebirds of Happiness Hand Towel Chart
#### DESIGN OPTIONS

| Fabric Count | Design Area | Cutting Dimension |
|---|---|---|
| 22 | 4⅛" × ⅞" | 14⅛" × 10⅞" |
| 18 | 1⅛" × 5" | 11⅛" × 15" |
| 14 | 1½" × 6½" | 11½" × 16½" |
| 11 | 1⅞" × 8¼" | 11⅞" × 18¼" |

### Tulips and Polka Dots Hand Towel Chart
#### DESIGN OPTIONS

| Fabric Count | Design Area | Cutting Dimensions |
|---|---|---|
| 22 | 1⅜" × 5" | 11⅜" × 15" |
| 18 | 1¾" × 6⅛" | 11¾" × 16⅛" |
| 14 | 2¼" × 7⅞" | 12¼" × 17⅞" |
| 11 | 2⅞" × 10⅛" | 12⅞" × 20⅛" |

### Tulips in the Wind Hand Towel Chart
#### DESIGN OPTIONS

| Fabric Count | Design Area | Cutting Dimensions |
|---|---|---|
| 22 | 1⅛" × 3⅝" | 11⅛" × 13⅝" |
| 18 | 1⅜" × 4½" | 11⅜" × 14½" |
| 14 | 1¾" × 5¾" | 11¾" × 15¾" |
| 11 | 2⅛" × 7¼" | 12⅛" × 17¼" |

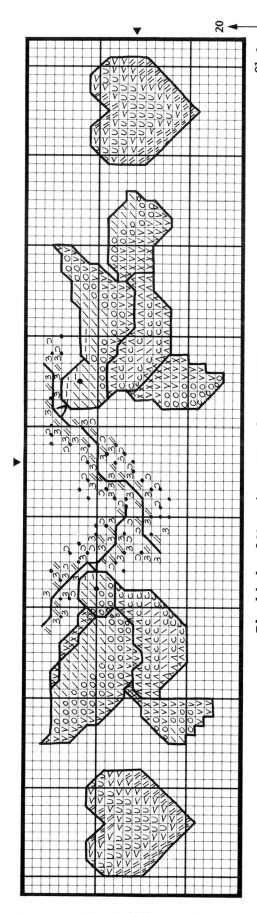

## Bluebirds of Happiness Hand Towel Chart
### COLOR KEY

| | DMC | Anchor | J. & P. Coats | Color |
|---|---|---|---|---|
| × | 312 | 979 | 7979 | Lt. Navy Blue |
| 3 | 319 | 218 | 6246 | Vy. Dk. Pistachio Green |
| 3 | 320 | 215 | 6017 | Med. Pistachio Green |
| ∨ | 322 | 978 | 7978 | Vy. Lt. Navy Blue |
| O | 334 | 977 | 7977 | Med. Baby Blue |
| ⁄⁄ | 367 | 217 | 6018 | Dk. Pistachio Green |
| ∪ | 368 | 214 | 6016 | Lt. Pistachio Green |
| C | 676 | 891 | — | Lt. Old Gold |

| | DMC | Anchor | J. & P. Coats | Color |
|---|---|---|---|---|
| ⁄ | 677 | 886 | 5372 | Vy. Lt. Old Gold |
| ‹ | 729 | 890 | 2875 | Med. Old Gold |
| — | 775 | 128 | 7031 | Vy. Lt. Baby Blue |
| ∪ | 776 | 24 | 3281 | Med. Pink |
| ⫽ | 899 | 52 | 3282 | Med. Rose |
| ∨ | 3325 | 129 | 7976 | Lt. Baby Blue |
| ‹ | 3326 | 36 | 3126 | Lt. Rose |
| ‹ | 3371 | 382 | 5382 | Black-Brown |

223

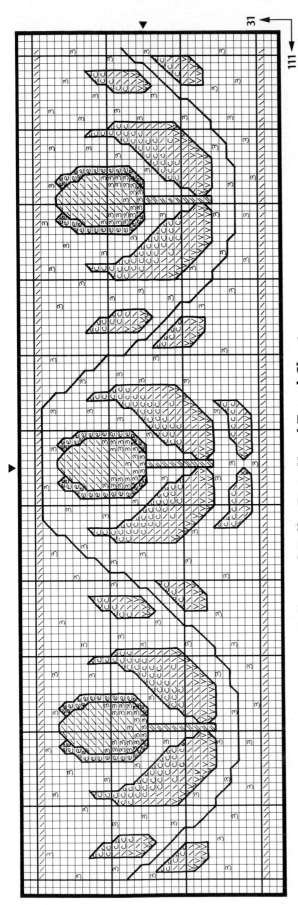

## Tulips and Polka Dots Hand Towel Chart
### Color Key

| DMC | Anchor | J. & P. Coats | Color |
|---|---|---|---|
| / | 501 | 878 | 6878 | Dk. Blue-Green |
| > | 502 | 877 | 6876 | Blue-Green |
| / | 503 | 876 | 6879 | Med. Blue-Green |
| C | 504 | 1042 | 6875 | Lt. Blue-Green |
| \ | 776 | 24 | 3281 | Med. Pink |
| e | 899 | 52 | 3282 | Med. Rose |
| | 3326 | 36 | 3126 | Lt. Rose |
| 3 | 3371 | 382 | 5382 | Black-Brown |

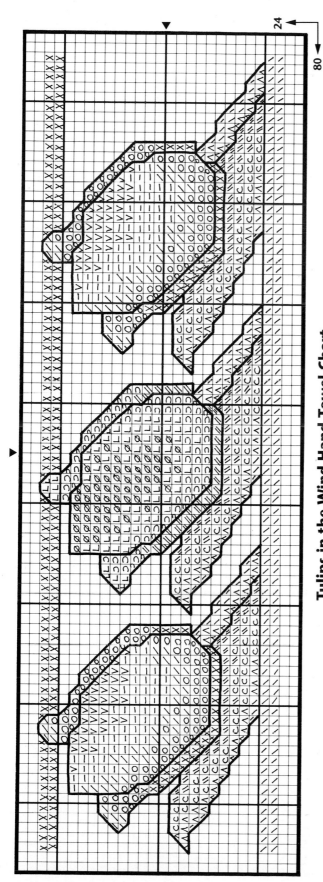

24

80

## Tulips in the Wind Hand Towel Chart

### COLOR KEY

| | DMC | Anchor | J. & P. Coats | Color |
|---|---|---|---|---|
| ⁄⁄ | 208 | 110 | 4301 | Vy. Dk. Lavender |
| ∩ | 209 | 109 | 4302 | Dk. Lavender |
| L | 210 | 108 | 4303 | Med. Lavender |
| ∅ | 211 | 342 | 4303 | Lt. Lavender |
| | 309 | 42 | 3284 | Deep Rose |
| ⁄⁄ | 319 | 218 | 6246 | Vy. Dk. Pistachio Green |
| ˅ | 320 | 215 | 6017 | Med. Pistachio Green |
| C | 367 | 217 | 6018 | Dk. Pistachio Green |

| | DMC | Anchor | J. & P. Coats | Color |
|---|---|---|---|---|
| ⁄ | 368 | 214 | 6016 | Lt. Pistachio Green |
| ⁄ | 776 | 24 | 3281 | Med. Pink |
| — | 818 | 23 | 3281 | Baby Pink |
| ˅ | 819 | 271 | 3280 | Lt. Baby Pink |
| | 890 | 218 | 6021 | Ultra Dk. Pistachio Green |
| × | 899 | 52 | 3282 | Med. Rose |
| O | 3326 | 36 | 3126 | Lt. Rose |

225

# OLD GLORY AFGHAN

*George and Martha, two of the most patriotic bunnies around, are center stage on this summer throw. Once you've finished cross-stitching, fringe the sides and drape it over a wicker chair to bring a country touch to your home.*

## SIZES

**Note:** Designs are over two threads on 18-count Anne Cloth
    Patriotic bunnies design area is 13¾" × 15¼"
    Stars and stripes heart design area is 3" × 3¼"
    American flag heart design area is 3" × 3¼"
    "U" design area is 4½" × 4¾"
    "S" design area is 4¼" × 4¾"
    "A" design area is 4¾" square
    Afghan measures 42" × 58", including fringe

## MATERIALS

* One 42" × 58" soft white 18-count Anne Cloth afghan*
* One skein of embroidery floss for each color listed in **Color Keys** (unless otherwise indicated)
* One spool of blending filament for each color listed in **Color Key**
* Size 26 tapestry needle

*See "Buyer's Guide" on page 240 for ordering information.

## DIRECTIONS

**1.** Prepare the edges of the afghan as directed in "Preparing Fabric Edges" on page 232. Find the center of the afghan and the center of each block in the top and bottom rows and mark them with pins. Find the centers of the **Patriotic Bunnies Chart,** the **"U" Chart,** the **"S" Chart,** the **"A" Chart,** the **Stars and Stripes Heart Chart,** and the **American Flag Heart Chart** by connecting the arrows.

**2.** Refer to the **Motif Placement Diagram** for placement of the center and border motifs in the afghan blocks. Matching the centers of the charts and afghan blocks, and using three strands of floss or blending filament, begin stitching at the center point, working each cross-stitch over two threads. Work out-

**Motif Placement Diagram**

ward until each motif is complete. Cross-stitch the "U," "S," and "A" motifs with very dark shell pink.

**3.** Using two strands of floss, backstitch Martha's dress, George's hat, and the red-and-white stripes in Martha's bonnet with very dark garnet, George's body with very dark beige-brown, and George's shirt with dark pewter gray. Backstitch the remaining areas with black-brown.

**4.** Work a French knot button on George's suspender and a French knot buckle button on Martha's shoe with three strands of black-brown. Refer to "The Stitches" on page 233 for instructions on making French knots.

**5.** To make the fringe, remove the selvage of the afghan. Zigzag stitch around the entire afghan through the center of the first row of whole blocks. Using a straight pin, remove the horizontal or vertical threads up to the

## COUNTRY TIPS
### *from Alma Lynne*

For a fancier look, weave ⅛"-wide red ribbon around the perimeter of this afghan, just inside the fringe. Or you can add a three-dimensional effect by sewing red star buttons onto Martha's bloomers and tiny white pom-poms onto George's knickers instead of stitching the stars and dots. Add button eyes and grosgrain ribbon suspenders for extra fun!

If you're an ambitious stitcher, continue the heart motifs checkerboard-fashion over the whole afghan. Or, pick up the star motifs from Martha's frock and scatter them about, using either red or blue floss to stitch them. If the project seems too overwhelming, leave off the "USA" and heart motifs and just cross-stitch the bunnies.

zigzag stitching. The afghan should have five full blocks across, with half-blocks on each side, and seven full blocks down, with half-blocks on the top and bottom. Beginning at the top left corner, gather 25 threads together and make an overhand knot. Continue clockwise around the afghan until you have knotted all the fringe.

### Stars and Stripes Heart Chart
#### DESIGN OPTIONS

| Fabric Count | Design Area | Cutting Dimensions |
| --- | --- | --- |
| 22 | 1¼" × 1⅜" | 11¼" × 11⅜" |
| 18 | 1½" × 1⅝" | 11½" × 11⅝" |
| 14 | 1⅞" × 2⅛" | 11⅞" × 12⅛" |
| 11 | 2½" × 2⅝" | 12½" × 12⅝" |

### American Flag Heart Chart
#### DESIGN OPTIONS

| Fabric Count | Design Area | Cutting Dimensions |
| --- | --- | --- |
| 22 | 1¼" × 1⅜" | 11¼" × 11⅜" |
| 18 | 1½" × 1⅝" | 11½" × 11⅝" |
| 14 | 1⅞" × 2⅛" | 11⅞" × 12⅛" |
| 11 | 2½" × 2⅝" | 12½" × 12⅝" |

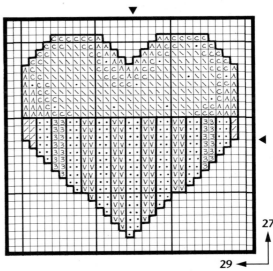

27

29 ◄

**Stars and Stripes Heart Chart**

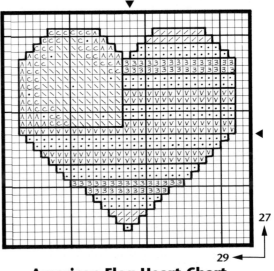

27

29 ◄

**American Flag Heart Chart**

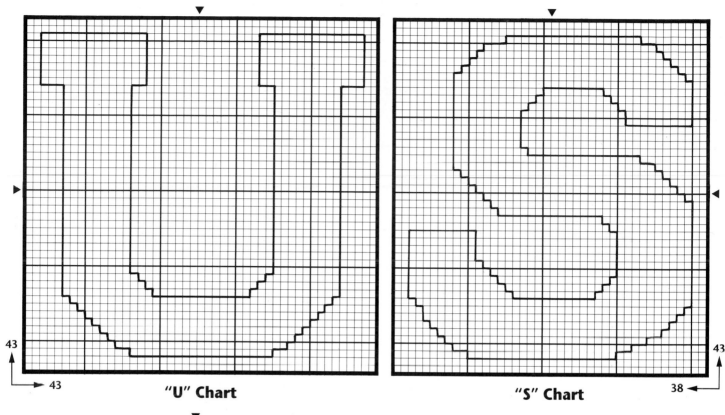

43

43

**"U" Chart**

43

38

**"S" Chart**

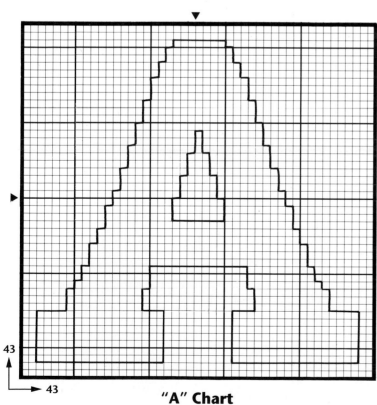

43

43

**"A" Chart**

### "U", "S", "A", Stars and Stripes Heart, and American Flag Heart Charts
#### COLOR KEY

| | DMC | Anchor | J.& P. Coats | Color |
|---|---|---|---|---|
| • | White | 2 | 1001 | White |
| / | 221 | 897 | 3243 | Vy. Dk. Shell Pink |
| V | 223 | 895 | 3240 | Med. Shell Pink |
| ∧ | 930 | 1035 | 7052 | Dk. Antique Blue |
| ⊂ | 931 | 1034 | 7051 | Med. Antique Blue |
| \ | 932 | 1033 | 7050 | Lt. Antique Blue |
| | 3371 | 382 | 5382 | Black-Brown |
| Ɔ | 3721 | 896 | 3242 | Dk. Shell Pink |

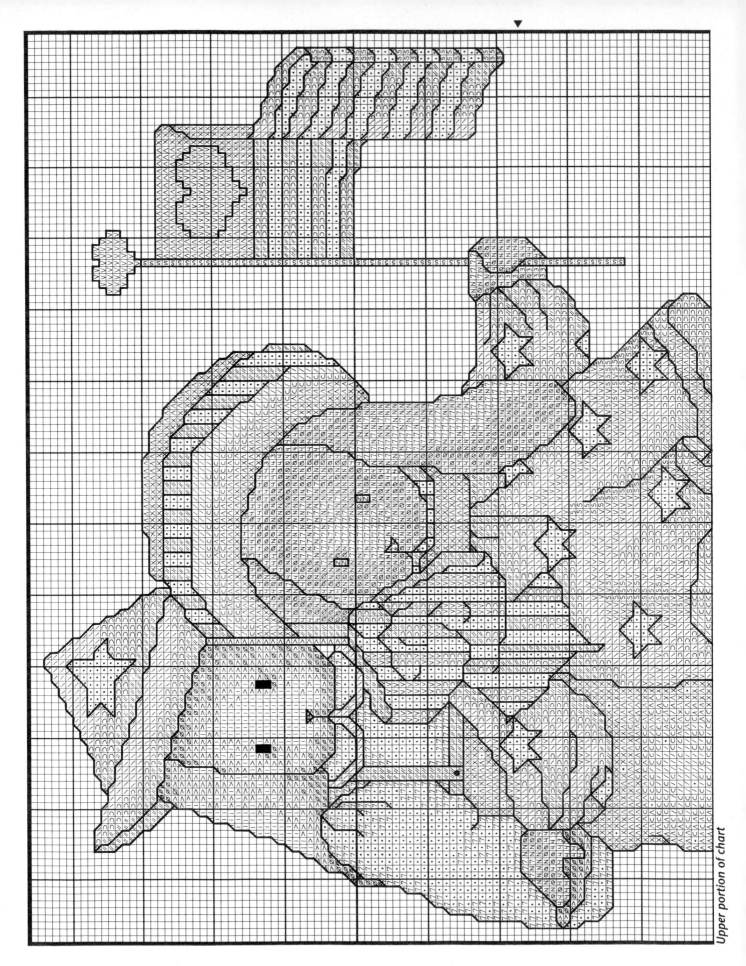

136

124

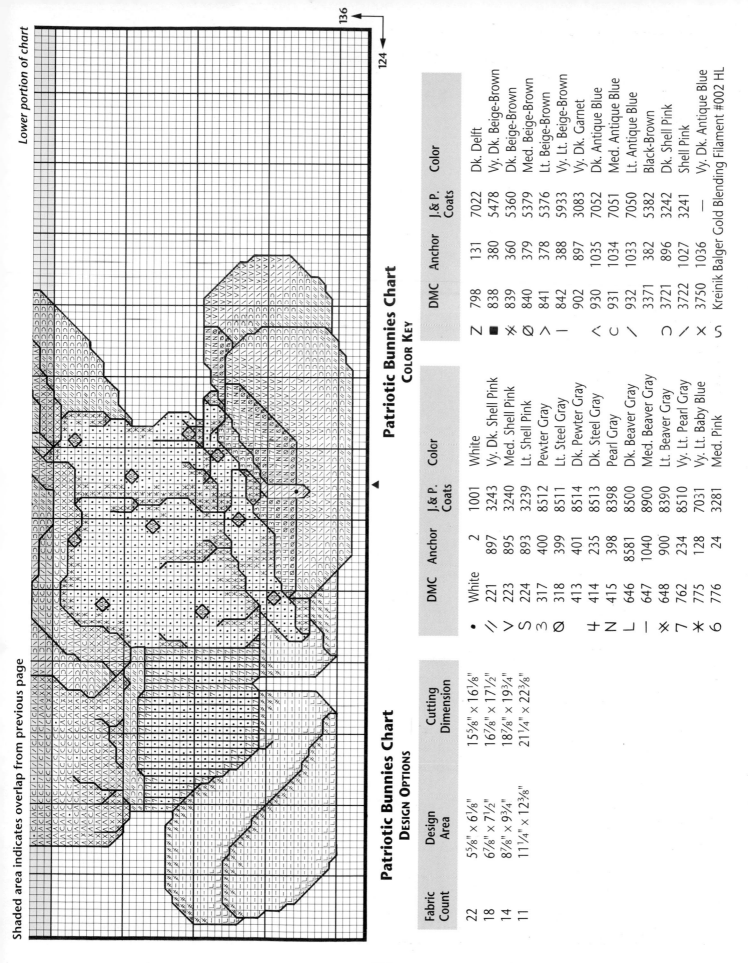

## Patriotic Bunnies Chart
### DESIGN OPTIONS

| Fabric Count | Design Area | Cutting Dimension |
|---|---|---|
| 22 | 5⅝" × 6⅛" | 15⅝" × 16⅛" |
| 18 | 6⅞" × 7½" | 16⅞" × 17½" |
| 14 | 8⅞" × 9¾" | 18⅞" × 19¾" |
| 11 | 11¼" × 12⅜" | 21¼" × 22⅜" |

## Patriotic Bunnies Chart
### COLOR KEY

| | DMC | Anchor | J.& P. Coats | Color |
|---|---|---|---|---|
| • | White | 2 | 1001 | White |
| // | 221 | 897 | 3243 | Vy. Dk. Shell Pink |
| V | 223 | 895 | 3240 | Med. Shell Pink |
| S | 224 | 893 | 3239 | Lt. Shell Pink |
| 3 | 317 | 400 | 8512 | Pewter Gray |
| ∅ | 318 | 399 | 8511 | Lt. Steel Gray |
| + | 413 | 401 | 8514 | Dk. Pewter Gray |
| N | 414 | 235 | 8513 | Dk. Steel Gray |
| L | 415 | 398 | 8398 | Pearl Gray |
| — | 646 | 8581 | 8500 | Dk. Beaver Gray |
| ✕ | 647 | 1040 | 8900 | Med. Beaver Gray |
| 7 | 648 | 900 | 8390 | Lt. Beaver Gray |
| * | 762 | 234 | 8510 | Vy. Lt. Pearl Gray |
| ✱ | 775 | 128 | 7031 | Vy. Lt. Baby Blue |
| 6 | 776 | 24 | 3281 | Med. Pink |

| | DMC | Anchor | J.& P. Coats | Color |
|---|---|---|---|---|
| Z | 798 | 131 | 7022 | Dk. Delft |
| ◼ | 838 | 380 | 5478 | Vy. Dk. Beige-Brown |
| ⋇ | 839 | 360 | 5360 | Dk. Beige-Brown |
| ⊘ | 840 | 379 | 5379 | Med. Beige-Brown |
| > | 841 | 378 | 5376 | Lt. Beige-Brown |
| | | 842 | 388 | 5933 | Vy. Lt. Beige-Brown |
| | 902 | 897 | 3083 | Vy. Dk. Garnet |
| < | 930 | 1035 | 7052 | Dk. Antique Blue |
| C | 931 | 1034 | 7051 | Med. Antique Blue |
| \ | 932 | 1033 | 7050 | Lt. Antique Blue |
| | 3371 | 382 | 5382 | Black-Brown |
| ⊃ | 3721 | 896 | 3242 | Dk. Shell Pink |
| / | 3722 | 1027 | 3241 | Shell Pink |
| ✕ | 3750 | 1036 | — | Vy. Dk. Antique Blue |
| S | Kreinik Balger Gold Blending Filament #002 HL | | | |

231

# LET'S START STITCHING

This section contains the basics of cross-stitch, duplicate stitch, machine appliqué, and dollmaking, with a bit of embellishing thrown in, so let's start stitching!

## CROSS-STITCH

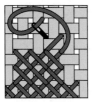

Counted cross-stitch is the most popular of all needlework skills and it isn't hard to master. You'll need to have the following supplies on hand.

**Fabrics:** Evenweave fabrics have been designed especially for embroidery and are woven with the same number of vertical and horizontal threads per inch. Cross-stitches are made over the intersections of the horizontal and vertical threads. The number of stitches per inch—the *count*—of any evenweave fabric determines the size of a finished design. The more stitches per inch, the smaller the design. The most common evenweave fabrics available are Aida, Hardanger, and linen.

**Premade Accessories:** You'll love the many premade accessories available with the evenweave fabric made as part of the construction. You'll find place mats, kitchen accessories, bookmarks, baby items, pillows, and bags; check for these items at your local needlecraft store.

**Needles:** Cross-stitch is done with a blunt-point tapestry needle. Your needle should slip *between* the fabric threads (not through them) as you stitch. Use a size 22 or 24 tapestry needle for 8-, 11-, and 14-count fabrics, and a size 24 or 26 for 16-, 18-, and 22-count fabrics.

**Embroidery Floss:** Any six-strand cotton embroidery floss can be used for cross-stitch. The floss can be divided; each project lists how many strands are needed. I list color numbers for the three largest floss manufacturers for each project. Each brand, however, has its own color range, so these suggestions are not perfect color matches. In addition to cotton floss, there are a variety of metallic and silky threads on the market.

Cut your floss into comfortable working lengths of approximately 18". Cut specialty flosses into 12" lengths. Use enough strands of specialty thread in your needle to equal the thickness of the floss recommended for the project.

When you stitch, the floss strands tend to twist; allow your needle to hang freely from your work. Do not carry your floss across the back of your work for more than $\frac{1}{4}$" since it tends to show through to the right side. If you are using dark floss on light fabric, end your length instead of carrying it across the back.

**Charted Designs:** Counted cross-stitch designs are worked from charts. Each square on a chart represents one cross-stitch. Each chart also gives you the number of horizontal and vertical stitches in the design. You'll notice two additional markings on most of the charts; the straight lines over or between symbols indicate backstitches and the large dots at the thread intersections indicate French knots. The symbol in each square on the chart represents the floss color used. Each chart is accompanied by a **Color Key,** which gives the floss color number. If a color name appears without a symbol, the color is only used for decorative stitches.

**Embroidery Hoop:** Counted cross-stitch can be done with or without a hoop. If you are working with linen, do *not* use a hoop because it permanently distorts the weave. If you choose to stretch a fabric in a hoop, use one made of plastic or wood with a screw-type tension adjuster. Placing the hoop over existing stitches will slightly distort them but a gentle raking with the needle will restore their square shape. Be sure to remove the fabric from the hoop when you have finished stitching for the day.

**Embroidery Scissors:** A pair of small, sharp-pointed scissors is necessary, especially for snipping misplaced stitches.

**Rustproof Pins:** You'll need rustproof straight pins to mark the center of your cross-stitch fabric. Be sure to remove them as soon as you begin stitching to avoid any stains or marks on your fabric.

### Preparing Fabric Edges

To prevent the fabric from raveling, overcast the edges by hand or zigzag the edges by machine. Or you may apply liquid ravel preventer (available at fabric stores) along the edges. Do *not* use masking tape—it leaves a very sticky residue.

### Starting to Stitch

Unless otherwise directed, work your design centered on the fabric. Follow the arrows at the bottom and side of a charted design to find the center; you may want to lightly shade the center square with a pencil for reference. Count the fabric threads or fold the fabric in quarters to find its center; mark the center with a straight pin.

Thread your tapestry needle with the amount of floss indicated. Bring the threaded needle from the back of the fabric to the front of the fabric. Hold an inch of the floss end against the back, then anchor it with your first few stitches. To end your thread or begin a new one, weave the floss through the backs of several stitches. Do *not* knot your floss.

## The Stitches

It's a good idea to practice your stitches if you haven't done any needlework lately. These directions will walk you through the four basic stitches.

### Cross-Stitch

A single cross-stitch is formed in two motions. Following the numbering in **Diagram 1,** bring your threaded needle up at 1, down at 2, up at 3, and down at 4, completing one cross-stitch.

**Diagram 1**

When working on linen, always begin to the left of a vertical linen thread, as shown in **Diagram 2.** Make sure this vertical thread is on top of the horizontal linen thread (rather than under it), as this will help to keep the first half of your cross-stitch "on top of" the linen weave.

**Diagram 2**

Work horizontal rows of stitches whenever possible, as shown in **Diagram 3.** Bring the thread up at 1, holding the tail end of the thread beneath the fabric; anchor it with your first few stitches. Bring the thread down at 2, then repeat to the end of the row, forming the first half of each cross-stitch. Complete the stitches on the return journey, making your cross-stitches touch by inserting the needle in the same hole used for the adjacent stitch.

**Diagram 3**

When stitching a vertical row, complete each stitch, then proceed to the next one. Be sure that all underneath stitches slant in one direction and all top stitches slant in the other direction.

### Backstitch

Work all backstitches after you finish the cross-stitches. Each project's directions will state which colors to use for backstitching. The chart will indicate where to place backstitches and how long each backstitch should be. **Diagram 4** shows how to make a series of backstitches. Bring your needle up at the odd numbers and down at the even numbers.

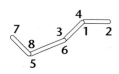

**Diagram 4**

### French Knot

Bring the thread up where indicated on the chart by the large dot. Wrap the floss once around the needle and reinsert it close to where the thread came up. Hold the wrapping thread tightly, close to the surface of the fabric. Pull the needle through, letting the thread go just as the knot is formed; see **Diagram 5.** For a larger knot, use more strands of floss.

**Diagram 5**

### Lazy Daisy Stitch

Referring to **Diagram 6,** bring the thread up at the center hole, loop the floss, reinsert the needle in the same hole, and bring it out two squares from the center (or as indicated by the chart), with the needle inside the loop. Pull the needle through, adjusting the size and shape of the loop. Stitch the loop down one thread farther from the center to secure it. Anchor the ending thread on the wrong side.

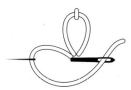

**Diagram 6**

## Washing and Pressing

Cross-stitch on any evenweave fabric is fully washable. When you have finished stitching, wash your piece in lukewarm water with mild

soap and rinse well. Do not scrub. Roll the embroidery in a clean towel to remove the excess moisture.

Place the embroidery face down on a dry, clean terrycloth towel. Press it carefully until the embroidery is dry and smooth.

## Design Options

In each set of directions, you'll find a **Design Options** table. This is a handy reference if you want to cross-stitch the design on a different count fabric than what's recommended. Find the fabric count on the table that matches what you'll be working on, then follow the line across to determine how large the design area will be. If this is suitable for your project, use the cutting dimensions to cut your fabric. The cutting dimensions allow for 5" of extra fabric around *each* side of your completed embroidery for ease in framing. If you are making the embroidery into a pillow, decrease the cutting dimensions according to your needs.

Each of these design options assumes that you will be stitching over one fabric square or thread, even though many of the models are stitched over two squares or threads. If you wish to stitch over two squares or threads, plan accordingly by refiguring the measurements. For example, if you have a design that is 50 × 50 stitches and you want to stitch it over one thread on 22-count fabric, your design area will be 50 ÷ 22 or 2¼" square and your cutting dimensions will be 12¼" square. If you want to stitch the design over two threads, you need to divide the fabric count by 2. In other words, your design area will be 50 ÷ 11 or 4½" square and your cutting dimensions will be 14½" square.

### DESIGN OPTIONS

| Fabric Count | Design Area | Cutting Dimensions |
|---|---|---|
| 22 | 2¼" × 2¼" | 12¼" × 12¼" |
| 18 | 2¾" × 2¾" | 12¾" × 12¾" |
| 14 | 3½" × 3½" | 13½" × 13½" |
| 11 | 4½" × 4½" | 14½" × 14½" |

## DUPLICATE STITCH

Duplicate stitching reproduces the stitch of the knitted fabric so that a completed design looks as if it were knitted into the sweater. Here are the supplies you'll need.

**Knitted Fabric:** You can use almost any knitted fabric for duplicate stitching. In addition to knitted sweaters, you'll find premade stockings, afghans, and of course, my original Dupli-Bands, which are manufactured just for duplicate stitching.

To figure the gauge of your purchased knitted fabric, count the number of stitches per inch, then the number of rows per inch, as shown in **Diagram 7**. It's best to count the stitches for at least two inches each way, then divide by two to get the average number of stitches per inch. For reference, stitches per inch is usually the first number and rows per inch is usually the second number given in a gauge specification.

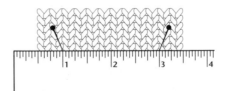

**Diagram 7**

**Needles:** Duplicate stitch is done with a blunt-point tapestry needle. Your needle should slip between the knitted stitches (not through them) as you stitch. Use a size 18 or 22 tapestry needle for most duplicate stitching, and a size 24 or 26 tapestry needle if the duplicate-stitch fabric is tightly knit.

**Embroidery Floss:** See "Embroidery Floss" on page 232 for general information. I recommend using all six strands when stitching on a 6 × 8-gauge knitted fabric. However, if you are using a different gauge, you will need to make test swatches to decide how many strands to use.

If you are concerned about floss colors bleeding when you launder your duplicate-stitched piece, presoak your floss in a solution of 1 tablespoon of white vinegar and 8 ounces of water before you stitch. Blot the floss dry.

**Charted Designs:** Duplicate-stitch designs are worked from charts in the same manner that counted cross-stitch is worked. See "Charted Designs" on page 232 for general information. Each square on a chart represents one V-shaped duplicate stitch. The finished size is determined by the gauge of the knitted fabric you've selected. Cross-stitch charts will be distorted when used with this technique, so look for designs specifically drawn for duplicate stitch.

**Embroidery Scissors:** See

"Embroidery Scissors" on page 232 for general information.

**Rustproof Pins:** See "Rustproof Pins" on page 232 for general information.

## Starting to Stitch

Each project gives directions for placing the design on the knitted fabric. Follow the arrows at the bottom and side of the charted design to find the center; you may want to lightly shade the center square with a pencil for reference.

## The Stitches

**Duplicate Stitch:** Locate the "V" on your knitted fabric that will be your first stitch. Following the numbering in **Diagram 8,** bring your threaded needle up at 1, down at 2, across the wrong side to 3, and back down at 4. Work your next stitch in the same manner.

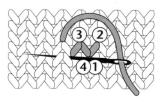

**Diagram 8**

Horizontal rows stitch much more smoothly than vertical rows. If you must stitch vertical rows, stitch from top to bottom.

To end your thread or begin a new one, run your threaded needle under the back of several completed stitches, then return in the other direction under other stitches to secure.

**Couching Stitch:** Lay the floss on the sweater in a curving line as shown on the project chart. Bring your working thread up through the sweater, over the curved line of floss, and back through the sweater, as shown in **Diagram 9.**

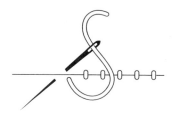

**Diagram 9**

## Washing and Pressing

When you have finished stitching, hand wash the completed duplicate-stitch piece in lukewarm water with mild soap; do not scrub. Rinse well. Roll the piece in a clean towel to remove the excess moisture; dry it flat.

To press, place your completed piece face down on a dry, clean terrycloth towel. Steam lightly, using a press cloth and lots of steam. Do *not* lay the iron directly on the piece.

## MACHINE APPLIQUÉ

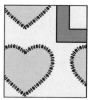

Since I can't find a lot of time for hand appliqué, I fuse my appliqué pieces in place, rev up the sewing machine, and zigzag away. You'll need the following supplies.

**Fabric:** Select washable fabrics if you are appliquéing on an item that will be laundered often. Light- to medium-weight cottons and cotton blends work best. Wash and dry all fabrics and clothing to remove sizing. Press as necessary.

**Fusible Webbing:** Fusible webbing can turn any fabric into iron-on fabric. Webbing consists of two parts—the webbing adhesive and its paper backing. Follow the manufacturer's instructions when fus-

ing because brands may require different heat settings or fusing times.

Because the fusible webbing is fused to the wrong side of the fabric, trace the mirror image, or reverse, of any asymmetrical design; symmetrical designs can be traced on either side. Trace the appliqué pieces onto the paper side of the fusible webbing using a graphite pencil. Cut around each tracing, leaving ¼" between each. Place the fusible webbing on the wrong side of the fabric, with the paper backing facing up, following the project directions to determine which pieces are cut from which fabrics. To fuse, iron over the paper backings with a hot, *dry* iron for a few seconds. Cut out each appliqué piece. Remove the paper backing.

Following the project directions for placement, fuse the appliqué pieces to the right side of the background fabric or sweatshirt, layering and overlapping them as shown by the dashed lines on the patterns. These dashed lines show the portions that appear underneath other appliqué pieces.

**Tracing Paper:** You can buy tracing paper at your local art store. You'll be using the tracing paper for tracing the appliqué patterns.

**Pencil:** Keep sharp pencils handy for tracing the appliqué patterns. Graphite pencils are ideal since colored pencils are difficult to see.

**Iron:** A clean iron is essential when using fusible webbing. Since even the slightest bit of misplaced webbing can ruin a project, clean the iron after each fusing.

**Scissors:** Quality dressmaker's shears can't be beat when cutting out fabric appliqués. Embroidery scissors also work well. Don't try to cut appliqué pieces with dull scissors because you will inevitably fray the appliqué's edges.

**Sewing Machine:** You do not have to own an expensive machine to make these projects. All you'll need is a basic machine that sews a straight seam and a zigzag stitch. Start each project with a new needle.

**Matching Thread:** Use thread that matches the appliqué pieces. Thread your bobbin with a neutral-color thread so you won't need to change the color for each appliqué. Always use good-quality thread to avoid breakage.

**Tear-Away Stabilizer:** Tear-away stabilizer is a nonwoven interfacing-like product that is pinned to the wrong side of the background fabric in the appliqué area. Use stabilizer for decorative zigzag stitching to prevent puckering. After completing the machine appliqué, gently tear the stabilizer away. In tight areas, you may need to start a tear with the point of your scissors.

## Getting Started

After cutting and fusing your appliqué pieces to the background fabric, pin the stabilizer in place. Set your machine for a closely spaced zigzag (satin) stitch. Loosen your needle thread tension so your bobbin thread will not be visible. Zigzag around the raw edge of each appliqué piece using matching thread; see **Diagram 10.** Machine appliqué the most underneath piece first and finish with the top piece. Change your thread to match each fabric color. Pull all

**Diagram 10**

loose threads to the wrong side of the background fabric and secure. Turn the appliquéd piece wrong side out before laundering.

## DOLLMAKING

I hope the darling bunnies, bears, angels, and Santas in this book will inspire you to begin dollmaking if you haven't already discovered how much fun it is!

## Preparing Patterns

Patterns are either full size or reduced on a grid. Trace the full-size patterns for use. To enlarge the patterns on a grid, enlarge the grid on a photocopy machine at the percentage given, or until the boxes measure 1".

## Marking Pattern Pieces

Mark around your patterns onto your fabric with a dressmaker's pencil, erasable marker, or graphite pencil. Mark the specified number of pieces needed on one fabric at a time, leaving at least ½" between pieces.

## Construction

There are two construction methods used for the dolls. The cut-and-sew method is the traditional way. The draw-and-sew method is used when patterns are small and difficult to maneuver.

**Cut-and-Sew Method:** A ¼" seam allowance is included in each of the patterns that use this method. After marking your patterns, cut them out on the marked lines; see **Diagram 11.** With right sides together, sew the pieces

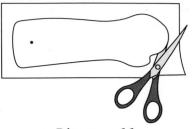

**Diagram 11**

together as directed.

Clip the curves as necessary. Use a narrow wooden dowel to aid your turning and stuffing. Stuff the dolls firmly (unless otherwise directed). Whipstitch all openings closed.

Some projects call for buttonhole twist thread to be used for assembling dolls. This is a heavy-duty thread that is more durable than regular thread. It is available in your local fabric store.

**Draw-and-Sew Method:** Use this method for sewing together pieces that are difficult to sew in the traditional manner.

Use two layers of fabric, having each layer large enough for all the pattern pieces needed. Place the right sides of the fabrics together and mark the patterns onto the wrong side of the top piece of fabric. Allow at least 1" between each pattern. Pin the fabric to hold the layers together.

Sew directly on the drawn lines, leaving an opening for turning on each; see **Diagram 12.** Cut out each piece, leaving a ⅛" seam allowance at the sewn edges and a ¼" seam allowance at the opening. Clip the curves as necessary.

Use a narrow dowel to aid your turning and stuffing. Be sure to stuff the dolls firmly (unless directed otherwise). Whipstitch all the openings closed.

Some projects call for buttonhole twist thread to be used for assembling dolls. This is a heavy-duty thread that is more durable

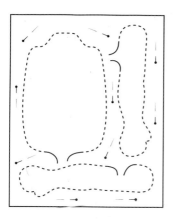

**Diagram 12**

than regular thread. It is available at your local fabric store.

## Hairstyling

When a hairstyle is indicated, the project's directions will instruct you to hand sew the twine, string, or yarn to the doll's head, forming a part down the center of the head.

## Facial Features

These dolls have drawn or embroidered facial features. Transfer the facial features onto the fabric using a black, razor-point, permanent pen or a dressmaker's pencil. Shade the eyes with colored pencils.

Some facial features are embroidered; specific directions are given for each project. The three embroidery stitches you'll use most are the satin stitch, the stem stitch, and the long stitch.

The satin stitch is a series of close backstitches that create a smooth, satinlike surface. Following the numbering in **Diagram 13,** bring your threaded needle up at 1 and down at 2. Bring it up again at a new 1 and down at a new 2, placing the stitches very close together.

The stem stitch is worked in a forward and backward motion

**Diagram 13**

along the marked line; be sure to keep the working thread to the right of the needle, as shown in **Diagram 14.**

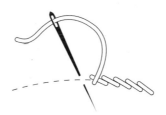

**Diagram 14**

The long stitch is just that—a long, straight stitch. Place the stitch as indicated by the markings on the individual pattern piece in the project directions.

## Bias Tape

Bias tape is a narrow fabric strip with prefolded edges. When I make dolls, I use it to replace traditional clothing facings since it reduces bulk in the seams.

To apply it, open out one fold and pin it to the seam allowance, aligning the raw edges, as shown in **Diagram 15.** Sew the bias tape to the garment using a ¼" seam allowance. Grade the seam allowances and clip the curves if necessary. Turn the bias tape to the inside and whipstitch the folded edge in place.

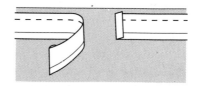

**Diagram 15**

## OTHER TECHNIQUES

I've included a few tips to speed along your needlecrafting. Take a few minutes to read this section before beginning your projects.

### Sewing

Browse through this section for professional sewing tips. This list of supplies to have on hand and terms you'll need to know should come in handy.

**Fabric:** I recommend using only 100 percent cotton fabrics. There are specialty fabrics used in the projects, like moiré taffeta and corduroy, that won't be 100 percent cotton, however. If you think your project will be laundered, wash and dry all fabrics to preshrink them.

**Thread:** Use a good-quality thread in a coordinating color for your projects.

**Sewing Machine:** You'll need a basic machine that sews a straight seam and a zigzag stitch.

**Scissors:** A sharp pair of dressmaker's shears should be in everyone's sewing basket. Remember to never use the same scissors to cut both paper and fabrics!

**Rotary Cutting Supplies:** Use a rotary cutter, rotary mat, and clear plastic ruler for cutting quilt border strips or pillow ruffles.

### Basic Construction

Even if you know the basics of sewing, here's a refresher course in some of the terminology.

**Seams:** All the projects in this book use a flat seam. Place two pieces of fabric to be joined with right sides together (unless otherwise instructed) and align the raw edges; pin to secure. Sew the pieces together ¼" (unless another seam allowance is specified) from

the raw edges, working a few stitches in reverse at each end to secure threads.

**Clipping and Grading:** Clip the curves of a seam once the seam line has been stitched. Cut perpendicular from the fabric edge to the seam line, being careful not to cut your stitches; see **Diagram 16.**

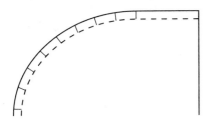

**Diagram 16**

Grade your seam allowances to reduce bulk. Trim away one seam allowance so that it is narrower than the other, giving a layered appearance; see **Diagram 17.**

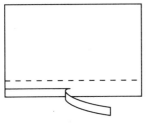

**Diagram 17**

**Whipstitch:** A whipstitch is used to join fabric edges when finishing a project. Insert your needle into one fabric edge at an angle, through the second fabric, back over the edge of the first fabric; pull the fabric edges closed. See **Diagram 18.**

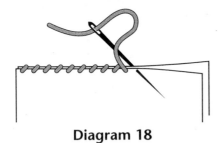

**Diagram 18**

**Cutting Bias Strips:** The projects that use piping include at least ⅜ yard of fabric for bias strips. There are two methods for cutting bias strips—the continuous-bias method and the simple bias strip method. Use your rotary cutter.

For the continuous-bias method, cut a square from the bias strip fabric. If you have ⅜ yard, your square will be about 12" after preshrinking. Fold the square in half diagonally and press lightly. Cut the square into two triangles along the fold line. With right sides together, sew the two triangles together using a ¼" seam allowance. See **Diagram 19.** Open the piece out flat; press the seam open.

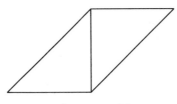

**Diagram 19**

Mark cutting lines on the wrong side of the fabric the width the project directions specify (usually 2"), marking parallel to the bias edge; see **Diagram 20.**

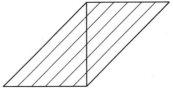

**Diagram 20**

Fold the fabric with right sides together, bringing the two non-bias edges together and offsetting them by one strip width, as shown in **Diagram 21.** Pin the edges together, creating a tube, and sew using a ¼" seam allowance. Press the seam open. Cut on the marked lines, as shown in **Diagram 21,** turning the tube as you cut.

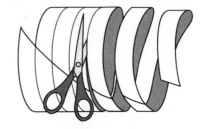

**Diagram 21**

For the simple bias strip method, square off the end of your fabric before cutting the bias strips.

Align the 45 degree angle line on a see-through ruler with the bottom edge of the fabric to make your first bias cut. Trim off the corner along the edge of the ruler. Move the ruler across the fabric, cutting parallel strips in the needed width. See **Diagram 22.** Sew the short ends of the bias strips together to make one long bias strip.

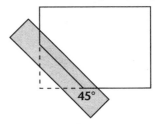

**Diagram 22**

**Making Corded Piping:** With wrong sides together, fold the bias strip in half lengthwise and insert the cording close to the fold. Using a zipper foot, machine baste the cording inside the bias strip, stitching as close as possible to the cording; see **Diagram 23.**

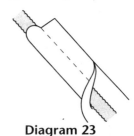

**Diagram 23**

**Sewing On the Piping:** Beginning in the middle of the

bottom edge, pin the corded piping to the right side of the pillow top, aligning the raw edges; do not sew yet. At the pillow corners, clip the seam allowance of the piping perpendicular to the seam to ease it around the curves.

Leaving about 2" free at the beginning and end, sew the piping to the pillow top along the basting line. To join the piping ends, pull back the fabric from one end of the piping. Trim the extra length off the cording so the raw ends butt; see **Diagram 24.** Turn ½" to the wrong side on one bias strip and unfold it to cover the cording and the other bias strip end, as shown. Finish sewing the seam.

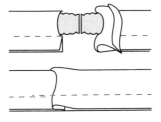

**Diagram 24**

**Ruffles:** Cut your ruffle pieces and sew them into a loop. Run a gathering thread around the ruffle and gather it to fit your pillow top. With right sides together, pin the ruffle evenly around the edges, using the pins as quarterpoint guides. Sew the ruffle to the pillow top, using a ¼" seam allowance; see **Diagram 25.**

**Covered Pillow Forms:** Sew two muslin pieces together using a ¼" seam allowance, leaving an opening along one edge. Clip the corners diagonally. Turn right side out and stuff. Whipstitch the opening closed.

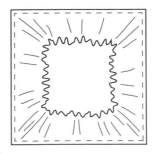

**Diagram 25**

**Assembling a Pillow:** With right sides together, place the pillow top and back together and sew around the outer edge, using a ¼" seam allowance; leave an opening along the bottom edge. Grade the seam allowances. Insert the pillow form into the pillow and whipstitch the opening closed.

**Patterns:** See "Preparing Patterns" on page 236 for general information.

**Marking Pattern Pieces:** See "Marking Pattern Pieces" on page 236 for general information.

## Froufrou

Froufrou is my special way of adding a personal touch to your garments.

**Materials:** Each project's directions will list the materials and the amounts you'll need for the froufrou. Don't let the suggested materials limit your imagination.

**Getting Started:** The froufrou on your garment needs to be treated delicately. I discovered an easy way to keep it neat—use Velcro so the froufrou can be removed before laundering! Cut the Velcro length in half and sew the loop (soft) side to each shoulder seam.

Cut the ribbon, lace, braids, trims, and fabric lengths as directed in each project's directions. Tie a half-knot in the center of each length, then tack the knot to the wrong side of the hook (scratchy) side of the Velcro length, alternating the ribbon and/or fabric colors when attaching them. Clip the ribbon ends diagonally. To add bells, slide the bell about 1" up on the ribbon end, then knot the end. To add floss skeins, tie one loop of the skein with a length of thread, then sew it to the Velcro strip. Press the Velcro lengths together and voilà! Instant froufrou.

## Tea Dyeing

Tea dyeing instantly antiques your projects. Use 100 percent cotton fabrics, as they absorb the color better than synthetics do. Tea dyeing is ideal for giving white fabrics a warm, well-loved look. Avoid dark fabrics since the tea will have little effect. Be sure to wash and dry your fabrics to remove the sizing.

You'll need a large pot so your fabric will dye evenly. Cut your fabric into ½-yard pieces, since larger pieces are difficult to maneuver. Steep ten tea bags in a gallon of boiling water for 20 minutes. Remove the tea bags and place the fabric in the pot. Continue to simmer for 10 minutes, stirring constantly. The color will lighten as the fabric dries.

Remove the fabric and rinse it in cold water until the water runs clear. Heat set the fabric by pressing it or tossing it in the dryer.

# BUYER'S GUIDE

**All Couped Up**
560 South State #B1
Orem, UT 84058
    Crepe doll hair

**Alma Lynne Designs**
611 West Broadway
Myrtle Beach, SC 29577
    Duplicate-stitch products,
    including Piper Glen afghans
    and Dupli-Bands

**Charles Craft**
P.O. Box 1049
Laurinburg, NC 28353
    Cross-stitch fabrics, including
    Soft Touch; prefinished acces-
    sories, including Cafe Check
    cross-stitch towels

**Daniel Enterprises**
P.O. Box 1105
Laurinburg, NC 28353
    Prefinished cross-stitch acces-
    sories, including Royal Lace
    velour guest towels and Tidy
    Tot eyelet bibs

**Gay Bowles Sales, Inc.**
1310 Plainfield Avenue
Janesville, WI 53547
    Mill Hill glass seed beads

**Janlynn Corp.**
34 Front Street
Indian Orchard, MA 01151
    Canvas tote bag (order #961-
    1011)

**Kreinik Manufacturing
Co., Inc.**
P.O. Box 1966
Parkersburg, WV 26102
    Metallic and pearl blending
    filament threads

**Lane Borgosesia**
4823 Centennial Boulevard
Colorado Springs, CO 80919
    Fur Luxe yarn

**Leisure Arts**
P.O. Box 5595
Little Rock, AR 72215
    Anne Cloth

**Rainbow Gallery**
13756 Victory Boulevard
Van Nuys, CA 91401
    Angora yarn #SB-1

**Wichelt Imports**
R.R. #1
Stoddard, WI 54658
    Cross-stitch fabrics, includ-
    ing Davos and Lugana

**The Wood Loft**
1661 Blaine S.E.
Grand Rapids, MI 49507-2048
    Bellpull hardware

**Zweigart**
Joan Toggitt, Ltd.
Weston Canal Plaza
2 Riverview Drive
Somerset, NJ 08873-1150
    Cross-stitch fabrics, includ-
    ing Aida, Annabelle, Cork
    linen, Davosa, Dublin linen,
    Linda cloth, Lugana, Pastel
    linen, Tabby Cloth, and
    Valerie

# SPECIAL THANKS

### ALMA LYNNE'S WARDROBE

**Foxy Lady Boutique**
Myrtle Beach Hilton
Myrtle Beach, S.C.

**Elaine's**
The Hidden Village
Myrtle Beach, S.C.

### CUSTOM FRAMING

**The Howard Gallery**
Myrtle Beach, S.C.

### PHOTOGRAPHY PROPS

**Antique Market Place**
Ronks, Pa.

**Audrey Nutes Antiques**
Chadds Ford, Pa.

**Carsons Country Stew**
New Holland, Pa.

**The Christmas Shop**
Paoli, Pa.

**Dilworthtown Country Antiques**
Dilworthtown, Pa.

**Donna Borgstrom Antiques**
Media, Pa.

**Laurie's Wicker Porch**
Uwchland, Pa.

**Village Peddler Antiques**
Chadds Ford, Pa.

**Wallace Antiques &
    Craft Shop**
Witmer, Pa.